WITHDRAWN

Nathaniel Hawthorne: New Critical Essays

NATHANIEL HAWTHORNE: NEW CRITICAL ESSAYS

edited by
A. Robert Lee

VISION
and
BARNES & NOBLE

Vision Press Limited
11–14 Stanhope Mews West
London SW7 5RD

and

Barnes & Noble Books
81 Adams Drive
Totowa, NJ 07512

ISBN (UK) 0 85478 4640

ISBN (US) 0 389 20281 9

Printed and bound by
Mansell (Bookbinders) Ltd.,
Witham, Essex.
Phototypeset by Keyset Composition,
Colchester, Essex.
MCMLXXXII

Contents

Introduction

by A. ROBERT LEE

> Only this is such a strange and incomprehensible world! The more I look at it, the more it puzzles me; and I begin to suspect that a man's bewilderment is the measure of his wisdom!
> —Holgrave in *The House of the Seven Gables;* Chapter XII.
> Imagine a ghost just passed into the other state of being, looking back into this mortal world, and shocked by many things that were delightful just before—more shocked than the living are at the ghostly world.
> —*Journal,* 16 May 1862.

Both these observations, the first a typically shrewd speculation by perhaps the most interesting of all Hawthorne's artist-figures and the second a jotting made only two years before he himself 'passed into another state of being', reveal something not only of his characteristic watchful sense of the world, but of the fictional art through which he sought to take its measure. For Hawthorne, like his daguerreotypist Holgrave, was nothing if not given to the contemplative temperament, a deeply inward artist whose idiom is nearly always one of concealment and subtleties of indirection and irony. His notion of the ghost affrighted by the world recently left behind also signals something of his frequent playfulness, the typical genial ease of surface to much of his tone. Yet to his own age neither the profounder reaches of Hawthorne's fiction, nor his lighter side, readily won great understanding. Rather he seemed essentially a regional literary son of New England, a solemn and straight-forward allegorist who had put to picturesque local effect the communal Puritan past.

To succeeding generations of readers, however, he has rightly come to be judged an altogether more capacious man of letters, a trenchant, subversive imagination who saw in humankind a species almost willingly prey to all manner of ruling illusion and folly. Both his romances and his stories explore, time and again, his great themes of hidden guilt, isolation, the will-to-power, sexual and creative power brought up sharp against the prevailing community standard. In this respect, Henry James's homage to Hawthorne, though not offered without reservation, as 'a natural, original genius', is apt and deserved. For Hawthorne belongs not only to the American Renaissance, the mid-nineteenth century outburst of ideas and expression prophesied in Emerson's *Nature* (1836) and 'The American Scholar' (1837) and whose major voices, besides his own and Emerson's, include those of Melville, Whitman, Thoreau and Emily Dickinson, but to the American literary tradition at large and far beyond. This latter version of Hawthorne, so dramatically first perceived by Melville in his 'Hawthorne and his Mosses' (*The Literary World*, August 1850), and later, in their different ways, confirmed by Henry James and D. H. Lawrence, is the Hawthorne this new collection of essays seeks to acknowledge.

Hawthorne, then, whether in *The Scarlet Letter* (1850) and his other principal romances, or in his short stories, or in the working *Notebooks,* or indeed in the influence he exerted upon Melville and other subsequent American makers of narrative, stands indisputably as a central presence in American literary culture. He at once looks back to the New England Puritan world established by his forebears, and yet was able to see in that world a wholly contemporary set of meanings, whether about power, authority, or the inner nature of human psychology and sexuality. He also points forward: in the striking modernity of his philosophical interests and in his strategies of voice and narrative which for many anticipate literary modernism, and even post-modernism. He remains enigmatic, too, despite inspired recent biographical efforts to unravel the man from behind the many self-masking identities he chose to assume before the public eye. The enigma persists over into his fiction, an author who makes us see but prefers not (or only in the minutest part) to be seen himself. It can hardly be thought surprising that both the literal historic nineteenth-century Hawthorne and Hawthorne the romancer and inspired storyteller continue to attract keen critical attention.

Each of these eleven essays (eight are British, three American) has been commissioned with a view to attempting

8

fresh critical soundings in Hawthorne. They are intended to comprise a sequence with a clear overall design. Brian Way's opening essay takes a broad view of Hawthorne's stories, stressing in detail the ways in which Hawthorne's apparent surface decorum conceals the rich 'subversive undercurrents' of his perceptions about the human pageant. By contrast, Harold Beaver concentrates on a single story, 'Roger Malvin's Burial', and in analysing its devious, engaging tactics of language and ambiguity is able to emphasize the features through which Hawthorne's creation of romance can best be recognized.

There follow in turn accounts of each of the four major romances, with two essays given over to Hawthorne's master-piece, *The Scarlet Letter*. My own, which was conceived to anticipate, and complement, Mark Kinkead-Weekes's, seeks to establish how, in 'The Custom-House', Hawthorne fashioned a narrative in its own imaginative right yet which cannily dis-closes his working procedures as a romancer and constitutes an indispensible pathway into the *The Scarlet Letter* itself. The emphasis in the following essay falls upon Hawthorne's 'framing' of *The Scarlet Letter,* the manner in which the main text takes up and amplifies those elements of romance which Hawthorne sets beguilingly before his reader in his picture of 'the moon-lit room' in 'The Custom-House'. Richard Gray, in his account of *The House of the Seven Gables,* attempts to chart the shifting currents of interest which mark out Hawthorne's second romance, the interwoven metaphor of the book as house and vice versa and the seeming discrepancy of tone to the book's ending. Keith Carabine concentrates upon the strange role Miles Coverdale is called upon to play as narrator in *The Blithedale Romance,* Hawthorne's surrogate imagined author unable to refuse the story he must tell in all its ambiguity and incompleteness. Graham Clarke moves away from the tradi-tional reading of *The Marble Faun* as an elaborated version of the Fortunate Fall and suggests that in his last completed romance Hawthorne makes the very volatility of art his subject. He plays off Hawthorne's frequent allusions to painting, sculpture and frescoes and Rome as the city of art *par excellence* against the book's own speculations about making and seeking to respond appropriately to the imaginative transformation of reality.

The four concluding essays range more widely. Arnold

Goldman examines Hawthorne's England, 'Our Old Home', as it came to be phrased, but argues that not only did it present him with a 'materiality' which contrasted with his own New England roots but ultimately yielded an unexpected imagery of death. Eric Homberger examines the dialectic of happiness and sorrow which marks out each of the romances, the hope of human bliss checked or at least modified by the awareness of human error. In his far-ranging account of Hawthorne's obsession with the workings of law and authority Eric Mottram uses both the longer and shorter fiction to map those essentially ninteenth-century notions of what makes for, and what threatens, credible human selfhood. Richard Brodhead's essay looks to Hawthorne as an influence, principally upon Melville, but also upon the course taken in his aftermath by a great deal of American fiction. It is this Hawthorne, the elusive and richly prophetic romancer in whose craft later writers have found their example, who properly offers a point of conclusion to the collection as a whole.

1

Art and the Spirit of Anarchy: A Reading of Hawthorne's Short Stories

by BRIAN WAY

Hawthorne's stories are more varied and often more wayward than his novels, and the impression of order—of the directing hand of the moralist and allegorist—is not always so apparent. In spite of his many explicit tributes to high ideals, and his consistent decorum of tone, the underlying spirit of his best tales is almost invariably subversive, mocking, even anarchic. His purely moral sketches ('The Threefold Destiny', 'The Sister Years' and 'The Lily's Quest', for instance) are insipid and banal. His best work results from the tension in him between the wish to affirm and the impulse to deny.

A striking manifestation of this trait is his tendency to attack and undermine what, on the surface, he appears to admire most. In his own personal attitudes and beliefs he often showed an intense, sometimes a perverse, spirit of contradiction. He cared passionately for the idea of an American identity, and recorded outrageously chauvinistic opinions in his English and Italian Notebooks, and yet during the American Civil War he fiercely disparaged the Federal cause and expressed a wilful indifference to the very survival of the Union. The same extremes are evident in his feelings towards women: he idealized their beauty and the delicacy of their minds, but he hated and feared women of strong intellect and overbearing

11

sexuality.[1] In his fiction, these and similar contradictions are never suppressed nor harmonized, but intensified so as to produce an art which subtly mocks its own deepest aspirations.

Before turning to Hawthorne's own work, it may prove helpful to consider one or two statements of this aesthetic principle as expressed by other writers. A particularly vivid instance occurs in D. H. Lawrence's *The Rainbow*, where Will and Anna Brangwen visit Lincoln Cathedral. Will is intoxicated by the triumphant assertion of the Gothic nave, but Anna finds most satisfaction in the little carved figure of the Lincoln Imp which seems to jeer at the whole grand design:

> These sly little faces peered out of the grand tide of the Cathedral like something that knew better. They knew quite well, these little imps that retorted on man's own illusion, that the Cathedral was not absolute. They winked and leered, giving suggestion of the many things that had been left out of the great concept of the church.
>
> 'However much there is inside here, there's a good deal they haven't got in', the little faces mocked.

Diabolical little faces also seem to peep out of the odd corners of Hawthorne's best stories with the same subversive intentions: they hint at the existence of a universe which is wider, more incalculable, more anarchic than that contained in the architectonic simplifications of art, philosophy or religion; and they imply a notion of art in which the grotesque is quite as important as the sublime or the inspiring.

Wallace Stevens presents a somewhat similar view, which further illuminates the case, in his poem 'A High-toned Old Christian Woman'. The woman (who is the silent recipient of his aesthetic monologue), like Will Brangwen, has just offered the mediaeval Gothic nave as the supreme example of what art should be aiming at. Stevens agrees up to a point, but reminds her that a chorus of satyrs parading their bawdiness uproariously before a classic peristyle may raise 'a jovial hullabaloo among the spheres' which is equally significant as art. Art indeed is particularly prone to take anarchic and unpredictable forms: 'this will make widows wince. But fictive things/ Wink as they will. Wink most when widows wince'. The idea that the essential spirit of a work of art may find expression as an impudent wink is close to certain elements in Hawthorne's fiction; and the disconcerting effect of laughter which is at once irreverent and cosmic, earthy yet rivalling the music of the spheres, is of central importance in some of his finest tales.

In Lawrence's *Studies in Classic American Literature,* we find not simply parallels with Hawthorne's method but direct comments upon it. His notorious discussion of the latter's duplicity —that tendency to hint at deeper and more disturbing truths than the surface of his writing appears to imply—is especially valuable. Lawrence condenses this theory into a derisive little rhyme: 'Old-fashioned Nathaniel, with his little boy charm,/He'll tell you what's what, but he'll cover it with smarm.'[2] In one sense this is monstrously unfair, but in another, it is perfectly accurate—to the extent that it draws attention to the existence of two conflicting levels of artistic truth in Hawthorne's fiction.

This pattern can be seen in a relatively simple form in 'Endicott and the Red Cross'. The Puritan Endicott's bold gesture of tearing the red cross from the royal banner is presented by Hawthorne as the first recorded public demonstration of American liberties, and an omen of the distant day when the Revolutionary War would set the country free, but the story is not chiefly memorable as a euphoric celebration of the national identity. Endicott claims to stand for civil rights and liberty of conscience, but his rule in Salem is harsh and over-bearing, and those subject to his authority—the wanton gospeller on the meeting-house steps, the Episcopalian in the pillory, the Royalist in the stocks, the adulteress with the scarlet letter on her breast, and even the gently reproachful figure of the minister Roger Williams—embody a satiric commentary upon his pretensions. One could say of him what Starbuck says of Captain Ahab: 'Horrible old man! Who's over him, he cries: —Ay, he would be a democrat to all above; look, how he lords it over all below!' Both Hawthorne and Melville were aware of the anomalies inherent in the national idea, but Hawthorne, at least, does not seem concerned to draw up any kind of moral balance sheet, to take the good with the bad in Endicott's character. He is much more interested in contrast than in synthesis: he does not wish to bring the story's diverse threads together, but to force its conflicting meanings as far apart as possible. This is why his most significant image is one of mocking reflection: Endicott's polished breastplate mirrors the people in the village street, particularly those who suffer from, or protest against his rule, so that a satirical allegory of his failings and inconsistencies is emblazoned on his own person. It is apparent that Hawthorne's art, far from reconciling these extremes, derives a grotesque vitality from their opposition, and it would not be too much to say that this is the source of all the dramatic and symbolic energy of 'Endicott and the Red Cross'. Without it, the tale would be a mere piece of nationalistic costume drama like the 'Legends of the Province House'.

There is a similar pattern of conflict in 'The Birthmark', but in this story the author's feelings seem to be far more deeply involved. However much Hawthorne cared for the idea of an American national identity, he was bound to feel personally implicated in quite a different way when he asserted the importance of the spirit of intellectual inquiry. Aylmer, it is true, is a scientist, but Hawthorne does not make the rigid separation between scientist and artist which is habitual to us: in his view, it is as necessary for the latter to uncover the secrets of the human heart as it is for the former to explore the mysteries of the universe. And so it follows that when he turns a mocking and disabused eye upon these activities, correspondingly powerful subversive forces are generated in his writing.

When he first conceived the idea for 'The Birthmark,' he saw Aylmer's quest as an unequivocally noble one. In a notebook memorandum, he wrote: 'a person to be the death of his beloved in trying to raise her to more than mortal perfection, yet this should be a comfort to him for having aimed so highly and holily.'[3] In the story itself, however, Hawthorne undermines this view of his hero so completely that it remains only as a fantastic mirage—a basis not for admiring Aylmer, but for measuring the scale of his illusions. His obsessive attempts to remove the one blemish which disfigures his wife's otherwise perfect beauty cost her her life—an outcome which can hardly be regarded with complacent optimism once the characters have taken shape. On the surface, Hawthorne seems to find a value in Aylmer's pallid intellectuality, but beneath, there is an undercurrent of hostility and ridicule which grows steadily in strength as the action proceeds. Aylmer is progressively devalued in every possible way: it becomes harder and harder to see his love for Georgiana as anything but a mockery of true feeling, and more and more difficult to take his scientific investigations seriously. Unlike Chillingworth and Rappaccini his overweening intellectual pride lacks all tragic dignity: he is fatuously self-deluded rather than grandly diabolic, and the story as a whole is not so much a transcendentalist fable as a savage farce. The folio volume in which Aylmer chronicles his researches is a record of empty ambition and humiliating failure, and there is a taint of absurdity in all the little experiments with which he seeks to impress Georgiana with his scientific skill: the miraculous flower withers in her grasp; and the daguerrotype in which he tries to capture her beauty succeeds only in reproducing with fearful distinctness the hated birthmark on her cheek. At the dénouement of the story this covert strain of ridicule becomes the dominant note: the sound of Hawthorne's perfunctory moralizing is drowned by 'the hoarse chuckling laugh' of Aminadab, the laboratory assistant who plays Caliban to Aylmer's Prospero.

At a deeper psychological level, 'The Birthmark' hints obscurely at Hawthorne's conflicting feelings towards women. Judith Fetterley, a recent feminist critic, has convincingly argued that to idealize feminine beauty as Aylmer does is to imply that woman as she actually exists is a monster.[4] This contradiction is at the heart of Hawthorne's vision of his two most striking women characters, Zenobia and Hester Prynne. It is clear from these portraits and from much other evidence to which I have already referred, that he both dreaded and desired the excitements of female sexuality: he dwells upon the attractions of these women with an almost prurient intensity, and at the same time punishes them for the power they exercise over the men who come within their influence. Of all the short stories in which this preoccupation appears, 'Rappaccini's Daughter' is by far the most successful.

This great and complex work has generally been discussed in terms of Hawthorne's reservations about the overweening curiosity and Faustian pride of the scientific investigator, and he certainly handles this material with impressive dramatic force. His profoundest imaginative energies, however, are

15

involved in the creation of Beatrice Rappaccini. It is the effect of her father's experiment on her, rather than the experiment itself, which concerns us most. By associating her from infancy with poisonous flowers, he has made poison her natural element and the central principle of her composition. Her physical presence is deadly to any being not imbued with the same essence, and yet, until she falls in love with Giovanni Guasconti, she is largely unaware of her sinister power, and she retains to the end a childlike innocence of character. During her final interview with her lover, at a moment of tragic self-discovery, she expresses what she now feels to be the truth about herself: 'For, Giovanni, believe it, though my body be nourished with poison, my spirit is God's creature, and craves love as its daily food.' Through love, she has acquired a new consciousness, a distorting mirror in which she sees her nature fatally divided between two mutually antagonistic principles: a divine spirit which inspires man, and a poisonous body which betrays him. Poison, throughout the story, is merely a metaphor for the power of sexual attraction. Giovanni himself, when he first sees Beatrice walking among the plants in her father's garden, thinks of her involuntarily as a beautiful but poisonous flower: 'For the impression which the fair stranger made upon him was as if here were another flower, the human sister of these vegetable ones, as beautiful as they—more beautiful than the richest of them—but still to be touched only with a glove, nor to be approached without a mask.' As he falls more and more under her influence, sexual desire, like a subtle poison, is instilled into his system, separating him, as she is separated, from the common run of human interests and feelings: ' "Accursed one", cried he, with venomous scorn and anger, "and finding thy solitude wearisome, thou hast severed me likewise from all the warmth of life and enticed me into thy region of unspeakable horror." ' Rappaccini himself is presented quite explicitly as the Adam of this sinister Eden: he has transmitted to his daughter not so much the secret influence of some vegetable poison, as the unregenerate physical nature of a fallen race.

This is undoubtedly Hawthorne's central theme, but it is presented with a marked degree of ambiguity and indirection even measured by the standards of his fiction. His deepest impulses are half-concealed beneath the circumstantial detail of a Gothic tale. He participates fully in Giovanni's growing sense of repugnance, and yet criticizes him for his coldness of heart. He does not contradict the horror and self-loathing with which Beatrice confronts the reality of her own body, and he accepts the rightness of her decision to die rather than live with the knowledge of that reality, and at the same time, portrays her as a tragically noble, almost saintly being. In Lawrence's terms, this is simply another case of Hawthorne's duplicity, but a more substantial explanation is surely needed to account for the indirections of a story as powerful as 'Rappaccini's Daughter'. It seems more accurate to say that Hawthorne is caught in the tension between two contradictory impulses: a determination to reveal what he has discovered, and a natural hesitation to be fully explicit about such disturbing psychological material. Ambiguity may become a necessary defence mechanism for a writer who has unearthed unpalatable emotions that threaten his sanity, or the coherence of the art form he is using, or the stability of his relations with his readers. This was certainly a common predicament of the American artist in the nineteenth century, and Whitman's 'Calamus' poems, in which the author feels impelled at once to reveal and to hide his homosexual inclinations, is an interesting parallel case. For Melville, the difficulty is not merely the result of contemporary cultural conditions, but is integral to the creation of the profoundest art, and a distinctive feature of the work of both Hawthorne and Shakespeare. Such a writer 'craftily says, or sometimes insinuates the things which we feel to be so terrifically true that it were all but madness for any good man in his own proper character, to utter, or even hint of them.'[5] In 'Rappaccini's Daughter', however, Hawthorne does not resort to this manoeuvre primarily as a form of self-defence, but uses it positively as a narrative technique which is essential to the success of the story. Viewed in this way, the insidious progress of the poison in Giovanni's system becomes a metaphor not only of his own involuntary surrender to the powerful sexuality of Beatrice, but also of Hawthorne's reluctant discovery of the true significance of his allegory.

Hawthorne betrays many misgivings about the role of the artist in 'Rappaccini's Daughter'. He begins the story with a disparaging account of its supposed author, a certain Monsieur de l'Aubépine, whose real identity (if we had any doubts on the subject) is indicated by the fact that his name is simply the French word for hawthorn. This ironic prefatory note helps us to recognize that Doctor Rappaccini's experiment places the work of the artist as well as that of the scientist in an equivocal light: his gesture of triumph when he sees Beatrice and Giovanni standing together at last in the same poisonous atmosphere is compared with the joy of a sculptor contemplating a completed statuary group. In view of Hawthorne's tendency to attack what he values most, it is not surprising to find that these and many other doubts are echoed in virtually all the tales about art and artists. Of these the best known are 'The Prophetic Pictures' and 'The Artist of the Beautiful'. I have preferred to discuss the latter since, unlike the former, it has been largely misunderstood, and is in any case more suited to my argument.

The principal character of the story, Owen Warland, after years of discouraging and secret toil, succeeds in embodying his conception of the beautiful in a marvellous contrivance, a mechanical butterfly which imitates the movements of the natural world, and surpasses it in loveliness. Most readers have seen this story as an ecstatic celebration of the romantic view of the artist, but Marius Bewley seems much nearer the mark when he speaks of the works Owen produces as 'horrid little things'.[6] Indeed at certain levels of implication, the tale is a ferocious satire on the transcendentalist aesthetic ideal. The vague and high-flown phrases in which Owen pictures his quest to himself bear the unmistakable stamp of transcendentalism, as does his notion that to imitate 'the beautiful movements of Nature such as the flight of birds' is to approach the essence of the beautiful. This image of flight is used frequently by both Emerson and Thoreau when discussing aesthetic problems, and Hawthorne's own generally derisive attitude towards transcendentalist thought is evident in many places, especially in 'The Celestial Railroad', though there the treatment is far more good-natured and relaxed than in the present instance. In 'The Artist of the Beautiful', he seems to be suspended between hatred and contempt for the enemies of art and for the portentous triviality of the artist himself. He condemns the 'cold unimaginative sagacity' of old Peter Hovenden, the practical businessman; and sees a subtler though no less dangerous betrayal in Peter's daughter Annie, whose promise of youthful fire fades rapidly into commonplace domesticity. Robert Danforth the blacksmith is a more complex case: Hawthorne deplores his earthy insensitivity, but at the same time sees in him Promethean energies which are entirely lacking in the effete Owen Warland. At the forge, Danforth 'spends his labour upon a reality', and there is no answer to his question, who would waste half a lifetime creating an artificial butterfly when he might catch a dozen such on a summer's afternoon. Owen's feelings, nevertheless, are sufficiently harrowing to give us a disturbingly authentic view of the agonies of the alienated artistic life. There can be little doubt that the conflict of values and emotions so habitual to Hawthorne reaches a unique level of intensity in this story. The dénouement is an extraordinary achievement, since it polarizes this conflict to an extreme degree and fixes it in the reader's mind. Owen takes the mechanical butterfly as a belated wedding gift to Annie, who has been married for several years to Robert Danforth, and now has a growing child. The toy is received by the family circle with a predictable mixture of scepticism and condescending admiration, but Owen's visit closes with a sudden and unforeseen disaster. Annie's child, wishing to play with the butterfly, snatches at it in mid-flight, and crushes it to powder in his hand. His action is both hateful and profoundly satisfying: it brings Hawthorne's antipathy towards the enemies of art to a point of climax, and at the same time it gives dramatic form to his suspicion that the artist is doomed to create much that is contemptibly trivial and insignificant.

A vein of equivocal humour is clearly an important element in the stories we have considered so far. In most of them it is an undercurrent, an aspect of the situation implied rather than stated, but in 'The Birthmark' Hawthorne brings it to the surface so that it becomes explicit and dramatic. The 'hoarse chuckling laugh' of Aminadab gives a sharp focus to sug-gestions diffused throughout the tale which might otherwise remain somewhat vague and ill-defined. Indeed it would not be too much to say that Hawthorne's understanding of the anarchic power of laughter is one of the most disturbing and creative of his gifts as a writer of fiction. Laughter in his work, far from being genial and benign, is a force that seems to sap the very foundations of things. Arthur Dimmesdale is consumed with interior laughter as he re-enters the town after his forest interview with Hester. He experiences an insane desire to whisper blasphemies into the ears of every passer-by: 'At every step, he was incited to do some strange, wild, wicked thing or other, with a sense that it would be at once involuntary and intentional, in spite of himself, yet growing out of a profounder self than that which opposed the impulse.' Hawthorne defines Dimmesdale's mental state with characteristic psychological precision: his anarchic impulse to destroy the respectable fabric of his relations with his flock wells up within him from an irrational second self which is only partially under his control. Even so, this interior world remains undetected until he meets the witch-lady Mistress Hibbins. She immediately recognizes him as a kindred spirit, and the real character of his hidden thoughts seems to become suddenly audible in her cackling laugh.

Hawthorne handles a somewhat similar situation in 'Egotism, or, The Bosom-Serpent'. This is, in general, a very weak story, especially towards the end, where it declines into sentimental fatuity, but there is a certain manic energy in the scenes where the madman Roderick Elliston bates and torments his fellow-townsmen. He believes that the hidden evil in every human heart takes the form of a serpent coiled within the bosom, and so he accosts each person that he meets by placing a hand on his victim's breast and enquiring with a mocking inflection in his voice, 'How is the snake, today?'

The essence of Hawthorne's anarchic comedy, however, is not to be found in derisive words and gestures like those of Roderick Elliston, but in the disturbing dramatic reality of laughter itself. Aminadab and Mistress Hibbins, as we have seen, function in this way, but their laughter is only a marginal element in the works where they appear, adding a touch of the uncanny to subversive meanings which do not originate with them. By contrast, the destructive power of laughter is a central motive—perhaps the central motive—in two of Hawthorne's finest tales, 'Ethan Brand' and 'My Kinsman, Major Molineux'. He stresses the importance of this preoccupation quite early in the former story: 'Laughter, when out of place; mis-timed or bursting forth from a disordered state of feeling, may be the most terrible modulation of the human voice.' This is the essential truth of Hawthorne's allegory, and it need hardly be said that Ethan Brand's laugh is far more real than his sin, which would otherwise be little better than a moral and theological abstraction. If any evidence is required to prove that he has discovered and committed the unpardonable sin, it is to be found in his appalling laughter, not in obscure references to a forbidden intellectual quest, nor in the even slighter suggestions of a wicked psychological experiment performed upon the woman who had loved him. In this way, the terrible modulations of his voice gave authenticity to a situation which might well seem totally unconvincing, as well as providing the necessary element of dramatic intensity.

Brand's laugh also supplies the basic structure of events which gives the story form. Apart from the epilogue, where Bartram and Joe find Brand's calcined heart and skeleton in the lime-kiln, the entire action is framed between the first and last occasions when he laughs. He announces his return to his native valley with a peal of slow mirthless laughter, and he laughs again at the moment when he flings himself into the hell-mouth of the burning kiln. The two significant intermediate stages in the action are similarly indicated. On arriving at the kiln, Brand explains to Bartram that his search has ended where it began: after wandering through the world for eighteen years, he has found the unpardonable sin in his own heart, and as he tells his story, his laughter breaks out in an 'involuntary recognition' of the 'infinite absurdity' of his quest. His sense of the absurd is provoked by the pattern of his wasted life, which he now grasps fully for the first time. He had thought he was engaged in a vast cosmic journey through time and space, whereas in fact he was travelling along the circumference of a circle—a movement which gives the illusion of constant progress, although it is in reality constricted, always returning upon itself. Hawthorne was clearly fascinated by the notion of the circle as an image of futility, and made use of it in at least one other impressive story, 'Roger Malvin's Burial'. The same

NATHANIEL HAWTHORNE: NEW CRITICAL ESSAYS

image, accompanied once again by Brand's terrible laughter, provides a weird climax to the most elaborate scene in 'Ethan Brand' itself. Learning of the exile's return, a collection of village worthies climb the hill to the lime-kiln, and a carnival atmosphere develops around his silent figure. At the height of the merrymaking, a stray dog, excited by the din, begins to chase its own tail:

> But, now, all of a sudden, this grave and venerable quadruped, of his own mere notion, and without the slightest suggestion from anybody else, began to run round after his tail, which, to heighten the absurdity of the proceeding, was a great deal shorter than it should have been. Never was seen such headlong eagerness in pursuit of an object that could not possibly be attained; never was heard such a tremendous outbreak of growling, snarling, barking, and snapping—as if one end of the ridiculous brute's body were at most deadly and unforgivable enmity with the other. Faster and faster, round about went the cur; and faster and still faster fled the unapproachable brevity of his tail; and louder and fiercer grew his yells of rage and animosity; until, utterly exhausted, and as far from the goal as ever, the foolish old dog ceased his performance as suddenly as he had begun it. . . .
>
> As may be supposed, the exhibition was greeted with universal laughter, clapping of hands, and shouts of encore. To which the canine performer responded by wagging all that there was to wag of his tail, but appeared totally unable to repeat his very successful effort to amuse the spectators.
>
> Meanwhile, Ethan Brand had resumed his seat upon the log; and, moved it might be, by perception of some remote analogy between his own case and that of this self-pursuing cur, he broke into the awful laugh which, more than any other token, expressed the condition of his inward being. From that moment, the merriment of the party was at an end; they stood aghast, dreading lest the inauspicious sound should be reverberated around the horizon, and that mountain would thunder it to mountain, and so the horror be prolonged upon their ears.

The frenzied circular movement of the 'self-pursuing cur' is an apt image of Ethan Brand's own journey through life; and the 'awful laugh', which wells up from the depths of his soul as he perceives the analogy, seems to embody the very spirit of un-reason. To the appalled villagers it seems possible that this dreadful sound might grow in volume till it fills the valley. Magnified by their terror, it threatens to become the clamour of a universal nihilism.

A similar atmosphere pervades the climactic scene of 'My Kinsman, Major Molineux'. A wild shout of anarchic laughter surrounds the tarred and feathered figure of the Major as he and Robin meet at last in horrified recognition. The tumult of the mob implies the annihilation of all rationality and order, and Hawthorne seeks once more to universalize this feeling. Just as the sound of Ethan Brand's laugh spreads outwards beyond the immediate circle by the lime-kiln, until its thunder fills the surrounding landscape, so the laughter of the Major's persecutors is faintly heard by the man in the moon. To his ears, the uproar is softened by distance, so that he reflects complacently, 'The earth is frolicsome, tonight', but if the public humiliation of the Major is a frolic, it can only be the frolic of unreason. Thus far the two stories have a great deal in common, but in certain other ways they are very unlike. One fact in particular makes the structure and organization of 'My Kinsman, Major Molineux' quite different from those of 'Ethan Brand': the latter is concerned with the intermittent laughter of a single man, the former with the collective mockery of a whole city. Consequently, where it was possible for Hawthorne to write 'Ethan Brand' as a series of episodes, each marked by an outburst of the hero's laughter, it was necessary for him to construct 'My Kinsman, Major Molineux' as a complex narrative flow.

The structure of this tale bears a distinct resemblance to musical form, though its reverberations, needless to say, compose a highly discordant form of music—a symphony of mocking voices, a subtle orchestration of many subversive inflections.

When Robin comes to Boston in search of his wealthy and influential kinsman the Major, he is full of confidence—a confidence based on moral and political certainties. He is 'a good youth', the son of a country minister, with firm ideas of right and wrong. Still more, he is 'a shrewd youth' (a phrase which acquires an increasingly ironic meaning as the story proceeds) who feels he has a clear understanding of men and of the relations that exist between the classes. He knows—or

23

thinks he knows—that society is an immutably ordered hierarchy of the high and low in which the Major occupies an unquestioned position. These certainties are undermined, first for the reader, and then for Robin, by the laughing voices which echo along the nocturnal streets of the city.

Almost all Robin's attempts to obtain directions to his kinsman's house are met with derision: the 'ill-mannered roar of laughter' which follows his enquiries at the barber's shop; the inn-keeper's laugh, 'like the dropping of small stones in a kettle'; the 'pleasant titter' of the prostitute; and the 'drowsy laugh' of the watchman. Nevertheless, he stubbornly ignores the implications of their mockery, and in his self-confident rationality has no difficulty in finding an explanation for everything. Even when he meets the leader of the riot disguised in his devil-mask of red and black, he feels that, after a few minutes philosophical reflection, he can account for the man's bizarre appearance, 'shrewdly and rationally and satisfactorily'. Soon after this encounter, Robin falls asleep for a moment on the church steps where he is waiting for the Major to pass by, and during his short sleep he has a dream experience which effects a radical displacement in his mind. He seems to see his family back in the country at evening prayer, and when he awakens, the city is so strange and alien to him that he does not recover his confident grasp of its reality. He begins to feel that he has passed 'an evening of ambiguity and weariness', and as this perception enters his thoughts, he becomes increasingly aware of the mocking echoes which have surrounded him since his arrival. As the mob approaches, these echoes are blended in 'a wild and confused laughter', a discordant symphony of voices which reaches a deafening climax when the procession draws level with him. 'The shouts, the laughter, and the tuneless bray' are 'the antipodes of music', the negation of all harmony and order. Heralded by this fearful din, the tarred and feathered figure of the Major is an image of pure terror, the ultimate contradiction of the sureties which have sustained Robin till now. His bewilderment is greeted by a general shout of laughter in which every voice he has heard is individually distinct; and when he himself joins in, his own laugh, like Ethan Brand's, is an involuntary recognition of infinite absurdity. It is no wonder that he emerges from his experience pale and shaken, totally disorientated in his new environment. It is equally inevitable that the story should have an open ending: it is unlikely that Robin will return to the certainties of his country home, nor can we be sure that his 'shrewdness' will enable him to put together a new world-view out of the fragments of the old.

As a footnote to 'My Kinsman, Major Molineux', it is interesting to observe that Hawthorne's treatment of anarchic laughter has a cultural significance as well as the psychological and metaphysical implications which I have considered so far. The story is finely balanced between fantasy and realism, so that although the uproar is heard by the man in the moon, it is also firmly rooted in its time and place—in the boisterous hilarity of an American popular uprising. Because of this richness of local detail, the tale functions at one level within the tradition of American humour. Constance Rourke defines the salient characteristics of that tradition as 'grotesquerie and irreverence and upset',[7] and all these features are prominently displayed in Hawthorne's work. The folk-culture of eighteenth-century Boston as he portrays it has the earthy idiosyncratic quality of a Breughel and the activities of the mob are by definition rebellious and subversive. This secure grounding in the cultural and historical realities of American life is an important contributory factor to the greatness of the story.

Hawthorne is concerned with anarchic laughter because it is a source of power; it releases immense disruptive energies in the world of men, and analogous dramatic energies in the world of art. Whether in life or in art, it has the intimidating effect of exposing a hidden reality, a sense of the absurd in which comedy and terror are inextricably mingled. Melville, as we have seen, argued that the capacity to reveal this buried truth, however obscurely or indirectly, is perhaps the greatest gift which an artist can possess. In some of Hawthorne's most interesting stories about the creative process, the operations of this special insight seem to flicker as unpredictably as laughter through the artist's mind and through the works he produces. The deeper meaning of these tales is usually concealed beneath a whimsical and playful surface, as if the author were unwilling fully to acknowledge the view of the nature of art which they imply. He seems to suggest that the profoundest creative powers are closer to the spirit of anarchy than to any controlling sense of reason and order.

These preoccupations appear in an attractively light and witty form in 'The Devil in Manuscript'. This excellent story has none of the wispy insubstantial quality which is so characteristic of most of Hawthorne's shorter sketches, but is on the contrary taut, concentrated and extremely well-written. Oberon, a neglected author in a small New England town, is determined to burn his manuscripts in a flamboyant gesture of disgust. As each bundle of papers catches fire, his imaginative conceptions seem to leap up in flashes of flame or showers of sparks. The last package evidently contains some more profound and subversive ideas: it blazes up in the form of a fiery devil who grins and glares into the room, and then vanishes up the chimney with a roar. A moment later, the alarm is sounded—the house is alight, and the conflagration spreads rapidly, threatening to engulf the whole town. In a state of delirious excitement, Oberon rejoices that he has forced his fellow-citizens to take notice of him at last, and his exultant phrase, 'My brain has set the town on fire!' has a double implication. At a simple level, it expresses his satisfaction that he is revenged upon an unresponsive public. More interestingly, it suggests the anarchic power of art to leap from mind to mind, just as the fire rages from roof to roof of the author's native town.

A more insidious kind of humour, and a correspondingly subtler conception of art appear in 'Feathertop', a superbly witty and intelligent story which has never received its due. This, the last of Hawthorne's tales, takes so weary and cynical a view of the process of artistic creation, that it is tempting to regard it as the author's farewell to the writing of short fiction. Mother Rigby, a New England witch, starts one morning to make a scarecrow for her corn patch, when, seized by a sudden impulse, she decides to bring the figure to life with the aid of diabolic powers. She breathes into it a semblance of animation by making it smoke her pipe. It walks, though with a hitch in its gait that reminds one of the dry sticks which make up its skeleton; and it talks, though only in the emptiest clichés. Its rags are transformed into fashionable clothes, and Mother

Rigby, consumed with bitter merriment, sends it to the town to deceive the people with its fine appearance. By this point in the story it is clear that her magic tricks are a burlesque of the process of artistic creation. As the result of a Faustian compact with the devil, she has breathed life into a thing of shreds and patches—a situation which, Hawthorne explicitly informs us, does not differ in essentials from that of any writer of romances. The tobacco smoke which Feathertop inhales—what enables him to mimic the movements of a living man—is a fine satiric detail: it is a covert reference on Hawthorne's part to that image of the wind of inspiration which recurs so insistently in Romantic aesthetic theory. Hawthorne himself calls the animated scarecrow 'a work of art', but in the context of the story this phrase has so ironic an implication that, far from dignifying the work of Mother Rigby, it merely serves to devalue the idea of art. There is indeed a strong undercurrent of suggestion that created fictions are no better than miscellaneous rubbish masquerading as reality, and this pessimistic reading is supported by the dénouement of the tale. Tired of his own existence, Feathertop returns to Mother Rigby's cottage, and expires at her feet. The witch is tempted to revive him, but she too is weary: her freak of fancy—as arbitrary as the artistic impulse itself—is extinct, and she decides that Feathertop will do best as a simple scarecrow after all.

In this way, Hawthorne's view of the fitful nature of creativity differs interestingly from that of most other nineteenth-century writers. Coleridge and Shelley, for instance, invoke the wind of inspiration with tragic fervour. Hawthorne, whose Romantic leanings are always qualified by his eighteenth-century rationalism, regards the impulse rather with an ironic detachment composed equally of amusement and apprehension. For him, the arbitrary inclination, the unexpected turn, the indirect approach, even the whimsical and the frivolous, are inescapable elements in the creative process. At the beginning of 'Monsieur du Miroir', a weak sketch which nevertheless contains some penetrating remarks on this question, he writes: 'Nor let the reader condemn any part of the narrative as frivolous, since the subject of such grave reflections diffuses its importance through the minutest particulars; and there is no judging beforehand what odd little circumstance may do the office of a blind man's

27

dog among the perplexities of this dark investigation.' From this point of view, Wakefield, in the story which bears his name, may be regarded as a sort of debased artist: he decides to play a little psychological experiment on his wife, a whimsical fancy only intended to last a few days, but which in the event projects him into an alienated unreal existence for twenty years.

The best of all Hawthorne's stories about the wayward nature of the artistic impulse, however, is 'Drowne's Wooden Image'. Drowne is a stolid and unimaginative woodcarver, a maker of ships' figureheads which, whether they represent George III, Britannia or Admiral Vernon, are all comically lifeless. But, just once in his career, inspired by the beauty of a Portuguese lady whom he has been commissioned to take as a model, he executes a work of genius. The power of creation seizes him mysteriously like witchcraft, playing havoc with his emotions, disrupting his relations with his fellow-citizens, and then leaving him as unpredictably as it came. He describes the moment of inspiration to his friend the painter Copley in terms which suggest both its sudden onset and its inexplicable character: 'A well-spring of inward wisdom gushed within me, as I wrought upon the oak with my whole strength, and soul, and faith.' There is a striking parallel between Drowne's account here and Kenyon's description in *The Marble Faun* of how he carved his statue of Cleopatra 'It is the concretion of a good deal of thought, emotion, and toil of brain and hand, . . . but I know not how it came about at last. I kindled a great fire within my mind, and threw in the material as Aaron threw the gold of the Israelites into the furnace, and in the midmost heat up rose Cleopatra as you see her.'

Although these statements are very much alike, there is no real similarity between Drowne and Kenyon, and it seems to me that Hawthorne's treatment of the former is far more interesting. Kenyon is presented more or less in accordance with the orthodox Romantic aesthetic: he is a committed artist, intelligent and earnest, rewarded for his pains with occasional moments of creative frenzy. Drowne, on the other hand, is a splendid grotesque, a comic folk-figure, who is normally as insensible as any wooden effigy in his workshop. His brief flowering as an artist is an inexplicable and absurd phenomenon. It is as if one of his own blocks of oak suddenly came to life—an image which Hawthorne actually uses with the greatest subtlety and humour. The wooden carving of the Portuguese lady becomes familiar to the townspeople as they see it taking shape under the strokes of Drowne's chisel, but they never see the model herself, nor even dream of her existence, since she is kept hidden by her protector Captain Honeywell. When she finally appears on the street, as if by supernatural means, it seems for a moment that Drowne's creative inspiration has achieved the ultimate triumph of breathing life into inanimate matter.

I began this essay by suggesting that the spirit of anarchy, which is so apparent in most of the best of Hawthorne's short stories, complicates his view of life, and underlies his conception of art. In 'The Devil in Manuscript', 'Feathertop' and 'Drowne's Wooden Image', this conception becomes more or less explicit: here one may say, echoing Wallace Stevens's felicitous phrase, that 'Fictive things wink as they will.' These subversive undercurrents, however, do not produce any effects of chaos or incoherence on the surface of Hawthorne's writing, and the paradox of his artistic success seems to lie in his ability to invoke the powers of unreason, and then contain them within the bounds of an aesthetic order. Lawrence's composite image of Lincoln Cathedral and the Lincoln Imp offers a precisely parallel case: the little face which leers from the stonework negates the principles on which the church is founded, but is nevertheless contained within its grand design. It is Hawthorne's particular achievement to hold this sense of balanced contraries before him more clearly than almost any other writer of fiction.

NOTES

1. Edward Wagenknecht, *Nathaniel Hawthorne: Man and Writer* (New York, 1961): see especially the chapters 'The Citizen' and 'The Fire in the Members'.
2. D. H. Lawrence, *Studies in Classic American Literature* (London, 1964), p. 91.
3. Quoted by Richard Harter Fogle, *Hawthorne's Fiction: The Light and the Dark* (Norman, Oklahoma, 1964), p. 128.
4. Judith Fetterley, *The Resisting Reader: A Feminist Approach to American Fiction* (Bloomington, Indiana, 1978), pp. 22-33.

5. Herman Melville, 'Hawthorne and his Mosses', *Works,* vol. 13 (New York: Russell and Russell), p. 130.
6. Marius Bewley, *The Eccentric Design: Form in the Classic American Novel* (London, 1959), p. 135.
7. Constance Rourke, *American Humor* (New York: Doubleday Anchor Books, 1953) p. 63.

2

Towards Romance: The Case of 'Roger Malvin's Burial'

by HAROLD BEAVER

In his review of Hawthorne's *Twice-Told Tales*, Poe made a notorious claim. He argued that in the 'brief tale' a writer must aim at 'a certain *single effect*' based on 'one pre-established design'. What is more: 'If his very first sentence tend not to the outbringing of this effect, then in his very first step has he committed a blunder.' How true is this of Hawthorne? His designs were certainly calculated; but his effects, far from single, are usually iridescent with ambiguity. The more obvious the allegorical pointers, the more open the (theological or scientific) clues, the more evasive seems the preconceived finale. Fiction, for Hawthorne, was by its very nature foxy: a way of presenting, but also of disguising, the truth. Fancy, magic, including all forms of spiritualism and the supernatural even, were ultimately will-o'-the-wisps on a frontier between history and the imagination. This shadow-land of 'romance'—this no man's land—he first explored, in the full power of his maturity, in 'Roger Malvin's Burial' (1832).[1]

I shall quote not only the first sentence, then, but the whole opening paragraph which acts as prologue to that tale:

> One of the few incidents of Indian warfare naturally susceptible of the moonlight of romance was that expedition undertaken for the defense of the frontiers in the year 1725, which resulted in the

31

NATHANIEL HAWTHORNE: NEW CRITICAL ESSAYS

well-remembered 'Lovell's Fight'. Imagination, by casting
certain circumstances judicially into the shade, may see much to
admire in the heroism of a little band who gave battle to twice
their number in the heart of the enemy's country. The open
bravery displayed by both parties was in accordance with
civilized ideas of valor; and chivalry itself might not blush to
record the deeds of one or two individuals. The battle, though so
fatal to those who fought, was not unfortunate in its consequences to the country; for it broke the strength of a tribe and
conduced to the peace which subsisted during several ensuing
years. History and tradition are unusually minute in their
memorials of this affair; and the captain of a scouting party of
frontier men has acquired as actual a military renown as many a
victorious leader of thousands. Some of the incidents contained
in the following pages will be recognized, notwithstanding the
substitution of fictitious names, by such as have heard, from old
men's lips, the fate of the few combatants who were in a condition
to retreat after 'Lovell's Fight'.

The first hiccup is 'naturally': 'One of the few incidents
of Indian warfare naturally susceptible of the moonlight of
romance . . .' Why 'naturally'? For something assumed to be
'natural', within a certain cultural convention, implies the very
opposite of 'natural'. Behind that opening, in fact, lurks a
gnomic code, as Barthes would call it, ready to identify what
constitutes 'heroism' as well as 'romance'. The very first move
assumes two interconnected responses: one, a general reaction
to an incident in the Indian Wars of 1725 that is still 'well-
remembered' and so 'naturally' remembered as heroic; two, a
specific authorial insistence that such an incident is 'naturally'
fit for literary elaboration. (The two purposes are semantically
linked by a transition from Latin to Anglo-Saxon: an expedition
'undertaken' for defensive purposes being naturally
'susceptible' of romantic purposes.)
  Further paradoxes abound around that central core. It was a
defensive expedition, yet fought 'in the heart' of hostile
territory—victorious, too, against all odds. Such defensive
attacks make a suitable subject for fiction, but only when subjected to 'the moonlight of romance', when viewed (that is to
say) in a certain reflected, or borrowed, light. The facts of the
frontier expeditionary force of 1725—the open, sunlit account,

so to speak—must be bounced off another cooler, inherently darker and foreign medium: the 'imagination' whose function, we learn, is to arbitrate, to be judicious, in an almost theatrical sense, by *casting* 'certain circumstances' into a *chiaroscuro* of moral light and shade. It is both a *visionary* quality, that 'may see much to admire', and *judicial* in the most orthodox way.

Without a vestige of history, there can be no heroic romance. The opening sentence both makes a symbolic notation of the convention and points to its infrequent applicability. For romance must be—in part, at least—responsible to the record: that little band of colonists facing odds of two to one. The gnomic code thus sketched is complex, though it has something to do with the relation of history to literature. Literature, in this sense, is concerned with a subject that is both 'natural' to remember and 'natural' to celebrate—'naturally' structured somehow for processing by the creative imagination. It operates 'naturally', it seems, on a frontier: not only on the colonial frontier of New England's Indian Wars, but on a symbolic frontier between sunlight and moonlight, on a romantic frontier between fact and fantasy, on a moral frontier between light and shade, on a judicial frontier between head and heart. Both the first sentence and whole first paragraph are resolved in an oxymoron which labels this defensive war, waged in the name of a bellicose Puritanism, 'Lovell's Fight'.

There can be no story, then, without history; but equally, as it turns out, no history without stories. At the core of the confusion are the contradictions inherent in the opening adverb ('naturally', of the first sentence) echoed by its complement ('judicially', of the second). Yet the two words seem almost interchangeable. For what is 'naturally susceptible' of romance is intellectually and morally susceptible. Just as imagination 'naturally' casts certain circumstances into the shade in order to highlight the effects of heroism. On this Anglo-Indian frontier nature and dogma not only meet, but are ineluctably intertwined. Not only is literary convention seen as an aspect of nature, but nature itself (in the final apocalypse of the withered oak bough) will take on the signs of literary convention.

The display of bravery, from the start, is judged 'in accordance with civilized ideas'. The codes of civilization (dogma or convention) are uppermost. Whatever the insistence on moonlight and that shadowed 'heart' of alien darkness, the bravery is 'open', not covert, and natural in that sense; yet it is somehow not 'in accordance' with *savage* ideas of valour. 'Civilized ideas' seems a pleonasm in this context. Civilization *is* ideas; ideas equal civilization. Indians, by their very nature, are excluded from the gnomic code (here announced under the name of 'chivalry'). If worthy of judicious admiration, their conduct—however incongruous or paradoxical the effect—must be incorporated within white conventions, white discourse, white pretentions to moral supremacy. The line between nature and culture may be shadowy, but there is only *one* standard of culture and that is constantly encroaching on and eroding and expropriating the preserves of nature. No Indian 'ideas of valor' are possible on this frontier, since Indian ideas are, by definition, a contradiction in terms and so incapable of moral distinction.

Such, naturally, are the aims of orthodoxy: to define what is 'natural'; then to pronounce itself, in the final stages of the take-over, as solely and wholly 'natural'. This is the origin here of a constant, ambiguous reversal of terms. If culture is natural, then nature too may be presumed to foreshadow or display the occasional orthodoxies of culture. It looks like a two-way traffic, but is actually a skilled, if nervous, game of solitaire in one man's hands, for whom savage warfare (in this instance) must be 'naturally' appropriated to the literary controls of romance. So the whole game of literature, it may be presumed, is 'naturally' structured for the conversion of sunlight to moonlight, fact to fantasy, heart to head.

Hawthorne is a master of that conversion, ambiguously pretending to be lost on that shadowy frontier, yet cumulatively resolving the tension in favour of 'civilized' values of his gnomic code. But never with commonplace assurance. Never with glee. He painfully perpetuates his dithering. He prefers to pretend that he is still lost. He dives back for cover into the dark. His saving grace is the *guilt* that he nurtures at his betrayal—at the necessary resolution—of these tensions on the American frontier. It lies at the origin of his style: at once orthodox in its loyalties (where 'the country' equals the Commonwealth of Massachusetts and 'peace' is interpreted solely in terms of the white settlements) and self-deprecatory in tone. The authorial voice, that is, attempts both to be assertive and to conceal that assertion by euphemism, denials, and double negatives: 'chivalry itself might not blush'; the battle 'was not unfortunate'; 'notwithstanding the substitution of fictitious names'. It dodges through the issues of chivalry and valour, colonist and Indian, history and fiction. It smudges the language with explicit negations and sonorous latinity: 'not unfortunate in its consequences to the country' that 'conduced to the peace which subsisted . . .' Yet it can chop through that studied assonance with one sharp phrase: 'it broke the strength of a tribe.' If the Latin suggests the imperial destiny of American settlement, then the Anglo-Saxon counters with the brutality of the facts.

But what are the facts? No names are given, not even of 'one or two individuals'. No Indian tribe is named. There is an insistence on 'history', on 'record', on minute 'memorials'; yet all that can be deduced is that in 1725 one Lovell was 'the captain of a scouting party of frontier men'. Even the concept of history is smudged by its juxtaposition (and identification) with oral tradition. A multiple metamorphosis is emphasized in tapering the larger considerations of the prologue to the exigencies of this tale. Only a remnant of a remnant survived: in the first place, the scouting party was small; in the second place, of that small band only a 'few combatants' were in a condition to retreat; in the third place, their fate was condensed to oral narratives, handed down from generation to generation; in the fourth place, that tradition is now the preserve of a minority of 'old men'; in the fifth place, it has been transformed yet again, by the intervention of the author, with his 'substitution of fictitious names'. If the tone, the language, the rhetoric is smudged, so finally, by this five-fold transformation and diminution, is the identity between fact and fancy, this story and history.

That slide area, linking history and fantasy, Hawthorne calls 'romance'. To oral tradition we are indebted to just four facts: that Lovell was the captain of a scouting party; that the New England frontiersmen were outnumbered two to one; that they broke the strength of an Indian tribe; and ensured peace for several years. That factual bundle is known and dated as 'Lovell's Fight' (1725). To imagination we owe a dim reflection of those facts, tangentially lit, known and dated as 'Roger

35

Malvin's Burial' (1832). Moonlit reflection, it turns out, is partly a matter of suppression, or possibly distortion ('casting into the shade'), and partly of fictitious substitution. For if the norm of history is a minute record (of 'military renown'), the norm of imagination is dictated by literary forms: both those of heroic epic ('open bravery . . . in accordance with civilized ideas of valor') and medieval chivalry. If an historical incident may be 'naturally' romantic, a romance must be 'judicially' imaginative. This shadowland on an ethnic frontier is cross-hatched with a deliberate confusion of genres; its aesthetic surface marked by relentless alliteration.

The 'moonlight' of the introduction is immediately followed by sunlight in the forest:

> The early sunbeams hovered cheerfully upon the tree-tops, beneath which two weary and wounded men had stretched their limbs the night before. Their bed of withered oak leaves was strewn upon the small level space, at the foot of a rock, situated near the summit of one of the gentle swells by which the face of the country is there diversified. The mass of granite, rearing its smooth, flat surface fifteen or twenty feet above their heads, was not unlike a gigantic gravestone, upon which the veins seemed to form an inscription in forgotten characters.

It is the art of romance that is moonlit, not the romantic narrative itself. This presents new antitheses, new symbolic doublings and superimpositions. After the prologue, the narrative proper is divided into four parts: 1: the wilderness (centred on the fate of Roger Malvin); 2: the return to the settlement (centred on Reuben Bourne and Dorcas Malvin); 3: the return to the wilderness eighteen years later (centred on Reuben Bourne); 4: death and resolution (centred on Dorcas Bourne). Its circular pattern of *aller et retour* is as artfully constructed as the flight of a boomerang. The whole story is based on a series of cycles, separated by roughly twenty years, like the Indian wars that periodically flare up and die. First young Roger and his friend escape Indian captivity near Montreal; then young Reuben seeks help for the dying Roger; then the fifteen-year-old Cyrus is shot on the very spot where Roger died.

The backward focus is itself ideological, implying a contrast between the expanding New England frontiers of the 1720s and the contemporary south-western frontier of the 1830s, between the reckless policies of President Jackson and the puritan values of barely a century earlier. For the literary frontier turns out to be a symbolic frontier; and as the symbolic frontier is superimposed on the historical (Anglo-Indian or ethnic) frontier, so a psychological frontier is superimposed on the symbolic frontier, a moral frontier on the psychological frontier, and a biblical frontier (evoking *Exodus*) finally on the moral frontier.

The key remains 'imagination', now metamorphosed into its eighteenth-century guise of 'fancy'. Reuben Bourne is the sleepwalker between the social world and the wilderness, where 'dreaming fancy' (of conflict) turns to the 'haunting and torturing fancy' (of an undiscovered crime). He is overcome by dreams. We first meet him mid-way between dreaming and waking, when a shout 'found its way in an imperfect murmur to his lips'. That self-contradictory shout, which is both soft and loud, is the psychological mark of the frontier. He is fully awakened only at the end when the trance is dissipated and transferred: to his son 'asleep, but dreamless, upon the fallen forest leaves' and his wife sinking 'insensible by the side of her dead boy'. Her final 'shriek' echoes his first deep 'shout', that final vision, his earlier 'vision of the conflict of which he was one of the few survivors'. For from a military no man's land Reuben Bourne has sleepwalked, it seems, into a moral no man's land. Or rather Hawthorne has transformed the historical frontier into a psychological, even criminal frontier.

That 'rock' is both tombstone and hieroglyph, the site both of 'burial' and suppression. That symbolism never shifts. It is rock-hard. As it first appears 'not unlike a gigantic gravestone' (in part 1), so it reappears, unresolved, 'not unlike a gigantic gravestone' (in part 3). Though inscribed with mysterious hieroglyphs that cannot be read, it demands to be read. It issues a challenge. The reader must try to decipher its lines. His is an interpretative quest. However impervious-seeming the tale, in its inturned recyclings and mirror imagery, it is the reader's task to penetrate that haunting fancy, which is art. The proferred meaning may not be the only meaning. The pre-established design may be to transcend a *'single effect'*. Far from being some kind of allegory, or biblical parable even, 'Roger Malvin's Burial' cries out to be read as a psychological text to

37

which a symbolic code is key. But then it is a countercode, as surreptitious and subversive ultimately as every other element of this tale, which turn and turn about subverts and is subverted by another.

The rhetorical figures which underline this subversion, creating a constant hover of uncertainty, are those of litotes or meiosis. The text is left forever ajar. It is never quite closed: the rock was 'not unlike a gigantic gravestone'; 'nor can it be affirmed that no selfish feeling strove to enter'; a 'brave man does not shrink in the battle'; 'I am a man of no weak heart'; though 'I will urge no selfish motive'; a mournful smile 'was not without its effect on Rueben'; 'no merely selfish motive . . . could have induced him'; 'friends are not far distant'; 'though no party may range so far into the woods'; this 'precaution was not unnecessary'; 'nor can it be denied that his intervals of industrious attention . . . were but scantily rewarded', etc. It is as if words were both used and not used, as if they were both presented and deleted, in a single ambiguous gesture that leaves both the initial gesture and its cancellation, both the name and its antonym, simultaneously legible. In Derrida's phrase, such terms are used *sous rature*: they are both visible and visibly rejected, both stated and contradicted, both presented and subverted, in an amalgam that is both 'x' and 'not-x', both concept (on some paradigmatic register) and its antithesis (or trace) that makes such a concept conceivable in the first place.

History and imagination, in apposition, are transformed, once the story opens, to a contrast of light and shade. Sunlit nature looks down on the shadowland of men: a cheerful hovering in treetops above is confronted by a weary stretching of limbs in leaves below. A grey-haired, muscular old man, who painfully rears himself up, confronts a smooth, flat, granite rock rearing to fifteen or twenty feet above his head; his deeply lined countenance is mirrored by an inscription. This cross-hatched area of symbolic interpenetration, of symbolic duplication and puns, I repeat, is the zone of 'romance'. It is a paradoxical zone between light and shade, between sleeping and waking, between visionary conflicts and conflicting visions, where an engraved stone that defies reading may mysteriously be turned to a 'gravestone'.

But nature, however sunlit, is also wild: a 'howling

wilderness', a 'trackless forest'. These shadowy men, however wounded, also represent civilization. The settlement offers its colonists the social stability of their hearths. Roger Malvin is prepared to die as long as he may be sure of eventual burial. For though the wilderness is a place of natural and savage bounty (of 'berries and other spontaneous products'), it is also a place of Indian bullets and concealment 'by the dense undergrowth'. Only society can transform the burden of a body to the weight of a dying wish. Only society digs graves: 'In the cities and wherever men dwell, they bury their dead in the earth; they hide them from the sight of the living.'

For the language of men is that of symbols (the bloodstained bandage as pledge of a vow) as well as of verbal signs (Roger's dying request, Reuben's promise, Roger's blessing and prayer). Above all, that of social rites: 'An almost superstitious regard . . . was paid by the frontier inhabitants to the rites of sepulture.' Yet even the frontier is symbolically marked. It is a semantic wilderness marked by both white and Indian hands. One inscription is that of the mutilation of corpses, though this record judicially withholds the brute facts of scalping and of castration. Another is Reuben's handkerchief, bound to the oak sapling, that links the treetops of the opening with men's hands, by converting a tree into a sign. Another is Roger's dying vow: 'I have loved you like a father,' he says,

> wherefore should I not rest beneath the open sky, covered only by the oak leaves when the autumn winds shall strew them? And for a monument, here is this gray rock, on which my dying hand shall carve the name of Roger Malvin; and the traveler in days to come will know that here sleeps a hunter and a warrior.

For if wilderness, in Roger's eyes, ultimately stands for exposure and candid exposition without sin or shame, settlement antithetically stands for rites of concealment, of suppression and self-suppression. *There* is the place of sin, with its shame of hidden promises and hidden corpses and hidden vows.

The frontier, for Reuben, is the ambiguous zone, a middle ground without sin exactly, merely the 'consciousness' of 'selfish feeling', of a 'selfish love of life'. Reuben acts as a deserter who distrusts his own motives (whether in contacting

Dorcas or a search party), while instinctively acknowledging the need for sacrifice and self-sacrifice. In this perverse moral zone 'a sort of guilty feeling'—'conscience, or something in its similitude'—caused Reuben 'to seek concealment from Malvin's eyes'. So he plays the voyeur, gazing 'earnestly', with a repressed Oedipal itch to see his 'father' die. He hides 'from the sight of the living'. In that repression he inaugurates his own self-burial.

Hawthorne's most obvious symbolism, counterpointing these rites of suppression and self-suppression, is that of the unclouded and clouded sun, of the open and secretive eye. In the wilderness the sun is unclouded; the prophetic vision in Roger's dying eyes kindles a light in Reuben's eye. But, homeward bound, the sun is clouded, just as Reuben had averted his gaze and received Roger's parting words 'with downcast eyes'. For a spontaneous moral bond, it seems, holds only in the wilderness and between males. The very prospect of home—of a return to women and domestication at the hearth and in the family—triggers the first in a long chain of the most devastating neurotic symptoms.

Part 2 opens with Reuben's collapse into total physical stasis: 'it was only through absolute incapacity of motion that he at last sank down beneath a tree.' Did he swoon? Was he speechless? Were no questions asked by the relief party? (The text yet again withholds the answers.) Once at home, he returns to another 'unquiet sleep'—to that wavering no man's land between waking and sleeping, life and death—in a state of shock: 'Reuben's recollections strayed drowsily among the perils . . .' But there was no avoiding the language of men: 'inquiries', 'definite answers', 'authentic particulars', gossip and praise. Confronted with the thought of desertion, he resorts to desperate self-concealment. His 'first impulse was to cover his face', later to sink back and hide 'his face in the pillow'. He confounds Dorcas's question by semantic evasion:

> 'You dug a grave for my poor father in the wilderness, Reuben?' was the question by which her filial piety manifested itself.
>
> 'My hands were weak; but I did what I could,' replied the youth in a smothered tone. 'There stands a noble tombstone above his head; and I would to Heaven I slept as soundly as he!'

Art, by this protestant ethic, is exposed as a self-protective device, an ambiguous cover for sin. *That* is the turning-point of Hawthorne's romance. Aesthetic ambiguity presents a threat precisely because it prefers symbolic coherence (of the text) over the truth (of events). Reuben's unspoken lie, by casting 'certain circumstances judicially into the shade', creates a fiction, something that never happened, Roger Malvin's burial.

Ellipsis, here, creates not only a fiction but a tale-within-a-tale which ironically bears the very title of the tale we are reading:

> The tale of Reuben's courage and fidelity lost nothing when she communicated it to her friends; and the poor youth, tottering from his sick chamber to breathe the sunny air, experienced from every tongue the miserable and humiliating torture of unmerited praise. All acknowledged that he might worthily demand the hand of the fair maiden to whose father he had been 'faithful unto death'; and, as my tale is not of love, it shall suffice to say that in the space of a few months, Reuben became the husband of Dorcas Malvin.

That 'incommunicable thought', concealed from her whom he most trusted and loved, is elevated to the status of a criminal offence. 'By a certain association of ideas, he at times almost imagined himself a murderer.'

Reuben Bourne is now consumed by the imagination, that dim reflection of events operating by suppression and substitution. His is no longer a 'dreaming fancy', but a fancy of art, a waking dream, 'a haunting and torturing fancy'. That 'shout—deep and loud in his dreaming fancy' is transformed to 'a voice audible only to himself'. He has wholly appropriated and internalized the rite of burial until Roger Malvin lies entombed in Reuben Bourne. Such is the force of the fiction which is 'Roger Malvin's Burial'. Away from the wilderness Reuben Bourne is necessarily locked in paralysis. No wonder he is changed 'into a sad and downcast yet irritable man'. With that corpse festering inside him, no wonder he declines into moody misanthropy with 'downcast eye'. Utterly inturned, utterly 'insulated', all surfaces become mirrors; all reflections, self-reflections: 'and he could no longer love deeply except where he saw or imagined some reflection or likeness of his own mind.' So the artistic imagination is revealed as a criminal imagination, the criminal imagination as a narcissistic imagination, especially in so close a relationship as that between father and son.

A two-month pioneering expedition cannot lift the doom. Felling and burning timber on this symbolic frontier, far from throwing 'sunlight into some deep recess of the forest', merely seals his doom. For the journey back is now a journey within. Hawthorne's 'howling wilderness' is now a psychological wilderness. Any attempt to push the frontier forward—for the preservation of life and liberty and the pursuit of happiness—had long been undermined. There was no exodus to Eden, no Promised Land where 'peace would throw its sunlight into the sepulcher of his heart.' The lapsed Puritan cannot hope to resolve his moral crisis by pioneering.

But the Bournes are trapped. They have nowhere else to turn. They are forced into pioneering. They are forced back to that twilit, visionary zone, which is the zone of romance.

> Oh, who, in the enthusiasm of a daydream, has not wished that he were a wanderer in a world of summer wilderness, with one fair and gentle being hanging lightly on his arm? In youth his free and exulting step would know no barrier but the rolling ocean or the snow-topped mountains; calmer manhood would choose a home where Nature had strewn a double wealth in the vale of some transparent stream; and when hoary age, after long, long years of that pure life, stole on and found him there, it would find him the father of a race, the patriarch of a people, the founder of a mighty nation yet to be. When death, like the sweet sleep which we welcome after a day of happiness, came over him, his far descendants would mourn over the venerated dust. Enveloped by tradition in mysterious attributes, the men of future generations would call him godlike; and remote posterity would see him standing, dimly glorious, far up the valley of a hundred centuries.

Such is the ironic voice of the text, contrasting its romantic ideal with Reuben as spurious dreamer. The vision is patriarchal: part Job, part Washington, part Daniel Boone. It is a pastoral vision for hunters 'on the bank of some unpolluted' brook, whose fancy has turned the wilderness itself into a 'dreamer's land of fantasy'. Into this perverse semantic zone (of the forest eclogue) the Bournes wander with their muskets and axes. It is a zone literally of sleepwalkers drifting away 'into a region of which savage beasts and savage men were as yet the sole possessors'. But it is also a psychological zone of the criminal's instinctive return to the scene of his crime, casting his eyes back 'as if in fear of some pursuer'. There the Bournes establish a home in the wilderness (that ultimate oxymoron) with its pot on the fire, its Massachusetts Almanac and Bible. The 'wild and romantic spot' reflects their uneasy, affectionate equilibrium. 'There is something chilling, and yet heart-warming,' the text proposes, 'in the thought of these three, united by strong bands of love and insulated from all that breathe beside.'

As the 'howling wilderness', on this symbolic frontier, had long been turned into a psychological wilderness, so the psychological wilderness is now reflected in the swelling landscape like 'huge waves of a petrified sea'. Everything is enfolded and duplicated. Where the rock reared its smooth flat surface and the dying Roger had painfully reared himself upright, the family now 'reared their hut'. Where Roger had lifted his hands 'in a fervent prayer', Reuben can now only repeat a desperate 'Pray Heaven . . . pray Heaven!' As a premonition of the moment of catharsis 'a pitying sound was heard in the forest; or did those old trees groan in fear that men were come to lay the axe to their roots at last?' Now the spell is to be broken, the branches creak and rustle as if the forest too 'were waking from slumber'.

But first the fiction must be repeated; the romance within the romance, restated. For it is not the exposure of Reuben's hypocrisy that will resolve Hawthorne's romance, as might be expected. Rather it is the resolution of the romance that will expunge the hypocrisy. The sin, such as it was, will never be confessed or revealed. Dorcas, who faints, will never discover the truth of her father's burial. Only art can refashion art. Only by a second fiction, however intricate, can the original fiction be neutralized and defused.

The text is circular. As the sleepwalker's steps, in their 'devious course', lead 'almost in a circle', so the tale comes full circle. Not only Roger Malvin's burial, but the whole wilderness is now internalized with a biblical flourish:

43

Unable to penetrate to the secret place of his soul where his motives lay hidden, he believed that a supernatural voice had called him onward, and that a supernatural power had obstructed his retreat. He trusted that it was Heaven's intent to afford him an opportunity of expiating his sin; he hoped that he might find the bones so long unburied; and that, having laid the earth over them, peace would throw its sunlight into the sepulcher of his heart.

That original stasis has been transformed to a total and impenetrable block. That original shout (in his dreams) that had turned to a 'voice audible only to himself' (of conscience) has finally—desperately—turned supernatural. Perhaps as the Israelites were led by the Lord through the wilderness, so the hardships of this journey were part of a divine plan to purge him of his iniquities.

His hunter's eye was still keen. Piercing 'behind a thick veil of undergrowth, he fired, with the instinct of a hunter.' At that moment the voice is released in 'a low moan'. For the shot acts both internally and externally. It is both mirror and hieroglyph, like the gravestone rock. 'As if reflected in a mirror, its likeness was in Reuben's memory. He even recognized the veins which seemed to form an inscription in forgotten characters.' Just as in Cyrus he had recognized only his own mirror image. The bullet that penetrates Cyrus ricochets, as it were, back upon himself in self-mutilation, self-penetration.

But there is yet a fourth mirror: the 'shadowy' oak which is Reuben's symbolic double. Just as the inscribed rockface and lined grey head of Roger Malvin had emblematically mirrored each other, so does the blasted oak, whose top was 'withered, sapless, and utterly dead', mirror the blasted soul of Reuben Bourne.

Part 4 returns to Dorcas and her forest pastoral. The clock turns back. For a second time the text moves to its appointed end. For the trap is closed: as much by the gloomy pines that 'circled round the spot' as by the imaginary walls of her forsaken home that 'seemed to encircle her'. For Dorcas, too, is subject to visions:

> The sun was now beneath the horizon, and the light that came down among the leaves was sufficiently dim to create many

illusions in her expecting fancy. Several times she seemed indistinctly to see his face gazing out from among the leaves; and once she imagined that he stood beckoning to her at the base of a craggy rock. Keeping her eyes on this object, however, it proved to be no more than the trunk of an oak fringed to the very ground with little branches, one of which, thrust out farther than the rest, was shaken by the breeze.

That anonymous song of the frontier cottage had been her last desperate attempt to bind the wilderness to the settlement. But its charming fiction of 'domestic love and household happiness' was just another romance-within-the-romance. Though an aesthetic fiction this time, not a moral fiction; and no longer to assuage the consciousness of guilt so much as that of love. Yet its 'magic' is as elaborately self-protective. Dorcas, torn by family affection, feels as lonely and vulnerable in the wilderness as Reuben torn by guilt. Both trust in the symbolic coherence and ambiguities of a text rather than confront the agonies of experience. Cyrus alone is without pretexts, protected by his 'sportive mischief' and laughter.

A gun's 'report' punctures that closed circle—that spell—as it had punctured Reuben's. But what for him was a kind of awakening, for her will be a kind of death. While for him 'the creaking of the trunks made a sound, as if the forest were waking from slumber', for her the wind's breath in the branches 'died away' (like Cyrus) 'in a hollow moan'. She is trapped in her husband's dream. She is trapped by his destructive conscience on that moral frontier. She is trapped, in that isolated all-male world, by her own man. 'From behind the trunk of every tree, and from every hiding place in the thick foliage of the under-growth, she hoped to discover' her laughing son. But the 'sun was now beneath the horizon. . .'

It is then she finds Reuben, like a cataleptic, tranced, for a second time seized by an 'absolute incapacity of motion'. 'How is this, Reuben?' she asks. 'Have you slain the deer and fallen asleep over him?' The question is doubly ironic: it is she who is to inherit that sleep; he who will soon awake. In this world of erroneous objects (an oak tree mistaken for Cyrus, Cyrus mistaken for a deer) Reuben Bourne finally lifts his downcast eyes and 'stared into her face'; and with that open stare—face to face—the trance is transferred. It is Cyrus who is discovered 'asleep, but dreamless'. It is Dorcas who sinks insensible to the ground.

So the spell is broken. The oak bough breaks and Reuben, its symbolic counterpart, breaks into tears. This is the moment of self-recognition and tragic awakening. In the final paragraph play is made with the concepts of redemption and expiation, suggesting the New Testament sense (of the Father and only begotten Son) as well as its Old Testament analogue (of Abraham and Isaac), perhaps even with a glance at Moses in the wilderness tapping 'water from a rock'. Is this biblical frontier, evoking *Exodus,* then the ultimate frontier? Is this the story's meaning? That self-destruction is purged by the destruction of a son (the genetic self) and by instinctive prayer? Or that the conscious sacrifice of the grandfather is atoned by the unconscious sacrifice of the son? Or that a voluntary self-sacrifice in one generation is expiated by an enforced self-sacrifice in the next? That the sins of the fathers descend upon their sons?

It all seems rather muddled and nonsensical. Abraham, after all, did not sacrifice Isaac. If Reuben 'trusted that it was Heaven's intent to afford him an opportunity of expiating his sin', he is pretty shabbily treated. Why is God not heard? Why does that 'supernatural voice' in which Reuben believed not sound? Why should the death of a son, upon a woodland altar, be read as a ritual of regeneration?

This urge of Reuben Bourne's to interpret that 'voice audible only to himself' as a 'supernatural voice' had long been anticipated by the text, with allusions to binding chains (of the spirit) and gnawing serpents (of the heart). The text actively intervenes to conspire with such interpretations. Just as it had earlier insisted on a version of patriarchal romance, so it now insists on this version of biblical romance, of temptation in the wilderness and expiation. For the biblical vision is also the patriarchal vision; the patriarchal, necessarily biblical. But both are spurious. If the patriarchal ideal, as evoked in this context, was clearly ironic, so are the biblical and allegorical ideals. There is no need to side with the text. To the contrary, there is every need to question the text. It asks to be questioned. Like those mysterious hieroglyphs on the engraved 'grave-stone', its rhetorical range of litotes, ellipses, oxymorons and

46

puns demands its own elaborate decipherment—though each may prove inscrutable, and though the inscription for decoding Reuben Bourne's and Roger Malvin's fate may resist, in the end, a *single* interpretation.

NOTES

1. 'Roger Malvin's Burial' first appeared in book form in *Mosses from an Old Manse* (1846). Poe's review of *Twice-Told Tales,* 'Tale-Writing', was first published in *Graham's Magazine* (May, 1842). Reuben, in Hebrew, means 'Behold a son!'; Dorcas, in Greek, means 'gazelle'; Cyrus, the mighty Persian king, was viewed by Isaiah as God's appointed agent (Chapters 40-8).

3

'Like a Dream Behind Me': Hawthorne's 'The Custom-House' and *The Scarlet Letter*

by A. ROBERT LEE

I have thus far omitted all mention of his *Twice-Told Tales*, and *The Scarlet Letter*. Both are excellent, but full of manifold, strange and diffusive beauties, that time would all but fail me to point out the half of them.
—Herman Melville, 'Hawthorne and his Mosses', *The Literary World*, 17 and 24 August, 1850.

This sketch of the Custom-house is, as simple writing, one of the most perfect of Hawthorne's compositions, and one of the most gracefully and humourously autobiographic. It would be interesting to examine it in detail . . . .
—Henry James, *Hawthorne* (1879).

1

If on publication *The Scarlet Letter* stirred an almost comic outburst of Mrs. Grundyism in Salem and other narrower New England circles, its reception on both sides of the Atlantic throughout the later nineteenth century was generally greatly more discerning. Given the mean local politicking which led to Hawthorne's dismissal in 1849 from his Surveyor's post in the Salem custom-house with the changeover from a Democratic to

48

Whig Presidency, and the unlooked for financial necessity it imposed on him to seek a serious livelihood from his writing (not to mention the upbraiding he ·received from many Salemites for having written a truly 'scarlet' book and treated with calumny and disrespect his fellow customs-men), he must have reacted with wry added pleasure to the praise his first major romance brought him. Though on occasion he would later proclaim himself grievously under-reviewed and misunderstood—this from a man who assiduously sought to disguise his true self in all manner of masks and ironies—not only *The Scarlet Letter* but his two earlier story-collections, *Twice-Told Tales* (1837) and *Mosses from an Old Manse* (1846), in fact won him wide approval, especially in America, as the testimony of, among others, Poe, Longfellow, Emerson and Evert Duyckinck, the astute editor of *The Literary World*, bears emphatic witness.[1] Even *Fanshawe* (1828), the early romance he wrote in college and which he came to think so abortive, was not without reviews. From the outset then, though few writers so consciously cultivated a manner of reticence and withdrawal, Hawthorne could in truth assume a steady and well-disposed readership.

No American acclaim, of course, could have been quite as startling, or as unstinting, as Melville's pseudonymous 'Hawthorne and his Mosses'. There, both to Hawthorne's and Sophia's delight, he found himself proclaimed 'a man of a deep and noble nature', 'this Portuguese diamond in our American Literature', an indissoluble New Englander by temperament and tradition yet a native man of letters to be spoken of with no less than Shakespeare and the wider community of established literary masters. Doubtless 'Hawthorne and his Mosses' reveals as much about Melville's own excited imagination in bringing *Moby-Dick* to completion, and his need to recognize and in turn be recognized for, a fellow voice of dissent from the prevailing Transcendentalist good cheer of the age, but it was an act, too, of formidable intuitive insight, a dramatic and rightly esteemed departure-point for nearly all subsequent estimation of Hawthorne. Although the mention of *The Scarlet Letter*—'full of manifold, strange and diffusive beauties'—amounts to no more than an aside, at once intriguing and almost cryptic, the review as a whole shows Melville drawn not only to Hawthorne's celebrated 'power of blackness', the dark, Calvinist accent to his view of mankind, but also to Hawthorne the artificer whose 'lights and shades' so dazzle and embroil the reader, evidence of the serious artfulness which shapes all of his best fiction.

In England, too, Hawthorne won admirers for his craft, and in perhaps unexpected quarters. Anthony Trollope found himself powerfully affected by the 'concentration of energy' at work in *The Scarlet Letter,* an imagined world of 'severe' ancestral Puritanism which he was drawn to possibly because it contrasted almost totally with his own 'beef and ale' novels, as he calls them, a domain to leave the reader 'entranced, excited, shuddering and at times almost wretched'.[2] And as if to bridge these tributes, though there is no evidence to suggest he read either, Henry James, shrewdest of all literary intermediaries between the New and Old worlds, despite his reservations about Hawthorne's 'symbolism', paid *The Scarlet Letter* his own considerable due. He clearly sensed in Hawthorne's achievement a foreshadowing of what the fiction he was writing himself might come to represent:

> The book was the finest piece of imaginative writing yet put forth in the country. There was a consciousness of this in the welcome that was given it—a satisfaction in the idea of America having produced a novel that belonged to literature, and to the forefront of it. Something might at last be sent to Europe as exquisite in quality as anything that had been received, and the best of it was that the thing was absolutely American; it belonged to the soil, to the air; it came out of the very heart of New England.[3]

These and the subsequent landmark commentaries of D. H. Lawrence, Van Wyck Brooks, F. O. Matthiessen and Q. D. Leavis, together with the vast contemporary scholarship on the strategy and detail of Hawthorne's romance-form and on his sources in New England lore and typology and the allegories of Spenser and Bunyan, have deservedly installed *The Scarlet Letter* as a great exercise of the imagination.[4] In this it also takes its place as part of the American Renaissance, the momentous literary efflorescence of the American 1840s and 1850s which includes, besides Hawthorne's own other stories and romances, Emerson's essays, *Walden, Leaves of Grass,* Melville's *Moby-Dick* and Piazza stories, and Emily Dickinson's poetry.

Yet oddly, in the light of this degree of attention, the critical focus has almost invariably ignored, or at best skimped, Hawthorne's 'The Custom-House', as if, though it runs to almost a fifth the length of the main narrative, Hawthorne's wonderfully disingenuous disclaimers are wholly to be believed and it serves indeed as no more than an antiquarian footnote, a beginning piece of pleasantry. To be sure, the famous definition of Romance and Hawthorne's 'moonlit room', especially when taken with his other Prefaces and the rich quarry of annotations in his different Notebooks, have not wanted for attention. But the utter organic importance of the whole piece—its delicate signalling of the tone of *The Scarlet Letter,* its concern with the kind of relationship a text like *The Scarlet Letter* bids to establish with its reader—has by no means met with full acknowledge- ment. 'Graceful' and 'humourously autobiographic' it assuredly is (there is an almost classically muted vein of Hawthorneian humour throughout), but James is rather typical in passing over 'The Custom-House' in favour of an account which begins with the throng awaiting Hester Prynne's emergence at the oak and iron-spiked prison door. That thres- hold cannot be thought other, on its own terms, than central, but it is not the first in the narrative. 'The Custom-House' is. And it behoves any reader to focus his attention with the greatest care and 'in detail' upon the way Hawthorne gets us, and himself, into his romance. For not to do so is to render *The Scarlet Letter* the same critical disservice we do *Moby-Dick* in turning too directly to 'Loomings', Melville's opening chapter, without taking meticulous account of his 'Etymology' and 'Extracts'.[5] Both writers use their prefacing brilliantly as attempts to create a reader, indicate the kind and aim of their fictions, and to set up a resonance which will echo and reverb- erate throughout the whole of the 'main' parts of their texts.

2

Strictly, even 'The Custom-House' is not the first item to be encountered in *The Scarlet Letter*. Hawthorne's Preface To The Second Edition, written amid the local hullabaloo caused by his 'official sketch'[6] in newspapers like the *Salem Register* which spoke of him as 'a despicable lampooner', the maker of 'calumnious caricatures of inoffensive men',[7] exhibits precisely the same engaging vein of irony which runs through 'The Custom-House' itself. In speaking of the 'unprecedented excitement' and 'public disapprobation' (1) brought about by his picture of official life in the custom-house, he both guys the irritation of his one-time Salem neighbours and their sheer uncomprehending of his book, and of greater importance still, calculatingly perpetuates the *persona* of himself as the unwitting literary man drawn through no fault of his own into the hurley-burley of public life, the scribbler stumbled into politics. Cartooning this 'Hawthorne' as a species of mad arsonist, some Jacobean revenger who might be imagined to have poured the blood of his chief victim over the dying embers of the custom-house he has just burnt down, in the same breath he insists on his posture as holy innocent, the creator of a sketch remarkable only for its 'frank and genuine good-humour' (1).

The good-humour we can take with at least a few grains of salt. The sketch is certainly in no way malicious; but its tone could hardly be thought other than rueful, the issue of an ironic sensibility not a little irritated by the whim of political manoeuvre. Hawthorne undoubtedly did have his sights trained on the Salem political spoils system. Yet in pooh-poohing the sorry provincial outcry 'The Custom-House' had aroused he resorts to exactly the same deflationary irony which first offended his townsmen. He at once plays up to, and gently derides, his accusers in suggesting that 'The Custom-House' might be omitted 'without loss to the public, or detriment to the book' (1)—something for which he has too often been taken literally—but that, in his own due consideration, it should remain in place because he could not have managed 'a livelier effect of truth' (2). Hawthorne knew well enough, and without doubt recognizably looks to the reader 'The Custom-House' so carefully endeavours to specify to know, that altogether subtler justifications than mere good-humour and 'effects' exist for the sketch's continued inclusion. But under the pretext of 'general accuracy' (1) and keeping faith with his original well-meant intention of doing little more than memorialize an endangered New England seaboard round of life, he alleges himself obligated to re-offer his sketch 'without a change of word' (2).

The Preface is disingenuousness writ small, Hawthorne as wide-eyed authorial innocent.

Typically, 'The Custom-House' proper begins with Hawthorne professing himself a figure of passivity, a private, normally unforthcoming man, 'disinclined to talk overmuch of myself and my affairs' (3). He speaks almost as if affrighted by the 'autobiographical impulse' which, 'inexcusably, and for no earthly reason' (3) has prompted him twice in his life to address the public, on the present occasion and earlier in 'The Author Makes the Reader Acquainted with his Abode', his Preface to *Mosses from an Old Manse*, a piece wholly as teasing and double-edged as 'The Custom-House' and the Prefaces to his three other principal romances. In recalling 'my way of life in the deep quietude of an Old Manse' (3), Hawthorne recalls both a literal sense of location, the house he had rented from the Emerson family in 1842, but also the inward chamber of his creative imagination in which were conceived and nurtured his story-mosses. Thus, in again reaching out, a man 'possessed' let us remember, to 'the few who will understand him' (3)—on the evidence of 'Hawthorne and his Mosses' he would surely have counted Melville among that number—his own 'circle of existence' finds completion. But even so, and however much is revealed by the author and understood by his reader, there remains an 'Inmost Me' (4), the private reaches of the actual historical self, in Hawthorne's case the self which he appears never to have wholly disclosed even to Sophia. Perhaps Melville's observation late in his own life when visited by Hawthorne's son, Julian, in 1883, that Hawthorne 'had all his life concealed some great secret, which would, were it known, explain all the mysteries of his career',[8] did indeed contain a kernel of truth. At any rate, the self to be disclosed in 'The Custom-House', from the outset, will be a writerly self, a self fashioned ultimately by the 'Inmost Me', but essentially different and derivative from it. The 'true relation with his audience', then, can be itself no more than a fiction, an agreed contract of intention and goodwill between the two consenting parties. The 'rights' (4) of each are so preserved. Hawthorne will 'play' author and the reader his assigned part.

This benign charade, and it is charm with a fundamental strategic purpose, continues as Hawthorne purports to offer in

53

what follows the 'Proofs of the authenticity of the narrative therein contained' (4). He will blend the life of the custom-house into the life of his narrative, 'a faint representation' (4) based on actuality to give latitude and longitude to his story of the scarlet A. The story, waiting only to be extricated from deep within the custom-house, attends patiently across space and time its teller. And in that capacity, Hawthorne declares himself with disarming guile to be writing 'in my true position as editor' (4). The first in a sequence of assumed identities, this 'editor' is further evidence of Hawthorne's careful self-veiling in both 'The Custom-House' sketch and the main narrative. The reader will indeed be left with an 'edited' text, a story so thoroughly ordered and composed as to allow all the main interpretation to seem to fall upon his own critical shoulders.

In no clearer fashion could the main procedures of *The Scarlet Letter* have been indicated: as the reader defines so, more than usually, will he himself be defined, whether in the matter of the dazzling A itself (both the gorgeously embroidered red and gold version worn by Hester and the vegetal green version assumed by Pearl), the triangle of Hester, Roger and Arthur, the dialectical scaffold and forest scenes, or the individual moments of intense picturing like Hester's first visit to Governor Bellingham's in which the A dilates and contracts as it is mirrored upon the breast-plate of the armour (106) or Hawthorne's Gobelin tapestry of David, Bathsheba and Nathan undoubtedly insinuated into the minister's room by Chillingworth (126). Yet the description of life in this custom-house, if our 'editor' is to be taken at his apparent word, offers no more than 'a few extra touches' (4), a minor site for the discovery for the A. By now we should be referring to Hawthorne as 'Hawthorne', the author as himself an inspired fictional creation. Little wonder that Melville, no mean authorial confidence-man himself, could speak in his *Literary World* review of Hawthorne as the master of 'soft ravishments'.

3

'A spacious edifice of brick' (5), tracks, points of exit and entry, sailors 'outward bound' and 'recently arrived' (6), 'custom' of every kind both human and commercial, in these and similar terms Hawthorne begins his picture—'scene' is his word—of the daily round at the Salem custom-house. His language, at once evocative in detail of life in the port and amid the wharfs, nevertheless carries other resonances, which link directly into the main text. This house of custom, with its collectors, history, secret recesses and architecture, its sense of present and pastness, will serve, albeit obliquely, as the analogue of *The Scarlet Letter* itself, a most geometrical house of fiction, with its perfectly spaced three scaffold scenes, its juxtaposed pictures of forest and town. The text constantly proposes analogies with buildings, a many-chambered edifice like the custom-house.

And from the first chapter onwards the reader cannot but be struck by the recurring allusions to tracks and thresholds: spatial, as the ones which lead into and out of the forest and prison; temporal, as the rose which stays alive through history and embodies the link between Hester and her antinomian ancestor Ann Hutchinson; and sexual and moral, as in the iron line which divides Puritan and forest realms. One enters into the custom-house through a threshold, and departs only to cross a subsequent threshold into both the story of Hester Prynne and into history, the Puritan past. At a more general level it is hard not to be aware that these Puritans have themselves crossed the Atlantic threshold, set up and lived to other thresholds, and that only Pearl will manage to re-cross the original threshold back to the Europe whose ambassadors are the Spanish sailors at the close of the book.

Hawthorne cannot forbear, either, a characteristic piece of playfulness with the idea of the custom-house as a house of the nation, an America-in-small, its entrance guarded by 'an enormous specimen of an American eagle' (5). But no guardian prince of Nature this creature; rather it can bite its own, an 'unhappy fowl', fierce, mischievous, out of sorts. Or so it has come to seem to the Hawthorne the sketch will later reveal to have been dismissed from office, a 'federal eagle' (5) apt to 'fling off her nestlings' (5), a thing of claw, beak and 'barbed arrows' (5). In so dallying with this emblem Hawthorne anticipates his similar, more serious, equivocation in matters like the A, or the day and night-time scaffold scenes, or his use of literal mirrors and pictures.

By peopling the custom-house with 'a row of venerable

figures' (7), the custom-house officers, Hawthorne takes his reader increasingly back into time, to a slow, almost static, Matthew-like Biblical dimension. The customs-men resemble as much Greek choric presences, however, as Hebrew tax-collectors. Their general office could as easily be a morgue, a place of fossil lawbooks and Acts of Congress, as a site of day-to-day activity. It is here, amid time, age, and venerable infirmity, that Hawthorne conjures up the one-time author of *Mosses from an Old Manse,* by now virtually a dimly remembered figment of the imagination, and even as he is invoked no longer a customs-man but swept from office by 'the besom of reform' (8). A victim, then, of time and change, he can but dwell broodingly upon this Salem of his forbears, an attachment as he calls it 'of dust' (9). As *The Scarlet Letter* takes the reader back across time to the Puritan Settlement, so 'The Custom-House' prepares the way by taking its reader to Hawthorne's first ancestor, William Hathorne, and to his son, John Hathorne, Salem magistrate in the witchcraft trials of 1692. The son, 'a bitter persecutor', notorious for his severity towards a Quaker woman, thus blends Hawthorne's history into the history of Hester Prynne, Hawthorne or his family lineage as the personification of the Puritan severity which has struck hard and punitively at the defiant selfhood incarnated in some other Hester. It is this history which Hawthorne takes upon himself to exorcise, the writer not only as Editor and local historian, but the voice of latterday atonement. 'The Custom House' and *The Scarlet Letter* are so made to fuse in historical points of reference, Hawthorne's family history paralleling and interwoven with the triangular betrayal of Hester, Dimmesdale and Chillingworth in seventeenth century New England.

Yet though exorcised for their more brutal crimes, these ancestral Puritan forbears still issue chastisements from out of the seventeenth century. Who better than the historic originals to condemn art, speak dismissively of mere story-telling, especially to an heir who has strayed from the sermon and tract into the modern idolatrous distraction of fiction-writing? Where they, both his own ancestors and the Puritans of the book, however, could see unambiguously, in one-to-one terms and to a stern, unyielding standard, Hawthorne 'sees' equasively, through more shifting graduations of moral vision.

To find the right 'sweet moral blossom' (48) poses no simple task: who will with confidence judge Roger as against Arthur, or see only saint or sinner in Hester, or accept Pearl unworryingly as the subversive free spirit she threatens to be? Every circling parade of possible judgement which Hawthorne puts before the reader undercuts that original singularity of Puritan judgement. And as Hawthorne himself 'sees' more and more in relative terms, so his reader: for the reader, too, must seek to set one interpretation against another, whether of the great central A, the day and night-time faces of the community, the interplay of revelation and concealment, forest outlawry as against the conformism of the community standard.

In thinking back to the father-and-son continuity which has sent successive Hawthornes to sea from Salem (his own father died on a voyage to the Dutch East Indies in 1808), to a Salem for him become drear in its familiarity—the unchanging perspective of its Main Street, the almost conspiratorial predictability of the weather—Hawthorne seeks from his reader an unusually close sense of his own claustrophobia, New England as at once his necessary place of origin yet a place of imprisonment whether as geography, daily habit, or time. His own need to break free, take fresh root, would in life lead him increasingly to Europe, to the consulship in Liverpool and to Italy. Between him and Hester, his fictional creation, there are thus clear parallels: she too experiences the tension between closure and escape, outlawry and acceptance as a woman and artist. Throughout *The Scarlet Letter* Hawthorne expands brilliantly and with a great symphonic resonance upon these tensions, the conflicts between unchanging patterns of behaviour and dissent, the moral law of the community as set against the law of the forest, iron as against oak, free growth as against the community's black 'flowers', the covered head as against the unfettered expression of sexuality. 'Salem' in 'The Custom-House' is utterly akin to the 'Boston' of *The Scarlet Letter*; as cultures both lack the ease of a flexible metropolitan style, a larger and denser social perspective. That feeling of enclosure is located very precisely in the custom-house. The customs-men—General Miller, the Chief Collector, the 'certain permanent collector' (16), the various others only passingly referred to, even the one efficient soul about the place—all belong to a kind of living museum, their different styles and energies, as it were, boxed in and preserved for Hawthorne's authorial inspection. He shows himself perfectly aware that he, too, could go a similar way, into inertness, mere routine, dwelling almost lovingly upon their various infirmities and fads, upon gout, rheumatism, near-paralysis, the memory of far-off meals, even implied flatulence, all of which dramatize change as if all it brought were pain, time as a body subject always to demeaning illness. The writing of *The Scarlet Letter*, among other things, will therefore be for Hawthorne a matter of escape, art as health.

But first he must be forced by circumstance to break free from the place of custom in which he has become imprisoned. General Miller, 'our gallant old General' (20), the benign, geriatric figure with his 'I'll try, Sir!' (23), personifies in his slowness of gait the pace of Hawthorne's own custom-house life. Affected by imaginative dullness, his slowed-down creativity, Hawthorne must again, as he did in *Mosses from an Old Manse*, try to make the past live. In evoking the General's 'toilsome progress across the floor' (20), he appears to be suggesting his own creaks and pains in activating his tarnished imagination and signalling to the reader something of the reading-pace with which he is to proceed. *The Scarlet Letter* will not be a book in which the reader will meet great action, but rather a work of contemplation, a succession of emblematic scenes and exchanges each requiring attention as assiduous as their very composition.

The movement back from custom-house employment to the literary life causes him to recall his circle of New England *literati* who, both at Brook Farm where he bought stock, hoped to take Sophia and lived from April until November 1841, and at the Old Manse, had been regular visitors and companions. Among them are Emerson, a 'subtile influence' (25); Ellery Channing, nephew of the great Unitarian preacher with whom he shares his name, poet, and Thoreau's first biographer; Thoreau himself; George Stillman Hillard (his name was actually Hilliard), lawyer and literary man; Longfellow, Hawthorne's one-time classmate at Bowdoin college; and Bronson Alcott, most frenetic of all the Transcendentalists. He professes that life in the custom-house, by way of contrast with these, was no less

than a relief. Somehow, he recognizes, deep within the daily
round of duty, the creative spirit was biding its time, yet equally
it was at risk—a 'gift, a faculty, if it had not departed, was
suspended and inanimate within me' (26). Recall of the past,
both the Salem of his family roots, the more immediate past of
his time with his New England contemporaries, and the happy
coincidence of being able to bracket himself with Chaucer and
Burns as fellow literary customs-men (Melville after 1866
would become another), pushes him more and more towards a
re-awakening of his inner creative faculties. The account of his
individual circumstances, factual though it is by origin, also
gives a superb metaphoric glimpse of how Hawthorne's creative
psychology seems to have operated, in powerful alternating
rhythms of deadness and revival. Paradoxically his hibernation
in the custom-house, its very torpor, dust, voices, fixed rituals
and idiom, stirs this impaired creativity. From within the
custom-house, where history has been so ritually stored,
Hawthorne has the means to a story, Henry James's notion of a
'germ'. It is to the making of that story, and its departure-point
in the discovery of the A amid dusty reams of old paper,
'rubbish' as he calls it, that Hawthorne now proceeds, the artist
at last taking sway over the 'materiality' about him.

4

'The past was not dead', 'the habit of bygone days awoke in
me' (27)—so Hawthorne adverts to his former life as a writer,
his proven capacity of reviving the past imaginatively. From the
ground floor of the custom-house, he moves to a second storey,
noting that the edifice as a whole 'contains far more space than
its occupants know what to do with' (28). The space is both
literal, and imagined, an 'airy hall' (28) which serves both as a
store-house for 'bundles of official documents', 'rubbish',
'musty papers' (28) and a kind of fictional echo-chamber for the
past, a place of inner as well as outer memory and history. The
very talk of manuscripts nicely modulates between historical
transcripts of past 'custom' and literary transcripts. Within that
second storey, as if ransacking his memory and causing his
creative faculty to start into action, Hawthorne imagines
himself 'poking and burrowing' (29), 'unfolding one and

another document' (29), seeking like Faulkner's narrator in *Absalom, Absalom!* to make order of past disorder, sequence from what appears random. Among the details lies the 'small package' of the A, a bequest from an earlier time when 'clerks engrossed their stiff and formal chirography on more substantial materials than at present' (29). Hawthorne, too, is a chirographer, no Puritan 'clerk' however, more the frivolous romancer he so carefully has earlier parodied, a trifler, a fiddler as his admonitory Puritan ancestors have called him.

The package could hardly not excite. Bound in red tape (the perfect bureaucratic colour), under the seal of Governor Shirley, Massachusetts's Governor 1741-49 and 1753-56, and given over to one Mr. Surveyor Jonathan Pue, a name which in fact *does* appear in Felt's Annals though not as the figure so elaborately evoked by Hawthorne's designing imagination, the mystery stands before us and before its intending unraveller. Pue, the 'ancient Surveyor' (30), is no less than Hawthorne's spiritual bondsman. Both of them, ancient and modern, Puritan and son of a Puritan line, are bound as 'surveyors' and 'inspectors' of human custom, men whose shared destiny in their separate ways is to observe and transcribe. Within 'the mysterious package' (31) is contained 'a certain affair of fine cloth' (31), embroidered in gold whose glitter has faded, the expression of 'a now forgotten art' (31) and a talismanic object which readers of other American texts might compare with Melville's doubloon in *Moby-Dick,* Poe's raven, Twain's raft or Whitman's leaves of grass. It offers itself as a 'riddle' (31), 'a mystic symbol' (31), art itself which burns its holder, and whose circumstantial detail purportedly lies in the historic account passed down by Mr. Pue, the story of Hester Prynne, a woman regarded by her community as a nurse and 'noteworthy personage' (32). Hawthorne's willingness to authenticate his story by handing over to those who would seek it his 'proof' beguilingly mocks the too easy correspondence which vulgar realism frequently prescribes should exist between fact and image, life and art.

Within the 'deserted chamber of the Custom-House' (33), Hawthorne at last, and as if coyly, suggests he has 'the groundwork of a tale' (33), a departure-point for retelling the past. In a further sleight-of-hand, he takes on another identity, that of necromancer, the summoning force who speaks across the intervening centuries to the ghost of Surveyor Pue. Between them stands their bond, a pact to re-offer the story of the A. The great ease of Hawthorne's mock-solemnity, charming to a degree, should not, however, obscure the deeper tale he is telling. His antics with the ghost, the relics, the 'mouldy and moth-eaten lucubrations' (33), and his compact with the dead, serve to explain how he has re-found his creative powers, his return to his first calling of writer. But there is further necromancy to be done: pacing the custom-house, utterly given to contemplation, he makes vivid for us the onerous and mysterious task of making dead 'materiality' come to imaginative life, the transformation of 'fact' into 'fiction'. His necromancy must work not only upon Pue but upon the A, past events and figures whose combined resistance to his art taunts him like the death's-head grin of a skull. He speaks of his 'wretched numbness' (35), the 'tarnished mirror' (34) of his imagination, the haunting thought that in seeking employment in the custom-house he has for ever forfeited his birthright as an artist. His imagination has virtually become as intractable as the relics on the second-storey, a dead place. But given his pacing and contemplation, 'sea-shore walks and rambles into the country' (35), he finally crosses one more 'threshold' (35), that of the Old Manse. In two further chambers, first his study, then 'the deserted parlour' (35), amid solitude, effervescent transfiguring moonlight and stillness, the powers of his former alchemy slowly begin to make their hesitant return, his 'striving to picture forth imaginary scenes' (35) at last and irresistibly triumphing. It is in these conditions, night-time in a lonely room, that Hawthorne begins the transformation of his 'affair of fine cloth' into the narrative of *The Scarlet Letter*. The scene offers a most privileged glimpse into the workings of his most devious imagination.

5

Hawthorne's 'moonlit room' (35) and his classic definition of Romance I need not dwell upon: both have been energetically explored in critical discussion of his achievement and of its contribution to the larger tradition of American fiction. They take their place with comparable formulations to be found in Irving, Cooper, Simms, Brockden Brown, Melville, and pre-eminently, Henry James. But the detail of Hawthorne's imagery merits its own attention, for it again bears unusually closely upon *The Scarlet Letter* as a narrative whole.

Hawthorne's picturing of his moon-lit room is managed with extraordinary economy. He concentrates into one single vivid trope nearly every element he has sought to bring to attention in 'The Custom-House': the emblematic working of his romance-world in *The Scarlet Letter*, the 'unusual light' (35) which will 'spiritualize' (35) things and people throughout, the inter-mediate narrative terrain within which the story is to be set. By 'neutral territory' (36) the reader is to encounter neither the realist emphasis of the Great Tradition of the English novel nor outright fantasy, neither the factual house of custom nor a Gothic Otranto. Hawthorne's imagery of midnight and a trans-figuring light perfectly locates the atmospheric terms of reference of *The Scarlet Letter:*

> If the imaginative faculty refused to act at such an hour, it might well be deemed a hopeless case. Moonlight, in a familiar room, falling so white upon the carpet, and showing all its figure so distinctly,—making every object so minutely visible, yet so unlike a morning or noontide visibility,—is the medium the most suitable for a romance-writer to get acquainted with his illusive guests. There is the little domestic scenery of the well-known apartment; the chairs, with each its separate individuality; the centre-table, sustaining a work-basket, a volume or two and an extinguished lamp; the sofa; the book-case; the picture on the wall;—all these details, so completely scene, are so spiritualized by the unusual light, that they seem to lose their actual substance, and become things of intellect. Nothing is too small or too trifling to undergo this change, and acquire dignity thereby. A child's shoe; the doll seated in her little wicker carriage; the hobby-horse;—whatever in a word, has been used or played with, during the day, is now invested with a quality of strangeness and remoteness, though still almost as vividly present as by daylight. Thus, therefore, the floor of our familiar room has become a neutral territory, somewhere between the real world and fairy-land, where the Actual and the Imaginary may meet, and each imbue itself with the nature of the other. (35-6)

This passage is rightly celebrated as Hawthorne's most explicit account of the romance as he understands the form. But it offers itself, too, as precisely the thing it describes; each detail in the picture—the chairs, lamp, sofa, doll, hobby-horse etc—is at once a feature of the actual yet at the same time, bathed in Hawthorne's own transfiguring moonlight, changed into something imagined. In speaking of 'all the gleam and shadow of the picture' (36), he could hardly have found a better phrase with which to gloss the *chiaroscuro* and emblematic qualities of *The Scarlet Letter*. And as we are made to see in 'a familiar room' the very metamorphosising of these actual things into imaginary things, so in *The Scarlet Letter* we witness an 'actual' historic time and place marvellously transformed into a 'neutral territory', a world of people and events and behaviour subtly displaced from their literal bearings. But having for a moment illuminated his territory, and indicated how it cannot be regarded with any accuracy from a 'daylight' perspective, Hawthorne immediately draws back, careful not to allow his reader too firm a vantage-point. In the familiar, self-deprecating irony which marks out most of 'The Custom-House', he surmises how a better story might have been that of 'a veteran shipmaster, one of the Inspectors' (37), a story of sea-going adventure told perhaps by a custom-house Melville. Such was not to be for Hawthorne, however. Rather his attention lay snared in the American Puritan past and the deep flickering shadows cast by it for a literary New Englander dutifully bound by name and history to that legacy.

Even Hester Prynne's 'story' (34) might never have found expression, he goes on to confide, had not the quirk of politics deprived him of office. For having dwelt among ghosts—Surveyor Pue, his own Hathorne ancestors, Hester Prynne herself—he now imagines himself of their company, himself become a ghost, a beheaded phantom like Washington Irving's Headless Horseman. Hawthorne's teasing again plays lightly across the account of his dismissal, its geniality easing an otherwise painful memory ('The moment when a man's head drops off is seldom or never . . . the most agreeable of his life' (41)). We are urged to forgive Hawthorne all the more for his custom-house sketch, his autobiographical 'intrusion', by believing he writes under edict as one 'from beyond the grave', a decapitated surveyor, 'a politically dead man' (43). The real self, however, beset with paper, ink, steel-pens and his 'long-disused writing-desk' (43) speaks as the amanuensis of history, partly the live, actual three-dimensional Hawthorne, yet in equal part the Hawthorne of the moonlit room, a 'citizen of somewhere else' (44) in the sense of being a creative imagination. He finally affects to call upon a last voice to add to those of Editor, antiquarian, Parish pump scribbler, necro-mancer, chirographer, oath-swearer and unemployed customs-man, that of a man of peace, a high-toned giver of Christian benediction.

Life in the custom-house, both its literal features and its inward, contemplative significance for Hawthorne, indeed does lie 'like a dream behind' (44). It is a dream full of prophecy and vital sign-posts for the fable ahead. All that remains, as the reader turns his page, is to gather with the Puritan throng at the prison-gate and await the emergence of Hester Prynne whose tale, and the essential manner of its telling, have been so thoroughly anticipated in 'The Custom-House'.

6

Nearly all that is characteristic of *The Scarlet Letter*—Hawthorne's shadings of voice and masterly tactics of in-direction—he anticipates perfectly in 'The Custom-House'. Perhaps only his fun-poking, the gently barbed humour directed at his fellow Salemites, is less evident. For the sketch, like the romance of Hester Prynne which follows, ostensibly tells one story only to camouflage others. 'The Custom-House' indeed does portray something of mid-century Salem port life and Hawthorne's own minor political fray, but it conceals an array of subtler ends. However obliquely, it serves to define the Romance; to convey Hawthorne's sense of what for an American writer constitutes a usable past; to allegorize the deeply inward creative process whereby energies seemingly at ebb recover and are re-deployed; and to set up intimate writerly and readerly terms of reference whereby the ensuing fiction might most profitably be understood. 'The Custom-House' is thus at once in the service of *The Scarlet Letter*, its essential *prologomena*, yet freestanding, a preface yet altogether more than a preface, as delicate (and devious) as Melville's 'The Piazza' which he wrote to introduce his *Piazza Tales*. Both Hawthorne and Melville address their readers utterly as co-creators of the 'final' text, secret sharers in the making of their fictions.

It is a great and major part of *The Scarlet Letter*'s achievement that we speak of it as the most poised of his longer romances. In none of the others, certainly, is there the distancing ease to the overall pattern, the imaginative balance of each and all of the parts. In *The House of the Seven Gables, The Blithedale Romance* and *The Marble Faun,* and in the later posthumous story-fragments, Hawthorne turns increasingly to a death, in two cases to violent murder, not only as thematic high drama in itself but as a way of freeing his plots of the entangling knots which have threatened to choke them, to stifle their very imaginative life. Where, in other words, mystery hovers on the edge of mere mystification, or ambiguity on the edge of disfiguring obscurantism, Hawthorne uses the death of Zenobia and Donatello's act of murder as a way of releasing his story for other concerns and developments. Correspondingly, the later Prefaces, each far sparer than 'The Custom-House', take on a somewhat desperate air. Hawthorne seems to want to define Romance more provisionally, and with less of the confidence and imaginative colour of his 'moonlit room'. But where both the equations of these later romances look less certain, the note of 'The Custom-House' and *The Scarlet Letter* is entirely one of equipoise, 'the gleam and shadow of the picture' strikingly controlled and directed.

This equipoise—a matter of tone and the fine balance of the book's detail—lies as much as anywhere in the way *The Scarlet Letter* acts to fulfil all the promptings of 'The Custom-House'. I have suggested something of how, in Chapter 1, 'The Prison-Door', Hawthorne carries over to *The Scarlet Letter* his purposive language of thresholds, edifices, doors, houses and chambers, lines of demarcation and separate domain. But more still is indicated in the matter of continuity. The almost Augustan syntax and periodical sentence-structure of the opening chapter, and its self-effacing authorial voice, play effortlessly into the illusion that the reader, here in the main text as in 'The Custom-House', has essentially only his own mettle to fall back upon. For where in 'The Custom-House' Hawthorne affects to

speak as one driven by circumstance back to the pen—
'haunted' if we believe the Pue story—so in Chapter 1,
especially in the last paragraph, he speaks of offering his story
and its 'moral blossom' as a gift, a 'presentation' (48) he has not
the power to resist offering. This posture, so attractively
caricatured throughout 'The Custom-House', recurs in his 'we
could hardly do otherwise' of plucking one of the flowers from
the rose-bush as 'a sweet moral blossom' (48). And by tacitly
identifying Hester with this 'wild rose-bush' (48), and with
Ann Hutchinson, each a human counter to the ordering Puritan
trinity of prison, graveyard and church, Hawthorne again
emphasizes just how much he looks to in his 'understanding'
reader. For as 'The Custom-House' transports *its* reader from
space to time and from the present to the past, so the rose-bush,
and all it represents, does the same in reverse. By being 'kept
alive in history' (48) it yields not only a meaning for the
seventeenth-century Puritan and non-Puritan world but for
Hawthorne's own nineteenth century—and hence the contemporary—world:

> This rose-bush, by a strange chance, has been kept alive in
> history; but whether it has merely survived out of the stern old
> wilderness, so long after the fall of the gigantic pines and oaks
> that originally overshadowed it,—or whether, as there is fair
> authority for believing, it had sprung up under the footsteps of
> the sainted Ann Hutchinson, as she entered the prison-door,—
> we shall not take upon us to determine. Finding it so directly on
> the threshold of our narrative, which is about to issue from that
> inauspicious portal, we could hardly do otherwise than pluck one
> of its flowers and present it to the reader. It may serve, let us
> hope, to symbolize some sweet moral blossom, that may be found
> along the track, or relieve the darkening close of a tale of human
> frailty and sorrow. (48)

Hawthorne's deft equivocations also perfectly confirm the
persona he has created in 'The Custom-House'. At each turn, as
noted earlier, he appears to step free of responsibility for
guiding the reader to judgement. The style is deliberately
pitched to cultivate evasion, delicate authorial withdrawal,
typically in the posing of each alternative ('whether . . .
whether'), in the succession of subjunctive 'mights' and 'mays',
and in phrases like 'by a strange chance' and 'as there is fair

authority for believing'. A disavowal of the order of 'we shall not take upon ourself to determine' seems almost too explicit, the author positively unable to offer 'guidance' in the ways of his text or its moral import. Hawthorne's concluding sentence, too ('It may serve, let us hope . . .'), risks toppling into coyness, too knowing a reliance upon his reader's complicity. But like all that goes before it pulls just short; indeed, the whole paragraph works with absolutely the right degree of tact. It exemplifies, in local detail and at the very beginning of the story how, at an overall level, *The Scarlet Letter* will act to fulfil almost all the pointers established in 'The Custom-House'. For though both texts can, and too frequently have been made to, stand on their own, they stand infinitely to greater imaginative profit together, mutually re-enforcing and essential parts of the larger whole.

NOTES

1. Most of these reviews are to be found in B. Bernard Cohen (ed.); *The Recognition of Nathaniel Hawthorne* (Ann Arbor: University of Michigan Press, 1969).
2. Originally published as 'The Genius of Nathaniel Hawthorne', *North American Review*, CCLXXIV, September 1879, 203-22.
3. Henry James, *Hawthorne* (London: Macmillan, 1879).
4. See D. H. Lawrence, *Studies in Classic American Literature* (New York: Thomas Saltzer, 1923; Van Wyck Brooks, *The Flowering of New England: 1815-1865* (New York: Dutton, 1936); F. O. Mathiessen; *American Renaissance: Art and Expression in the Age of Emerson and Whitman* (New York: Oxford University Press, 1941); Q. D. Leavis, 'Hawthorne as Poet', *Sewanee Review*, LIX, Spring and Summer, 1951, 179-205, 426-58.
5. I have tried to show the importance of Melville's prefatory sections in 'Moby-Dick: The Tale and the Telling', in Faith Pullin (ed.); *New Perspectives on Melville* (Edinburgh University Press, 1978), pp. 86-127.
6. *The Scarlet Letter* (Ohio University Press, 1962). This and all subsequent page references are to the standard Centenary Edition.
7. The controversy in the *Salem Register* during March 1850, is usefully reprinted in *Studies in the Novel*, Nathaniel Hawthorne Special Number, Winter 1970, Vol. 2, No. 4.
8. Julian Hawthorne, 'Hawthorne at Lenox', *Booklover's Weekly*, 30 December 1901. Reprinted in Jay Leyda (ed.); *The Melville Log*, Vol. 2; 782 (New York: Harcourt, Brace and World, 1951).

4

The Letter, the Picture, and the Mirror: Hawthorne's Framing of *The Scarlet Letter*

by MARK KINKEAD-WEEKES

Most accounts of Hawthorne's masterpiece suggest that the letter killeth, but the symbolic picture giveth life. His art is seen as essentially the imaginative conversion of history into myth and emblem into symbol. The scarlet letter may begin in a firmly historical setting which defines a clear analytic meaning; but Hawthorne's imagination works on Hester in the opposite way from Governor Bellingham's armour, bringing the woman into focus so that she is no longer dwarfed by the emblem, and in the process her scarlet letter acquires a multiple suggestiveness. As Chillingworth, Pearl and Dimmesdale are brought into the picture, its complexity grows and deepens; type begins to grow towards character, typology is transformed into suggestive symbolism; until the exposure on the scaffold from which we began, becomes the negative night-piece at the centre of the novel, and then the fully developed picture of the tragic climax.

Yet surely the life of Hawthorne's picture is peculiarly affected by the nature of its framing? Critics get excited by the depth and resonance of symbolic interpretations and begin to talk of Hawthorne's darkness . . . but to return to the actual experience of reading, is to find that an essential peculiarity has been left out of account. There is something not only reserved, but cool and remote about the fiction. If we were tempted to speak of dark or tragic vision, is there not a question whether we have ever been disturbed, or moved to tears or gloom, or even (dare one ask it?) deeply involved at all? And though one cannot but be impressed by the solidity of representation and the depth of exploration which make *The Scarlet Letter* so much finer than even the best of the tales, is there not also a persistent impression of something static: the people statuesque, the scenes not drama but tableau? Grant that the fiction is ultimately symbolic rather than allegorical, yet there remains an insistent drive to figurative analysis, a tone of exposition, a tightness of structure calling attention to itself, an obtrusive artfulness. Most of all, the reader is made continually aware of an authorial persona, persistently interposing a highly artificial style between us and what we see. The great symbolic novelists seem (at least while we are reading) to plunge us into the mystery of life itself; but the more one reads Hawthorne, the more conscious one becomes of the deliberate artifice of his literary voice. The fiction is indeed a picture, something we look *at,* always aware that there is a frame all round, and even some transparent but intrusive medium in between. Yet we have to account for the fact that these qualities are of the work's essence, intrinsically part of its mysterious suggestiveness, not to be excused, or explained away, or silently passed by.

I think the clues to such an account are to be found in the Custom-House sketch, where indeed all criticism of Hawthorne would do well to start.[1] For he himself tells us there, with characteristic indirection, how to read him and what kind of art his is, based on necessary duplicities of stance.

We begin to see why he is at his best when writing about the historic past: both because it is obviously dead; and because it was really there, and remains startlingly alive. His art welcomes the distance of the past, precisely because it can be seen as framed, apart and quite different from the present. Old Salem is over and done with. But therefore (and a series of puns comes into focus) Hawthorne's art can begin not merely with anti-quarian imagination, but the the tolerance that the relativism of history brings: Mr. 'Surveyor' or 'Collector' of 'Customs'

69

Hawthorne is able to record a set of ancient 'customs' which Mr. Surveyor Pue had already collected a hundred years before, as an antiquity then already a century old. If Old Salem has little 'commerce' with the present day, it might seem that Hester's ancient Massachusetts would have even less. (We had better be careful how we talk of *Hawthorne's* sense of sin.) Yet it is the distance that allows objectivity, and the sardonic tolerance Hawthorne's *persona* also gives to those other decayed relics of the past, his fellow inspectors. It is clearly necessary to go on printing the Custom-House sketch as 'Introductory to *The Scarlet Letter*', in order to signal the ambiguous attitude of the author to his tragedy (which he takes care to tell us he was happy writing).

On the other hand of course, the past is not dead at all. It is still there in the blood he shares with his Puritan ancestors, though they would approve of him as little as he can share their values. Nevertheless they were very much alive, and remain so in him; and whatever he may feel about Salem, there is a sense in which he belongs there, made by it, and has to come to terms with the Quaker-beater and the witch-burner before he can quit for good and launch his children elsewhere. So Hawthorne must be the cultural critic of customs, not merely their collector and recorder; must tackle and evaluate the New England tradition on behalf of ninteenth-century America.

Moreover, although the future that the builders of the Custom-House looked forward to never materialized, and the upper storey became only a dump for records, it is there he pretends to have found other signs of life: not merely Mr. Pue's document, but the scarlet letter itself. Fiction though it be, this curiously secures the sense of 'fact' that Hawthorne always needed, like the topography of Old Boston, or the pigsty at Brook Farm, or the ruins of Rome. It is first and foremost a thing, a material object, of which 'each limb proved to be precisely three inches and a quarter in length.' Yet in its materiality, and because of its history, it can prove even more startlingly alive:

> My eyes fastened themselves upon the old scarlet letter, and would not be turned aside. Certainly, there was some deep meaning in it, most worthy of interpretation, and which, as it

70

were, streamed forth from the mystic symbol, subtly communicating itself to my sensibilities, but evading the analysis of my mind.

When thus perplexed—and cogitating, among other hypotheses, whether the letter might not have been one of those decorations which the white men used to contrive, in order to take the eyes of Indians,—I happened to place it on my breast. It seemed to me,—the reader may smile, but must not doubt my word,—it seemed to me, then, that I experienced a sensation not altogether physical, yet almost so, as of burning heat; and as if the letter were not of red cloth, but red-hot iron. I shuddered, and involuntarily let it fall upon the floor.

In the absorbing contemplation of the scarlet letter, I had hitherto neglected to examine a small roll of dingy paper . . .[2]

We do violence to abstract from this the one sentence about the mystic symbol in order to assert (on Hawthorne's behalf) the superiority of symbolism over analytic allegory, and of imaginative sensibility over intellect. For that will spoil both the humour and the characteristically indirect accretion of meaning. Hawthorne does indeed suggest how symbolic significance bypasses the mind, communicating before it can be understood. But he also shows the transcendental symbolist so comically taken aback by something obstinately literal, physical, hotly alive, as to lose his grasp of it altogether. Not only is the letter 'most worthy of interpretation', but it may need two kinds of hard-headedness—a sense of the literal and historic; and a willingness to 'cogitate hypotheses' (including apparently misleading ones) about the meaning of the letter— before it can be safely 'held'. And that is of course the point concealed within the jokey false hypothesis. Two kinds of 'Indian' may need to have their eyes 'taken' by that bit of rag: the pagan, still ignorant of certain meanings of the letter on 'election' day; and the 'Hindu' transcendentalist, who thinks the material and experiential only a veil of illusion over mystic streaming. It is necessary also to examine, more coolly, the letter, and a small roll of dingy paper concerned with history and with explanation. Yet the 'mystic symbol' communicating direct to the sensibilities, and the mysterious sensation of heat and danger on the heart, retain their roles in the whole flexible process from 'fastening the eye' to being able to hold the letter.

71

It is alive; but fully to grasp that life seems to require a complex stylishness of looking and of laying hold, in which elements of evasiveness (unsettling one position by others), and of equasiveness (balancing opposites), and of keeping one's distance, as well as touching the heart, all seem to be needed, in a constant succession.

Moreover, though the Custom-House in the 1840s provides a framing sense of separation and relativity in inspecting the past; the sheer life-energy of that sign of customs gone by also provides the measure of the torpor of the present. The favoured sons of Uncle Sam—the materialist, the organisation man, and even (alas) the ruined fortress—make Hawthorne's sardonic and political comment on the society which replaced the Puritans and the revolution, a society in which his fellow inspectors are quite at home and respected. Indeed, the public service and the business of such a society keep Hawthorne himself torpid; and it is only when his public 'head' is cut off that he can begin to live again, in the reclusive world of the writer. It is only there, now, that the liveliness of the Puritan letter can find at least some reflection, albeit no longer public or customary, in the mirrored chamber of the creative imagination.

Of Hawthorne's description of that chamber a great deal has been written. It is probably unnecessary to elaborate once more that definition of Romance in which the daylight kind of 'reality', solid and familiar, is so transfigured by moonlight which releases the mystery in it, without destroying the solidity, that 'the Actual and the Imaginary may meet, and each imbue itself with the nature of the other' (36). It is however worth emphasizing[3] how Hawthorne's prose enacts what it describes. Moreover the importance of that enactment is to make quite sure that *things* (not merely familiar and domestic but 'with each its separate individuality' (35)), and telling details ('a child's shoe; the doll, seated in her little wicker carriage'), will contribute as much as the moonlight to the magical effect. Surrounded by daylight materialism, Hawthorne may seem to put all the emphasis on the moonlight; yet he is actually very clear that it is the process of *mutual* transformation that is the point; the familiar made strange and remote; the mysterious made solid, individual, particular; and for that the material is as important as the moonlight. Indeed, were it not for this we should be merely in a cold white Platonic radiance which makes the figure in the carpet more distinct than the carpet, and in which actual objects are 'so spiritualized by the unusual light that they seem to lose their actual substance, and become things of intellect' (35). There is a clear implication that to spiritualize, intellectualize, image (all of which are interestingly made interchangeable, as though their operation was essentially the same) is not only to make strange and remote, but also to rob of life and colour, to neutralize. Ghosts may re-enter, but that is also because the room has become ghostly.

Which is of course why Hawthorne's house of fiction not only needs the doll in her little wicker carriage and the individual chairs, but also the counteractive firelight of the heart:

> It throws its unobtrusive tinge throughout the room, with a faint ruddiness upon the walls and ceiling, and a reflected gleam from the polish of the furniture. This warmer light mingles itself with the cold spirituality of the moonbeams, and communicates, as it were, a heart and sensibilities of human tenderness to the forms which fancy summons up. It converts them from snow-images into men and women. (36)

Ruddiness, warmth, tenderness, humanity—these, by a most uncomfortable implication, are what the spirit, the intellect, and the imagination empty out of life, in the process of releasing its more mysterious depths. For the first time we begin to see why Hawthorne *needs* to be evasive, equasive, and ambiguous in stance, continually shifting and successive in movement. It is not because he shares the celebratory sense of the Melville of *Moby-Dick,* of a rich and multiple abundance of meanings, which require many different points of view to explore or whale among, but which can all be fused and revealed together eventually, in one tremendous vision, by an equal eye. Rather it is defensive, counter-active, constantly aware that the truth-teller must walk as on a tightrope over reductions and devitalizations, and that no step can come down with committed weight, because all the footing is treacherous. How insure against the burning here, and the cold inhumanity there ?—except by keeping constantly on the move in a kind of strenuous simplicity, which constantly recognizes and passes over simplifications. Only by such a process can the letter be developed into the picture—or, rather, successive picturings—with sufficient interplay of counteractive kinds of lighting and shadowing to make sure that it will be fully imagined, intellectualized, spiritualized; yet also warmed by the heart; and yet again always remain stubbornly material, literal, individually detailed—for all are equally necessary, because each on its own will falsify.[4]

And even so, success will be indirect and perceived only out of the corner of the eye:

> Glancing at the looking-glass, we behold—deep within its haunted verge—the smouldering glow of the half-extinguished anthracite, the white moonbeams on the floor, and a repetition of all the gleam and shadow of the picture, with one remove farther from the actual, and nearer to the imaginative. (36)

Hawthorne's conception of Romance, and of *The Scarlet Letter* in particular, is not the picturing of the human living-room itself, seen by moonlight and by firelight, but the reflection of that picture in a mirror. The frame is not the exterior walls of man's dwelling in daylight and society, but the interior verge of the mirroring consciousness. The full mysterious suggestiveness is not to be found in the picture itself, nor even in its reflection in the mirror; but only for a moment, in the sidelong glance, does something *further* appear 'deep within its haunted verge'. And yet the 'something further' is absolutely dependent upon the actual and the picturing of the actual, though it is a step further 'away', nearer to the imaginative but never imaginary, for even the artist's dream must be a looking-glass and look like truth.

The real strangeness of this lies in the duplicity of duplication: how reflection can mirror and yet make a difference; or how what is double can yet remain one, and the same. Yet the phenomenon is a simple fact of life. We all have some acquaintance with the mysterious 'Monsieur du Miroir' who provided Hawthorne with an early sketch.[5] And in Hawthorne we must above all hold onto both sides of the paradox, for that is what distinguishes his kind of mirroring from the Platonic, or Paterian, or Freudian kinds with which it is too frequently confused. Once we take the direction of the Custom-House and the point of the evasive and equasive style, it is clear how the

Platonic man, who has escaped from the cave of shadows but can still only glimpse reflections of the Forms in water; or the Paterian man, who sees the inchoate street given significant form focus and intensity only by being aesthetically mirrored in the work of art; or the psychologist, who interprets every reflection in the mirror as only a language for the interior complexes of Narcissus; are all to be found in Hawthorne, but must therefore be, if adopted separately, reductive splittings and rankings of what he struggled always to hold together and to equate. In Hawthorne's mirror the objects in the room only 'seem to lose their actual substance, and become things of intellect' (35, my italics); and though that continual seeming is proof of how strongly he was drawn to transcendental idealism, he no less strongly asserts the earthly and material against the Idea.[6] Similarly, it is indeed the work of Art—whether capital A, picture, or mirror—that holds together, intensifies, beautifies what would otherwise remain incoherent; yet the last subversive sentence of 'The Artist of the Beautiful' insists that Hawthorne's artist had caught 'a far other butterfly' than his work of art, and that what he was really after was 'Reality'.[7] And though, of course, *The Scarlet Letter* will be a mirror of Hawthorne's interior—a 'psychological romance' in a modern sense rather different from what he meant by the phrase—yet the shoe and the doll speak, not of him, but of themselves and of his daughter in another room; and it was not for nothing that Roderick Elliston denounced the serpent lurking in the fountain, which he had nourished in his bosom by 'diseased self-contemplation'.[8] We must hold onto Hawthorne's insistence on the heart and the truths of feeling as against Idea and Image; onto his sense of history and its relativism as against any kind of timeless absolute; onto the wicker carriage and the piece of material with limbs exactly three-and-a-quarter inches, as against any kind of transcendence or subjectivity. *And vice versa.* For it is the need to concede some validity to all, that makes each necessarily partial and treacherous. Hawthorne's mirrors focus analytically and spiritually[9]; hold the history of generations[10]; bring out the inner spectres of the mind[11]; reveal secret truths hidden by appearance[12]; impart an 'ideal beauty' to the world they exactly reflect[13]; and afford glimpses of the preternatural or supernatural.[14] But they only do any of these in the degree that they do all; so that not one can be *the* significant mirroring, and none will do on its own.

He was drawn towards the old Typology precisely because it seemed a way of seeing one dimension reflected in another, or transfigured by another, without damaging the validity of each in its own terms or denying the difference between them. The Old Testament is transfigured by the New; but the New comes not to cancel but to fulfil its predecessor, and they can be both two in history and one in truth. Similarly the things of the world reveal the divine but remain themselves the while; not merely vehicles for supernatural tenors, or illusive shadows of the real, but equally concrete, moral, metaphysical, spiritual; yet differentiated, each in its appropriate dimension.

But of course Puritan typology had become old-fashioned because the Puritan certainties had gone—and liberal unitarianism had led to Emerson.[5] How was it possible, now, both to have a sharp sense of doubleness, and yet not fracture the kind of differentiated unity that Hawthorne still aspired towards? That he should have christened his firstborn Una, after Spenser's heroine, is surely significant. But in the mid-nineteenth century, how pit Una against Duessa, daughter of Arch-Imago, and earn her final restoration, even with the aid of an embattled protagonist and a red badge? The answer had to lie, it seems, in *style*. Having seen why Hawthorne's prose had to be evasive and equasive in its apparent simplicity, always moving on to ensure different angles; we may begin to glimpse also the reasons for wanting it to have the containing qualities of a mirror: surface polish, impermeability, coolly imperturbable, distancing. It is the silvering of the glass that stops it being transparent and makes it reflect, turning vision back to the beholder so blandly that it is with him that any sense of difficulty must seem to lie. The polish of the style insists that it is public, artful, Augustan; rather than personal, confessional, Romantic. It will not let us through to the author himself or ever pretend to be a window on a real world; but always reminds us of the medium, between. It holds the reader at a distance, not encouraging emphatic assurance or emotional involvement; indeed, making him aware that he is reading, and responsible himself for what he reads-in. Yet there is more to all these appearances than there seems on the surface. The cool distance, the air of objectivity, the bland accommodation so willing to reflect all possibilities within the same frame, do convey an equable inclusiveness and a whole greater than its parts, and furthermore, do begin to suggest something hauntingly deeper, when the lights are right.

We can perhaps test these hints of how to read, and try to show something of the counteractive processes at work, by reflecting on the two most famous reflections of *The Scarlet Letter*, and how they move in opposite directions, to the same end.

Before we are allowed to see Hester and Pearl in Governor Bellingham's armour, Hawthorne has made us double-minded. There are the two time-schemes of the Custom-House: the time of the story when the Elizabethan Hall is bright and modern, and the time of the narrator when the old houses are mossy, crumbling away. Again the two are linked, by the history-book, placed on the centre table as such gilded volumes always are, 'to take the eye', in 1630, 1850, 1980. Once again the sense of history releases the sense of relativity: the portraits gaze down with definite and severe views, but we do not. Even Puritanism has more than one 'face'; we take in the 'cheery' effect of the broken glass and cabalistic figures which decorate the facade with such brilliance, and the luxuriant oak-leaf carving on the chairs. There is not even a sharp division between fiction and fact, for Governor Bellingham was a real person, and we are not surprised to discover that Hawthorne has described a recorded house.[16] And here again are the sunshine in which things are solid, the vision made strange in white light, the warming by the heart, the composing into a picture, and the mirroring in consciousness. How important that large pewter tankard is, 'at the bottom of which, had Hester or Pearl peeped into it, they might have seen the frothy remnant of a recent draught of ale' (105). In its marvellous redundancy, this cannot merely betoken 'that the sentiment of old English hospitality had not been left behind'. The tankard might have done that, but the froth (just for our eyes) guarantees a material world, authentic in its own terms that require no translating into others, and are indeed the grounds of authenticity. Yet the white radiance of Governor Bellingham's armour transfigures, makes strange, spiritual, intellectual, image-inative. The armour, also, is a solid thing; and it speaks historically of 'the exigencies of this new country' where the Puritan lawyer must be soldier and Indian-fighter too. But it holds further dimensions—'Let your light so shine . . .', 'Put on the whole armour of God . . .'—in which Hester and Pearl must come into extraordinarily different focus. Now we become aware of false Duessa and true Una together. Material swells into Emblem; person into Type; the significance of breaching the Laws of God and Man is magnified—this, though more intensely, is what we have been seeing over six chapters, which develop the effects of Hester's sin on her, and on the child she dresses to duplicate the scarlet letter. Yet we cannot fail to see now, also, in this white 'intellectual' lighting, how the figure takes over from the carpet: the woman is dwarfed by the emblem, the child reduced to imp-image. So the scene has become a *locus classicus* for arguing that Hawthorne isn't *really* an allegorist, for what we see is clearly an optical distortion in its 'exaggerated and gigantic proportions'. And it is true that this 'moonlight' needs to be counteracted, both by a more colourful sense of nature, and by a warmer sense of the heart. So we have to 'come along' with Hester and Pearl, to look at cabbages, and the 'vegetable gold' of the huge pumpkin, and the red roses, and see that nature can be tamed into fruitfulness, though not without difficulty. And a far more complex and humane reading of the scarlet letter will come from Dimmesdale's plea, so that the 'hollow armour' can ring with truths of the heart; and the Letter become a 'red symbol' (paradoxical, multiply suggestive, and equasive) of 'ever-recurring agony, in the midst of a troubled joy' (114). So, when little Pearl lays her cheek against Dimmesdale's hand, while her mother looks on in wonder, the picture that forms in that moment may seem to hold so rich and complex a symbolism that it must *replace* the optical illusion. Yet it cannot do so. For the earlier focus is indelible. Governor Bellingham's armour has established Hester-and-the-A in the imagination, once and for all. Years after one has read and half-forgotten the book, that impression stays on the retina. The A *is* Hester now, not merely pinned on her as it was in the beginning. Moreover, if one process of the book turns letter into symbolic picture, another insists on writing the letter materially into flesh and sky—and critics who complain of this as a mistake have mistaken Hawthorne. Pearl is as much the 'eldritch scream', a weird uncanny creature, as the fatherless little girl, and will become so again the next minute. One kind of perception succeeds and is added to, but does not replace another. *Our* mirroring consciousness must contain both, holding together the sense of their duality, and the sense in which they are nevertheless mysteriously one.

Even if the whole point of Bellingham's armour were merely to show up the distortion of subordinating the woman to the letter; the reflection of Pearl in the brook would establish the equal distortion of trying to free the woman from the letter altogether. Hawthorne starts now where he had ended before, with nature, the heart, and human relation, and exactly reverses his previous process. Although we are still aware of allegoric readings—the Wood or Error, the moral wilderness, the realm of the Black Man—and of lighting that seems emblematic, so that the brook seems to run from the heart of darkness with its tale of sorrow, and Hester cannot come within the gleams of sun; yet, as we read, the vision becomes material and realized, more and more an 'actual' forest with great trees and lichened boulders, a brook that sounds as it does because of dead leaves and fallen trunks, a realistic dapple of sun and shadow, and a squirrel that drops a last year's nut with a toothmark in it. Moreover the narrator deliberately exposes (as he goes too far with Pearl and the wolf) the note of fancifulness in his fabling and pathetic fallacy. So the predominant experience this time is of nature emerging from beneath allegory to provide a context in which the man and woman begin to recover the natural feeling of their hearts, and even their natural, sexual, relation. It is delicately and convincingly done, step by step from the first halting and embarrassed beginnings to that astonishing moment when Hester takes off the letter and her cap—and it is as though we had never seen her before:

> By another impulse, she took off the formal cap that confined her hair; and down it fell upon her shoulders, dark and rich, with at once a shadow and a light in its abundance, and imparting the charm of softness to her features . . . Her sex, her youth, and the whole richness of her beauty, came back from what men call the irrevocable past . . . (202)

With the Letter, Hester discards both 'human law' and the 'higher truth'. Isolation has developed in her the power of the freethinker to criticise all systems of value external to the self; and what she claims is no less than the freedom of the heart to create its own identity, its own life. As the whole dimension of half light (or moonshine) goes, what more natural than that the material world should flood with golden sunshine. Logically, history must go too. Time, place and milieu become indifferent, save as the heart chooses and:

> The past is gone! Wherefore should we linger upon it now? See! With this symbol, I undo it all, and make it as it had never been! (202)

The embroidered letter becomes a thing again, among withered leaves, by the water.

But Hester mistakes. The brook remains a threshold which insists that there are dimensions beyond what she asserts as the only realities. And when the apparently anarchic child of wild nature drifts back to it, it reflects duality.

> Just where she had paused the brook chanced form a pool, so smooth and quiet that it reflected a perfect image of her little figure, with all the brilliant picturesqueness of her beauty, in its adornment of flowers and wreathed foliage, but more refined and spiritualized than the reality. This image, so nearly identical with the living Pearl, seemed to communicate somewhat of its own shadowy and intangible quality to the child herself. It was strange . . . (208)

In the reflection is everything Hester had sought to deny: the other realm, strange, shadowy, intangible, spiritualized. But though Pearl is two, the two are also one and authoritative. Both point imperiously at the scarlet letter and passionately demand its resumption. In one dimension this is valid in terms of child psychology, feeling, and character; but in another it asserts that Hester cannot *be* Hester without her past, without full consciousness of the terms that she herself has accepted, without the full *chiaroscuro* of sun and shadowlight. When Pearl crosses the brook the picture of man, woman and child forms again, but when she kisses her mother, this time, we see why she kisses the scarlet letter too, and why she washes off Dimmesdale's kiss in the brook. Not until he, also, can unite his duality into integrity, and she be manifested as the 'hieroglyph' which unites him with Hester, can the final picture be formed, reflected in its contrastive but necessary lightings, and only through that wholeness capable of releasing what haunts the verge.

What, then, has finally to be read into the climactic tableau of woman, man and child (which has been redeveloped again and again and again, so that we shall get more into it each time)? What is the role of the fourth figure looking on? What finally is the 'meaning' of the Letter A? Of course if one could answer these questions in what remains of this article, *The Scarlet Letter* wouldn't be worth writing about. My purpose in attempting, now, a rather brutal summary of the main families of interpretation will be merely to indicate the twin hazards, as I see them, that are the Scylla and Charybdis of Hawthorne criticism. On one hand lies the rock of exclusive interpretation which tries to make one reading stand out as definitive, so that the others become subordinate or misleading. On the other is the whirlpool, much more fashionable now, which makes Hawthorne so radically ambiguous that the A's 'significance lies in undecidability', it 'so refuses to stand reliably for any one thing and thus draws all significance into itself that all referents disappear into the function of symbolizing'.[17] Between *the* code, and deconstructive indecipherability, is there a way?

Reading through the eyes of a collector of customs, we see Adultery, and final Atonement. Sin breaks the sinners' bonds with God and society; a breach that can only be healed by full public confession, showing that not only sin but its companionship have been recognized and renounced. But this they cannot do; Hester because she cannot renounce her love and indeed wishes to take Dimmesdale's sin on herself; he because he is a coward, but also because he cannot bear to forfeit the chance of doing good as a priest. But though there is no penitence, there is penance, and some attempt at atonement. Hester is tortured by the shame of the letter, but learns to accept it, and tries to atone by good works. Dimmesdale tortures himself and is tortured by Chillingworth; he too tries to do good. But there is no redemption by works; for sin in cutting off from God, cuts off all possibility of good.[18] God has given Hester the scarlet letter, and the child, to save her from the Black Man;

and to Dimmesdale, Chillingworth; but redemption cannot be won by private pain. Dimmesdale tries to repeat the opening scene with himself in his place, but darkly and in secret—and the heavens still manifest Adultery. Hester in the forest tries to escape the letter and seek happiness with her child and lover in the wilderness or across the sea, but there is no escape in places. Only when Dimmesdale, realising the full horror and wickedness that come through isolation from society and God, gains the courage to repeat the night scene in the full light of day and before all the people, are the broken links healed, the confession made, the election secured, while the fiend's agent recoils helplessly and withers. Dimmesdale dies blessing God in the words of the Lord's Prayer; Hester finds peace and her place in society; Pearl's errand as messenger of anguish is fulfilled and she can make a life elsewhere. Only the old man who has done the devil's work and become satanic, refusing to forgive or be forgiven, remains damned.

Hawthorne is a fair customs-man, and grasps the Puritan position, but he is clearly critical too, even though it compares favourably in some respects with the torpid or transcendental present. He cannot accept their theology of sin, or inhumanity towards sinners, or refrain, for all his tolerance, from underlining the grimly repressive and joyless nature of their world. Yet they had hold of certain truths: the darkness of man's heart and the reality of evil; the destructiveness of isolation and the importance of society. They took life seriously as a battle of good and evil, and had a serious view of responsibility. Their sense of guilt caused terrible pain, but also mutes satire to respect. (Dimmesdale is a weak, even morbid character, but it is his self-torture that holds the imagination. If he could ever cease to feel guilty he would be a nonentity.) But we see how far the critic of customs diverges from Puritanism when we see the Puritan hard-line put into the mouth of Chillingworth. He it is who tells Dimmesdale that there can be no hope of good works; and Hester, with fatalistic determinism, that her sin has created a dark necessity from which none of them can escape, so 'Let the black flower blossom as it may!' (174). But as the complex persons come into focus from behind the stigma of Adultery, Atonement becomes more meaningful, and the Letter gains another A. Not only is the sinner Able, able to bring good out of

evil; but it even becomes possible to see the evil as the source of
the good, a *felix culpa*. By accepting punishment and guilt,
Hester is educated and strengthened by suffering, and acquires
a power for good beyond the scope of the rebel of the opening.
Her isolation remains dangerous, but she keeps her heart alive;
while Chillingworth commits the only unpardonable sin, the
violation of the sanctity of the heart in punishment and revenge.
Even more clearly, Dimmesdale gains power for good through
evil. As we listen with Hester to his last sermon we do not need
to hear the words, for the voice itself holds the point. It is the
base note of pain, the sound of the heart in guilt and sorrow,
that underlies all, and 'It was this profound and continual
undertone that gave the clergyman his most appropriate power'
(244), so that his most guilty suffering produces his greatest
power for good. The humanization of Pearl makes the same
point: her wildness is the product of her parents' sin and of the
isolation that causes, but it is through proving able to suffer,
and for the first time to weep for her parents in sympathy, that
she becomes a woman capable of happiness and good. The final
tableau is paradoxically an ignominious triumph of the heart.
The story remains dark, but relieved by glowing light. The
scarlet letter has changed from a lurid emblem of burning and
destructive evil to the crimson of the rose of love; not wild, but
the 'moral rose' Hawthorne promised at the prison door, to
'relieve the darkening close of a tale of human frailty and
sorrow' (48).

But what about Adam, America, the new Eden?—and what
about the sense of loss and waste? To the Puritan the forest is
the Black Man's; to the moralist it is a moral wilderness; but we
have been made to see the wild rose at the prison door and the
natural joyousness and vitality of the child in the wood. If there
be weeds at the prison door also, Pearl insists on placing flowers
and burrs and seaweed, equally, against the scarlet letter, as
nature pointing up repression. Must the black weed be emblem
of evil, outgrowth of some sinful heart? Is Pearl imp, scarlet
fever, small image of the Scarlet Woman? Or is her spontaneous, impulsive, natural life the most telling measure of the
waste of the Hester-that-might-have-been, whom we see only
for one instant? Pearl insists on the resumption of the letter, but
that is because it has become part of her mother, second nature

by a lifetime's acceptance; Hester and Dimmesdale can only achieve integrity by being 'true' to the selves they have become. Yet Hester's moment of radiance underlines the tragic loss and waste and denaturing, indelibly. Good may come from evil, and a moral rose from suffering, but Dimmesdale can only achieve his kind of selfhood at the cost of life itself, and Hester will never be fulfilled. She may dream of a better society, a healthier relation of man and woman, but she can be no Angel or Apostle of that revolution, as she glances sadly at the scarlet letter. Whether the darkness be relieved by the glowing light of atonement, or personal integrity and at-one-ment, that point of light is gloomier than the shadow.

Moreover (A is for radical Ambiguity) if Hester's integrity is defined by what is 'right' for *her*, then relativity becomes more than a mere consequence of historical perspective. And there comes hauntingly into focus the possibility that it is not only Puritan morality that represents natural impulse, but any morality. (Every human 'settlement' must build a prison.) There follows the further possibility that it may not be only vengeful probing into the sanctity of the heart that is an unforgiveable violation, but the activity of moral analysis itself. It is one of the strangenesses of the book that the child and the old man who might seem most tiresomely emblematic and least satisfactory as characters, should nevertheless be so disturbing—and one begins now to see why. The child is created out of Hester's rebellious feelings, out of 'the *freedom* of a broken law' (134, my italics). Her ebullient wild vitality creates a sense of what it would mean to be quite outside society, law, morality—to be anarchically free. All kinds of natural growth mock the scarlet letter. There can be no moral sympathy. Relationship, even that of a child to its mother, follows no law or responsibility other than the spontaneous ebb and flow of the child's own feelings. A tragic view of life, or grief, are to be met with uncompromising hostility. Any social judgement or restriction is to be fought against, and the child trains herself for war by sowing dragon's teeth all round. There is no God; she has simply grown out of nature as a wild rose on a bush. And graves are to dance on. Such imaginative anarchy works two ways. It is above all in her growing response to Pearl, that Hester's acceptance of the necessity of suffering and repression is validated. But Hawthorne has also created, haunting the verge of his coolly imperturbable mirror, an objective correlative of absolute relativity.

Chillingworth's unpardonable sin is clear enough: how the probing that begins as justice becomes a violation and ends with destructive evil and withering because it becomes obsessed with evil and blind to all else. Moreover this obviously connects with Hawthorne's persistent worry about the analytic artist who dessicates himself in isolated observation of others, and dries up the springs of his own humanity. But the disturbance goes deeper. For, as Dimmesdale observes, Chillingworth is as necessary to him as Pearl to Hester. In terms of motive, Chillingworth's profession of the scientist distilling wholesome medicine out of the black weeds that grow from the buried heart is savagely ironic. But in 'authorial' terms that is just what he does. If Dimmesdale be a moral hero, Chillingworth is needed both to bring about and to analyse his progress. Chillingworth is Hawthorne, applying the torture that will bring the red letter out of the dimmest dale of the heart until it writes itself into the flesh in agony; analysing remorselessly; finally bearing witness to the terrible cost to the character, and maybe the author too. For if it be unpardonable to violate the heart for immoral reasons; in a world without moral certainty it may not be pardonable to violate the heart by analysis at all.

Yet for all the multiplicity of readings, it is surely not necessary to decide between one, and undecideability? For if none can be *the* one, it is not because they are all false but because there is so much truth in each. Nor indeed—and there has been some flabby thinking here—are they mutually contradictory. All have points of convergence, and of divergence. So of course has an A, which is two-in-one. Read in one direction the arms move further and further apart; read in another they come together to a point, and are held together by an arm (Hester and Arthur on the scaffold, and Pearl). Both in detail and overall, Hawthorne's art seeks to differentiate without destroying unity, and to unify with the greatest diversification. The A 'holds' all the readings; but they not only contrast, it is the contrastiveness that creates the intensity. Having started from the letter, the whole book comes to a point again finally in the cryptic heraldry of the closing lines, whose 'meaning' can only be suggested by our full imaginative response to the climactic picture, with the whole weight of the work behind us. But the final impression is not of 'meaning' so much as contrastive intensity, 'so sombre is it, and relieved only by one ever-glowing point of light gloomier than the shadow.' The field of vision is black; to say otherwise is sentimental. But it *is* relieved by an ever glowing point of light. But that point of light *is* gloomier than the shadow. The light makes the blackness blacker. The sable makes the light glow. And that circling rhythm of contrasts, not allowing any position to stand, always moving on, shifting angles and lightings and equating oppositions in constant succession, is the essential process of Hawthorne's style both as he tells us in the Custom-House and as we find in detail in the book. There is no question of exclusion or superiority, or of turning one thing into another. Nor is there contradiction. It is a process of trying to get it all in. Only when the picture has been redeveloped again, and again, and again, can it be fully reflected in all its detail, but with a mysterious superadded wholeness, in our mirroring consciousness. Hawthorne's praise of Thoreau suggests what he wanted his own art to be:

> so true, minute, and literal in observation, yet giving the spirit as well as letter of what he sees, even as a lake reflects its wooded banks, showing every leaf, yet giving the wild beauty of the whole scene. (19)

In such a mirror, spectres (such as relativity) which might scandalize in daylight can be entertained without undue disturbance; but the really haunting glimpse from the corner of the eye has everything to do with *verges*, and with *wholeness*. For it is at a verge, a threshold, that different worlds meet, emphasising both their difference and the line of their unison. Hawthorne's imagination was intensely and minutely aware of things of this world, as (also) thresholds to another. His art is not a symbolism drawing all referents into itself but a hieroglyph, a sacred writing (letter *and* picture *and* mirror), a verge to a wholeness that can only be hauntingly reflected, beyond, within. We have to reckon with both a literalness, and a numinousness, that have gone out of fashion.

NOTES

1. For a fuller account of the Custom-House as house-of-fiction, and of its Collector as *persona* of the artist, see A. Robert Lee's essay in this volume.
2. *The Scarlet Letter* (Ohio State University Press, 1962), pp. 31-2. This and all subsequent references to Hawthorne's works are to the standard Centenary Edition.
3. As A. Robert Lee does, p. 63 of this volume.
4. It follows, also, that deficiency of one produces hypertrophy of another, and hence the characteristic modes of failure in Hawthorne: the work unleavened, or cold, or sentimental-coy, or fanciful, or excessively formal and artificial. On the other hand, *The Scarlet Letter* has two kinds of strength by no means so characteristic of the other romances: a strength of story, and (remarkably) of dialogue between Hester and Dimmesdale— though these, being what is framed, lie unfortunately outside my concern with Hawthorne's framing.
5. *Mosses from an Old Manse* (Ohio State University Press, 1974). 'Monsieur du Miroir' dates from 1837.
6. See, most explicitly, 'The Hall of Fantasy', in *Mosses*, especially pp. 182-85.
7. *Mosses*, p. 475.
8. 'Egotism; or, The Bosom Serpent', *Mosses*, p. 283.
9. See the discussion of Governor Bellingham's armour, and of Pearl reflected in the brook, below.
10. *The House of the Seven Gables* (Ohio State University Press, 1965), p. 20.
11. *The Scarlet Letter*, p. 145.
12. 'Dr. Heidegger's Experiment', *Twice-Told Tales* (Ohio State University Press, 1924), p. 237.
13. *The American Notebooks* (Ohio State University Press, 1972), p. 360.
14. *The Scarlet Letter*, p. 172; *Seven Gables*, p. 281.
15. Both the continuity, and the differences, between Puritan typology and the Emersonian view of Nature, are brought out in Sacvan Bercovitch (ed.), *Typology and Early American Literature* (University of Massachusetts Press, 1972), especially pp. 242-43.
16. Charles Ryskamp, 'The New England Sources of *The Scarlet Letter*' in John C. Gerber (ed.), *Twentieth Century Interpretations of 'The Scarlet Letter'* (Prentice-Hall, 1968), pp. 26-7.
17. Eric J. Sundquist, *Home as Found* (Johns Hopkins University Press, 1979), pp. 109, 113.
18. Thomas Hooker, 'A True Sight of Sin' in Perry Miller (ed.), *The American Puritans* (Doubleday, 1956), especially pp. 159-62.
19. *American Notebooks*, p. 355.

5

'Hawthorne: A Problem': *The House of the Seven Gables*

by RICHARD GRAY

Shortly after *The House of the Seven Gables* was published, Herman Melville, who had received one of the complimentary copies, wrote to congratulate its author. 'The contents of this book,' he declared enthusiastically,

> do not belie its rich, clustering, romantic title. With great enjoyment we spent almost an hour in each separate gable. This book is like a fine old chamber, abundantly, but still judiciously, furnished . . . There are rich hangings, wherein are braided scenes from tragedies! There is old china with rare devices . . ., there are long and indolent lounges to throw yourself upon; there is an admirable sideboard, plentifully stocked with good viands; . . . and, finally, in one corner, there is a dark black-letter volume in golden clasps, entitled 'Hawthorne: A Problem.'[1]

Melville then went on to praise the book both for its 'genialities' and for its representation of what he called 'a certain tragic phase in humanity', but in a sense he had already said all that was necessary. For there seems little doubt that he was at once excited and puzzled by his friend's second novel, and that his way of expressing this was to adopt its dominant image—fleshing this image out with references to abundance and inclusiveness, and falling back eventually on that enigmatic figure of a 'dark black-letter volume'. 'Hawthorne: A Problem':

that phrase could perhaps be applied to any one of the novels, with their mixture of daring and evasiveness, their pervasive irony, their play with opposites, and their various attempts to conceal or neutralize what one critic has called 'the dangerous knowledge that lies at the bottom of (their) plots'.[2] It seems, though, a particularly appropriate way of summing up the story of the Pyncheons and the Maules—not because that story is, as James claimed, 'a magnificent fragment'[3] or, as others have argued, totally incoherent, but because it raises so many issues, of varying degrees of seriousness, not all of which the author seems willing to pursue.

'Hawthorne: A Problem': the most immediate problem, really, is one of tone and attitude. What exactly *are* Hawthorne's feelings about, say, Holgrave's conversion to conservatism? How dry *is* the author's humour when he says that Phoebe, his little sun-goddess, was obeying 'the impulse of Nature, in New England girls by attending a metaphysical or philosophical lecture or viewing a seven-mile panorama'?[4] And what, most obviously, are we to make of that extraordinary ending in which, it appears, even the Pyncheon hens are redeemed and begin 'an indefatigable process of egg-laying' (273)? In one respect, it is easy to say what Hawthorne's relationship to his story is; for *The House of the Seven Gables* is probably his most personal novel, in that it draws most heavily and immediately on his own experience and family memories. Maule's curse, for example, derived from a family tradition that Judge John Hathorne—Hawthorne's ancestor and a judge at the Salem witchcraft trials—had been cursed by one of his victims. 'I am no more a witch than you are a wizard,' the accused was supposed to have declared, 'and if you take away my life, God will give you blood to drink.' In fact the curse, whatever its precise wording, had been directed at a colleague of Judge Hathorne's, Nicholas Noyes: but that did not inhibit the family legend. Nor did it prevent Hawthorne from attributing the subsequent decline of the family, more than half seriously, to this chilling event. Again, another victim of harsh Puritan justice meted out by one of John Hathorne's fellow-judges was actually named Maule. A family dream of lost opportunity, just like the Pyncheons', had actually grown up over some deeds to a large tract in Maine, acquired in the

89

seventeenth century and then unaccountably lost. And the conflict between Judge Hathorne and another person he had helped to persecute, named Philip English, was laid to rest in almost exactly the same way the Maule-Pyncheon feud is: a great grand-daughter of Philip English, apparently, married a grandson of the Judge, and the old English house, the largest and most imposing in Salem, then passed into the hands of the united families. By the time young Nathaniel was born, the house had been abandoned and its furniture disposed of, but it was still standing during his boyhood, grand, empty, decaying—an ironic reminder of former wealth.[5]

So the legends of the Hathorne family provide one strand of personal involvement, giving a measure of historical anchorage to the Gothic paraphernalia of missing deeds, inherited curses, dark mansions, and internecine violence. Another strand is provided by Hawthorne's own immediate experience, the various friends and acquaintances on whom the major characters of the novel are partially modelled. Judge Pyncheon, for example, is based on a Reverend Charles W. Upham, whom Hawthorne described as 'the most satisfactory villain that ever was',[6] after Upham had been instrumental in depriving the author of his post in the Salem Custom House. Hepzibah, a ghost feeding upon memories, is a distorted reflection of Hawthorne's mother, who became something of a recluse after her husband died. Clifford and Holgrave are, as one commentator puts it, 'manifestly expressions of two aspects of Hawthorne's own character . . . the man of action and the man of beauty.'[7] Phoebe, in turn, recalls Sophia Hawthorne, the author's wife, in her diminutive size, her practicality, her cheerfulness and apparent redemptive power—and in her name; for Hawthorne gave Sophia the pet name of Phoebe during the early years of their marriage.

This reliance on personal material does have one clear result: at times, Hawthorne assumes an extraordinary intimacy of approach with his characters. He speaks to them directly, in love or hatred, almost as if he were one of them. Indeed, apostrophe, a vivid and often exclamatory form of address, is one of the characteristic devices of the novel: whether the author is chaffing Hepzibah, arguing with Holgrave, or revealing an almost embarassingly personal sympathy for

Clifford. The heavy sarcasm that Hawthorne directs at the Judge, or the hymns of affection he sings to Phoebe: these are really only extensions of the same mode he uses in, say, his little essay on the pleasures of breakfast that begins Chapter VII; the sketches that punctuate the narrative (sometimes drawn from his own Notebooks);[8] or in his references to his own childish memories of the old Pyncheon house. Of course, *The House of the Seven Gables* is by no means unique in this respect; a similar tone is adopted in many of the tales and sketches and in "The Custom-House" chapter of *The Scarlet Letter*. But nowhere in Hawthorne's novels is this personal note so obviously and pervasively present.

Almost immediately, however, a qualification is necessary. Hawthorne did draw heavily on personal experience and family legend, when writing *The House of the Seven Gables*, and this often seems to abridge the gap between tale and teller. But it would be wrong to claim that his attitude towards his second novel was unambiguous, unaffected by doubts and a characteristic lack of certainty about his aims. For a great writer, Hawthorne was unusually lacking in self-confidence—something that is especially noticeable when one looks at why and how the Pyncheon story came to be written. *The Scarlet Letter* had been well received. Sales, however, had not been overwhelming; and more than one critic had complained about its lack of 'geniality', expressing the hope that his next book would be relieved by 'touches of that beautiful and peculiar humour', in which (it was claimed) Hawthorne excelled 'almost all living writers'.[9] This, as it happened, corresponded with Hawthorne's own doubts about his first novel, and with his general feeling that an author could hedge his bets with his public by offering variety, something for everyone—or, as he put it, firing buckshot at them rather than one lump of lead. So he set about accommodating himself to this criticism, with its implicit ideal of Shakespearean abundance, and as a result found himself falling into all manner of difficulties, trapped (to use his own figure) in a sort of Slough of Despond where he could find neither firm ground nor direction. Admittedly, he could be simple and positive about his new book. For instance, in an often quoted letter to Horatio Bridge, Hawthorne avowed that *The House of the Seven Gables* was 'more proper and natural' for him to write than *The Scarlet Letter*, 'more characteristic of my mind . . . and, I think, more sure of retaining the ground it acquires.' Yet only three months earlier he had written to Bridge, "I should not wonder . . . if the romance of the book should be found somewhat at odds with the humble and familiar scenery in which I invest it.'[10] And earlier still he had confessed, in a series of letters to his publisher, James T. Fields, that his second full-length novel required more thought than his first, that time and again it teetered 'on the utmost verge of precipitous absurdity', and that he had to work hard to 'pour some setting sunshine' over the final chapter because the logic of the narrative was leading him where he did not wish to go. As he admitted ruefully to Fields, 'it darkens damnably towards the close.'[11]

'A man living a wicked life in one place, and simultaneously a virtuous and religious life in another.'[12] Nobody who could jot that down as an idea for a story, or who could declare to his wife that he had led 'two . . . different lives simultaneously',[13] can ever be easily explained. But it would seem that in writing *The House of the Seven Gables* Hawthorne was guided by what he believed his public and critics wanted, and what, to be fair, a part of him wanted as well. As far as public and critics are concerned, he appears to have been wrong: the book was never even as popular as *The Scarlet Letter*, and the reviews were more or less evenly divided when it came to comparing the second novel with the first.[14] And as for the author himself: his mixed feelings about the work while it was still in progress find their issue in its shifting and equivocal idiom.

This, in fact, is all that can be said about the book's general tone: that it shifts, changes emphatically, while remaining qualified by an irony which is itself constantly varying in degree. To an extent, Charles Dickens acts as an influence here; Hawthorne was, we know, reading Dickens while he was writing *The House of the Seven Gables* and he seems to have been deeply affected by the sheer variability as well as the idiosyncrasies of the English writer's voice. The famous opening description of the old Pyncheon house, for example, a choice example of what might be termed urban Gothic, seems to echo this passage from Chapter I of *Barnaby Rudge*:

With its overhanging stories, drowsy little panes of glass, and front bulging out and projecting over the pathway, the old house looked as if it were nodding in its sleep. Indeed, it needed no very great stretch of fancy to detect in it other resemblances to humanity. The bricks of which it was built . . . had grown yellow and discoloured like an old man's skin; the sturdy timbers had decayed like teeth; and here and there the ivy, like a warm garment to comfort it in its age, wrapped its green leaves closely round the time-worn walls.

At some remove from this, there are the street scenes, where Hawthorne was aiming at what he called "the minuteness of a Dutch picture',[15] or the elaborately mock-heroic humour which envelopes figures like Ned Higgins or Jaffrey Pyncheon. Here, again, Dickens hovers in the background. One thinks, for example, of Mr. Pecksniff, standing by the fire, warming his hands 'as benevolently as if they were somebody else's' and his back 'as if it were a widow's back, or an orphan's back', when reading a passage like the following:

> With a bow to Hepzibah, and a degree of paternal benevolence in his parting nod to Phoebe, the Judge left the shop, and went smiling along the street. As is customary with the rich, when they aim at the honors of a republic, he apologised, as it were, to the people, for his wealth, prosperity, and elevated station, by a free and hearty manner towards those who knew him; putting off the more of his dignity in due proportion with the humbleness of the man he saluted . . . (118)

The book accommodates other modes besides the Dickensian, however. Thus, in many ways, the anthropomorphism of the house recalls *The Fall of the House of Usher* rather than *Barnaby Rudge*. Inextricably involved with the fate of its owners, the Seven Gables, like Poe's House of Usher,[16] is a peculiarly centripetal figure, almost forcing us to draw comparisons between outer and inner, the structures of architecture and the structures of the mind or self. One illustration of this is provided by the description of the dead Judge. Sitting alone in an inner chamber, as Hawthorne presents him he cannot help but recall this earlier portrait of a guilty conscience—which occurs in an analysis of the Judge himself and yet obviously has a more general application:

93

... an individual ... builds up ... a tall and stately edifice, which, in the view of other people, and ultimately in his own view, is no other than the man's character, or the man himself. Behold, therefore, a palace! . . . With what fairer and nobler emblem could any man desire to shadow forth his character? Ah, but in some low and obscure nook . . . may lie a corpse, half decayed, and still decaying, and diffusing its death scent all through! (201-2)

At another moment, Hawthorne can draw away from this sort of portentousness to a sardonic humour worthy of Mark Twain—as when he suggests that 'of all events which constitute a person's biography, there is scarcely one . . . to which the world so easily reconciles itself as to his death' (269); while, at others, he can resort to coy humour (as in his descriptions of Hepzibah), or a rather uneasy and equivocal kind of romanticism (as in his account of the evening when Phoebe and Holgrave pledge their love for each other). Always, Hawthorne is careful to avoid limiting himself. His main fear seems to have been of finding himself caught at one particular pitch, which would then, as he put it, 'go on interminably';[17] hence his difficulties, apparently, while writing the book, and hence our difficulties if and when we try to characterize the narrative voice.

Before leaving this problem of tone or voice, there are two things perhaps worth mentioning. In the first place, it seems fair to say that it is the sheer fluidity of this voice which makes *The House of the Seven Gables* seem all of a piece and yet such a puzzle—rather, that is, than the famous device of 'alternative possibilities'[18] whereby every major occurrence is provided with both a natural and a supernatural explanation. And, in the second, it is this again which makes it just about impossible to tell how the author felt about his admittedly disappointing conclusion. A great deal of often elephantine fun has been had at the expense of the final chapter. Critics have fallen over each other in their attempts to deal ironically with the abrupt death of the younger Jaffrey Pyncheon and the departure to a bright new house on the other side of town. The point to be made, though, is that in all this they have been anticipated by the author himself. The death of the Judge's son, for example, is announced in as cheeky and cavalier a fashion as, say, the death

94

of Antigonus in *The Winter's Tale*—or, for that matter, the conversion of the wicked Duke Frederick in *As You Like It*. Alice Pyncheon floats heavenward as easily as any *deus ex machina*. And, along with the reader, one minor character is left scratching his head as 'Old Maid Pyncheon' and her relatives depart, declaring with mock naïveté, 'it is all very well; but if we are to take it as the will of Providence, why I can't exactly fathom it' (277). The aplomb is evident, the author's tongue is evidently in his cheek. The only question to be asked—and it is one that, in the end, cannot be answered—is just how firmly it is planted there.

Further discussion of the final chapter must be postponed for a while, though. For the moment, it is worth examining the second major problem that *The House of the Seven Gables* raises, which has to do with its structure, its centre of consciousness or organising principle. 'I should not wonder,' Hawthorne wrote to Fields his publisher, 'if I had not refined upon the principal character a little too much for popular appreciation.'[19] Unfortunately, he did not go on to say who he, at least, thought this principal character was. Ever since then critics have simply added to the confusion. Phoebe, says one, is Hawthorne's spokesman; Clifford Pyncheon, declares another, is the character Hawthorne is referring to; while still others have plumped for Holgrave, Hepzibah, or Judge Pyncheon.[20] No one, as yet, has had the temerity to propose Uncle Venner or Ned Higgins as a centre of consciousness. But there have been attempts to solve the problem, or at least shelve it, by suggesting that all the major characters are simply reflections of Hawthorne himself or, more generally, that they represent conflicting aspects of the same single mind.[21]

Another comment by Hawthorne, however, suggests a further possibility. It occurs in a letter he wrote to Fields just before *The House of the Seven Gables* was completed. 'I am hammering away a little on the roof,' he said, 'and doing up a few odd jobs that were left incomplete. Then I must read it to my wife.'[22] This is the figure of the house that Melville found so convenient, whereby building a dwelling and building a narrative become interchangeable activities, and the Pyncheon house provides the organising principle of the book. The author, this figure suggests, is like an architect or builder, taking fragments from his surroundings and constructing a shelter out of them, something which mediates between what Hawthorne himself termed 'cool solitude' and 'the sultry heat of society'.[23] Part of this was suspected by at least one contemporary critic, Evert Duyckinck, who asserted in his review of the novel, 'The chief, perhaps, of the dramatis personae is the house itself.'[24] But even Duyckinck did not seem to realize quite how far this idea could be taken, or just how intimate the relationship is between architectural and fictional structures—the habitation of the major characters and the space inhabited by author and reader for the duration of the tale.

To some extent, the importance of the house can be gauged from the opening description. Within the space of a few pages, the 'venerable mansion', the aspect of which, the narrator tells us, has always affected him 'like a human countenance' (11), is established as a living presence, an organism which somehow incorporates within itself the entire story of the Pyncheon family. The organic metaphor, as Fogle has pointed out,[25] is then developed over the entire narrative: the hearth, apparently, is the house's heart, its timbers are as 'oozy' as any human skin, the windows are the eyes looking out on the 'mighty river of life' (147). And so on. What the reader will hardly guess from the opening pages, however, is that the house is not just a symbol, or, more accurately, a comprehensively developed emblem, but a kind of emblematic frame in which all the metaphors of the narrative are implicated. To use another analogy: in this respect, it functions rather like one of the author's own imaginary mirrors, reflecting the various images that Hawthorne devises and uniting them, making them part of one vital design. So, it is at once heart and head, 'a part of nature' (30) thanks to its association with the Pyncheon elm and Alice's posies and an artifact of culture. With its principal entrance like a church door it describes all that is good in inherited beliefs, while its Gothic ornamentation, of course, and its situation—withdrawn in pride from the rest of the street— project all that is corrupt and evil. With 'storm and sunshine' (11) playing over it, its frowning exterior reminds us of the outward appearance of most of the Pyncheons, while its interior, as a passage already quoted amply suggests, commemorates their guilt-ridden consciences. Within its walls are contained some of the principal emblems: the portrait of the old Colonel, the chair in which both the Colonel and the Judge die, and the mirror which reflects the history of the Pyncheon family. While the other emblems in the book are defined ultimately in terms of their relationship to it: the street with its small 'portion of the world's great movement' (142) passing along outside, the garden, an Eden as full of sunshine and shade as the house itself, and the train which Clifford in a moment of ill-founded optimism sees as the human habitation of the future.

Nor is it only the metaphors which are placed in this way; the major characters are as well. Hepzibah, for example, is introduced to us on the morning when she has decided, somewhat reluctantly, to reopen the shop that one of her ancestors set up under the front gable 'about a century ago' (311); and her timid, equivocal attitude towards the world around her is ultimately defined by that activity. Needing the sort of involvement she has never had, yet at the same time fearing it and slightly despising those to whom such involvements come easily, reaching out hesitantly and then drawing back in a mingled gesture of self-defence and pride: what she does at the entrance to her shop is what she does, essentially, throughout the book. Similarly, the dangers implicit in what Hawthorne calls Holgrave's 'speculative and active' (187) temperament, his desire as he himself puts it 'to look on, to analyze' (191) people as if he were an uninvolved spectator: all this is located for us by his habitual position within the house, 'in a remote gable—quite a house by itself, indeed—with locks, bolts, and oaken bars on all the intervening doors' (33) between himself and others. The parlour containing the chair in which 'many a . . . Pyncheon had found repose' (209) belongs, without a doubt, to the Judge: his image is there from the beginning, in the portrait of his 'iron' predecessor, and eventually, inexorably, that image takes him over. Phoebe belongs to the garden, just as surely as the flowers with which she is associated. And Clifford will probably always remain, in the reader's mind, by the arched window: watching the Italian organ-grinder, perhaps, blowing soap bubbles ('little impalpable worlds,' Hawthorne calls them, 'with the big world

97

depicted, in hues bright as imagination, on the nothing of their surface' (152)), or trying desperately to leap down into the street and join in. The portraits of him there, in his different moods, capture nicely his remoteness, his pathetic love of beauty and his pursuit of imaginative release—as well as his longing to recover, somehow, the years and pleasures he has lost.

Image, character—and also plot: the narrative, as it emerges, is an elaboration of the house, a dramatization of its different aspects. Hawthorne's strategy is to lead us, as it were, through the house and its surrounds, sketching their appearance and figurative implications. This is suggested by, among other things, the headings to several of the chapters: 'The Little Shopwindow', 'Maule's Well', 'The Pyncheon Garden', 'The Arched Window', 'Clifford's Chamber', 'Alice's Posies'. Far more important than this, though, is the essentially static character of the narrative, which the characters enter by entering the house. At the very beginning of *The House of the Seven Gables*, the author and reader anticipate this movement, when together they cross what Hawthorne calls—introducing a word that reappears again and again—'the threshold of our story' (36). From then on, different members of the Maule and Pyncheon families are continually crossing thresholds, coming to our attention—to adopt another image used remorselessly by Hawthorne—by coming on stage. Hepzibah, for example, emerges before our eyes at the threshold of her chamber and then, having been treated to a suitably mock-heroic intro duction, crosses the threshold into her shop. Clifford appears in a similar way, though with an added touch of melodrama: we hear steps in the passageway, which pause at the head of the staircase and then 'twice or thrice in the descent' (94), the doorknob turns slowly, there is a final pause at the threshold of the parlour, and then in he comes. Phoebe arrives at the threshold of the mansion like a visitor from another world but, as it turns out, a welcome one. Judge Pyncheon, on the other hand, is always an unwelcome arrival and has to force his way over the threshold. Figuratively, in doing this he crosses the threshold from life to death; while later, we are led to believe, all the other major characters cross the threshold in another direction, towards 'hope, warmth, . . . joy' (266) and a new life.

Even the minor characters are not excluded in this respect—nor, indeed, can they be, given that they *are* a part of the story: little Ned Higgins is constantly crossing the threshold of the shop, in search of new culinary delights, while Uncle Venner's position, just on the periphery of the action, is nicely caught in a childhood memory—of the times he used to sit, as a child, at the threshold of the mansion.

The shape of the house precedes all the action, then. The characters belong to it, in the sense that they and the emblems accompanying them are defined by it, and to the extent that what happens to them is literally or figuratively a product of their being there in that particular place. Very rarely does the action move away from the mansion and its immediate environment, and when it does the movement is invariably abortive. Hepzibah and Clifford try to go to church, which is not that far away, but they only get as far as their own front door. Even when they do get further, in their memorable flight on the train, Clifford's mind is still held captive by the house, and, inevitably, following a familiar pattern in Hawthorne's writing, the escape is followed by a return.[26] Characters, like Clifford again, may dream of a world elsewhere, departure 'to the South of France—to Italy—Paris, Naples, Venice, Rome' (102). But they cannot, because it is the house that gives them identity, imaginative shape and the scope for action: which, of course, is just another way of saying that the house is an analogue of the book.

Until the final chapter: what happens here, really, is that Hawthorne tries to continue the story after it is finished. The Judge is dead, the house is defunct, and with these events the novel has reached its imaginative conclusion. But at least one part of Hawthorne wants a 'prosperous close',[27] some setting sunshine; so he cannot resist tacking on a happy ending. Admittedly, as I have suggested, that ending is hedged about with ironies, as is the ending to *The Adventures of Huckleberry Finn*: but, like the final chapter of Twain's book, Chapter XXI of *The House of the Seven Gables* constitutes a kind of betrayal. For Hawthorne has made his characters live on after the framework which gave them their being has ceased to exist. 'The dead man . . . was forgotten' (267), the narrator declares; Clifford and Hepzibah bid farewell 'to the abode of their forefathers with hardly more emotion than if they had made it their arrangement to return thither at teatime' (277); and they and their friends set off for a new life which requires little definition because it has nothing to recommend it, either to characters or author, beyond the promise it offers of sudden escape. On a biographical level, it is as if Hawthorne is commemorating his own earlier departure from what he called the 'haunted chamber'[28] of his youth—or trying, by a process of sympathetic magic, to engineer his release from that feeling of self-imprisonment which he tended to associate with the figure of the house. Formally, he is withdrawing from the world of the book while still continuing to write—as James sensed, starting a completely new story and not a very good one at that. And, on yet another level, he is retreating from the issues raised by the tale, that sense of history and temporal interdependence which characterizes the earlier chapters, into an historical world where past, present, and future remain dissociated.

Which brings us to the third problem raised by *The House of the Seven Gables*, the problem of what is commonly called its theme or subject. What is the book about? What issues does it explore and what conclusions, if any, does it reach concerning them? It is easy enough to see that certain things come in for close scrutiny during the course of the narrative, such as the battle between old and new, aristocratic Pyncheons and plebeian Maules; the consequences of pride and the possibility of redemption; and the conflicting claims of solitude and society.[29] But do these constitute the real stuff, the conceptual core of the novel? In his Preface Hawthorne offers one possible answer, an apparent reading of his own story, when he suggests that the history of the Pyncheons illustrates how 'the wrongdoing of one generation lives into the successive ones, and, divesting itself of every temporary advantage, becomes a pure and uncontrollable mischief.' But this reading is presented in a typically ironic and equivocal way. Many writers, he tells us with mock naïveté, 'lay very great stress upon some definite moral purpose, at which they profess to aim in their works.' He does not wish to be thought 'deficient in this particular', and so he is offering his 'moral', for those who want one, at the very beginning. In any case, he declares, adding a strong cautionary note,

> When romances do really teach anything, or produce any
> effective operation, it is usually through a far more subtle
> process than the ostensible one. (viii)

This, surely, is a clue; and, acting upon it, perhaps it would be
best to accept Hawthorne's 'moral' provisionally, while placing
it in the context of the entire narrative. The idea that 'the
wrongdoing of one generation lives into successive ones' pre-
supposes a fairly specific notion of history, the relationship
between past and present. Looking at the actual story of the
Pyncheons and Maules, however, it becomes clear that there is
more than one notion at work in it, that past and present are
entangled in often contradictory ways, and that these entangle-
ments seem to preoccupy the narrator. One way of putting it
would be to say that the moral itself seems to be the subject of a
'subtle process' of investigation and, in a manner characteristic
of Hawthorne, generates far more questions and hypotheses
than it does answers.[30]

Of course, there *is* a great deal in the story which reinforces
the assumptions implicit in the 'moral', suggesting a somewhat
static idea of history. According to this idea, the present simply
repeats or mirrors the past; and Hawthorne suggests as much
himself, in the opening chapter, when he declares, 'we are left to
dispose of the awful query, whether each inheritor of the
property—conscious of wrong, and failing to rectify it—did not
commit anew the great guilt of his ancestor' (24). This sense of
repetition is registered in things both large and small—in the
Original Sin of the Pyncheons, for instance, and in the sound of
blood apparently gurgling in their throats. And it receives
appropriately emblematic expression in the mirror which
dominates one of the rooms of the mansion, in which, so we are
told, 'the departed Pyncheons' can be seen 'doing over again
some deed of sin' (24-5). Even the 'freshest novelty of human
life', Hawthorne remarks caustically at one point, is made up
out of 'old material' (12); even Holgrave's rejection of the past
has been repeated by 'the hopeful of every century since the
epoch of Adam's grandchildren' (159). There is nothing new.
History is a series of echoes and reflections: which is perhaps
why Hawthorne often allows us to see the image or reflection of
a character before we see the character himself. Certainly, it is

one reason why incidents and character-types recur throughout the novel, producing a peculiar sense of *déjà vu*.

Over against this notion of history, though, is another, essentially dynamic and progressive, which seems to deny Hawthorne's 'moral'. This is most clearly articulated in the story of Holgrave and Phoebe. Holgrave reads Phoebe his account of one of her ancestors, Alice Pyncheon, who was apparently hypnotized by Matthew Maule (a carpenter and grandson of the supposed wizard), humiliated and then destroyed. When he finishes reading, Holgrave, who is, of course, a Maule himself, discovers that in imitating Matthew's gestures while telling his tale he has inadvertently hypnotized Phoebe and now has her potentially under his control. The narrator underlines the parallel, just in case the reader should miss it: Holgrave, he tells us,

> could establish an influence over this . . . child as dangerous, and perhaps as disastrous, as that which the carpenter of his legend had acquired and exercised over the ill-fated Alice. (187)

But it is underlined only to be erased. Holgrave refuses the opportunity, because he respects Phoebe's individuality, and, instead of a symbolic rape, there is eventually a marriage. So the past can apparently be denied; the destructive consequences of earlier crimes may, as a matter of moral choice, be evaded; in sum, progress would seem to be possible.

Other things reinforce the possibility of progress: Holgrave's gardening, for instance, which involves the uprooting of 'rank weeds (symbolic of the transmitted vices of society)' (81). And that progress, it is clear, can be down as well as up: the Pyncheon breed of hens illustrates this—a race that has degenerated, we are told, 'like many a noble race besides, in consequence of too strict a watchfulness to keep it pure' (83). But quite as important in this respect is the double-edged character of much of the narrative, clues which point equivocally towards both repetition and change. The analogy drawn between the aestheticism of Clifford and earlier Pyncheons is one example of this: is the point here their difference or their similarity? Or take the comparison between Judge Pyncheon and his ancestor the Colonel. The Judge is certainly like the Colonel, as the portraits of the two indicate:

they have the same features, in some ways, the same lust for power, and the same ability to switch between public and private faces. And yet there are also differences, Hawthorne tells us: there is 'less beef' (109) on the Judge, he has lost 'the ruddy English hue' and acquired 'a certain quality of nervousness, . . . a quicker mobility . . ., and keener vivacity'. 'In compliance', as the author puts it, 'with the requirements of a nicer age' there is a difference in moral texture too: the Judge is much smoother than the Colonel, a suave hypocrite rather than simply and roughly two-faced. The differences, which to some extent correspond with Hawthorne's general notion of what distinguishes the American race from the English,[31] are summed up in a way that is not entirely unserious:

> This process . . . may belong to the great system of human progress, which, with every ascending footstep, as it diminishes the necessity for animal force, may be destined gradually to spiritualize us, by refining away our grosser attributes of body. (110)

One is left wondering again, just what is the relationship between past and present? Is this a significant change or merely a change of costume?

In a sense, Hawthorne forces us to ask such questions because he is constantly raising the issue of time and historical relationships himself. The meditation on time which accompanies Clifford and Hepzibah's flight on the train is well known; so, too, is the contrast between time as duration and time as a system of measurement which frames the portrait of the dead Judge. Less well known, but more important perhaps, are those moments when the author seems to be trying to achieve some sort of resolution between his two versions of history. Holgrave, for instance, appears to offer one possible solution, when he explains how he feels now, in his newly redeemed state, about houses and the past. 'I wonder', he says (referring to the Judge's house to which they are about to move),

> that the late Judge . . . should not have felt the propriety of embodying so excellent a piece of domestic architecture in stone, rather than in wood. Then, every generation . . . might have altered the interior, to suit its own taste and convenience; while the exterior . . . might have been adding venerableness and

103

permanence which I consider essential to the happiness of any one moment. (273-74)

Essentially, this is a compromise position. The notion of recurrence, previous generations shadowing and structuring the present one, is still there, certainly: but it is qualified by a recognition of the need for, and indeed the inevitability of, gradual, specific change.

It is tempting to see this as Hawthorne's final word on the matter, reinforced as it is by other remarks. Clifford's declaration on the train, for instance, that 'all human progress is . . . in an ascending spiral curve' (227) implies the same, basically melioristic position, and so do the narrator's own gently critical comments on Holgrave's earlier radicalism. A case could be made, too, for saying that the form of the book illustrates this idea. Everything in *The House of the Seven Gables* invites our active collusion. That fluidity of tone mentioned earlier, the Gothic paraphernalia, the emblems and characters that seem to melt into one another and then into the ambivalent figure of the house, the equivocations and the pervasive irony: all these things represent, as Frank Kermode puts it, 'evasions of narrative authority, and imply that each man must make his own reading'.[32] But make it, one must add surely, within certain fairly clear limits which are laid down by the house/book. The House of the Seven Gables, dwelling and narrative, is in this sense Holgrave's 'piece of domestic architecture', structuring our perceptions, leading us along specific lines of imaginative inquiry, but allowing us at the same time a good deal of freedom of interpretation according to our 'taste and convenience'. Our individual versions of the story, and our personal visions of the mansion, consequently re-enact that compromise between recurrence and change which Hawthorne and his young daguerreotypist seem to be seeking.

And yet, there is still that final chapter. Suddenly, we are back with an optimistic, progressive notion of things. The Judge is dead and quickly forgotten; the house is abandoned; Clifford, Hepzibah and company all change for the better. Nearly everyone, including the narrator, seems to wash his hands of the past. Holgrave's remark about houses, when placed in its proper context here, only tempers our disappointment; it looks to be little more than a tattered flag held aloft while the author sounds the retreat. One comes away, in fact, with the feeling that Hawthorne was finally unwilling either to remain comfortable in his unbelief or, alternatively, to articulate a possible resolution. As far as the possibility of a resolution is concerned, an interesting comparison could be made with one of Hawthorne's own favourite novelists, Sir Walter Scott, who resolved a similar conflict between two different ways of looking backward with the help of the speculative school of Scottish historians;[33] Hawthorne was notoriously distrustful of all speculative schools and apparently reluctant, on this occasion as on others, to plunge himself into what he once referred to, in one of his sketches, as the dangerous current of a theory. Perhaps of more relevance here, though, is the dilemma explored in some of the later works, which offer a revealing parallel with *The House of the Seven Gables*. I am thinking, in particular, of the material relating to England: *Our Old Home, The English Notebooks*, and the 'American Claimant' manuscripts. In all of this work, the leading figure—who is either Hawthorne himself or a fictional surrogate—is faced with the problem of defining his relationship, as an American, with his English past. Quite frequently, the Hawthorne figure feels as detached from his ancestors as Holgrave does at first; this finds expression in a continual harping on the differences between old world and new, aristocracy and democracy, and an almost neurotic obsession with American superiority. But then again, the author tells us, he is often conscious of 'an unspeakable yearning towards England'[34]—and a sense of *déjà vu* so powerful that he feels he has *become* his own ancestor. There is no attempt made to reconcile these two responses. They simply alternate with each other. The present is sometimes an echo or repetition of the past, and sometimes a separate world 'disjoined by time and the ocean'.[35] As a result, in the abortive versions of the novel, Hawthorne seems unable to bring together what he terms 'the two ends of the story'.[36] We never know, quite simply, whether the American claimant will accept his rightful inheritance or feel compelled to reject it.

In one sense, then, the final chapter is unclear because little attempt is made by the author to bring together and resolve earlier positions. In another sense, however, it is far too clear, too obvious and straightforward, because this avoidance of a resolution seems to issue, not from Hawthorne's innate scepticism and subtlety of imagination, but from a simple desire to leave us with a 'moral'. Admittedly, that moral is not the one offered, in such a benign and disingenuous manner, in the preface to the story, but it is a moral all the same. Admittedly, too, touches of irony and equivocation are still there. But the irony no longer feeds into the substance of the narrative, helping to shape our responses; it floats on the surface, as it were, never really impeding the basic impulse of escape. And the equivocations do not require us to participate any more, to rebuild and recreate meaning as we read; they simply qualify, in a modest way, what are essentially a series of ready-made answers—and, perhaps, help to alleviate Hawthorne's embarrassment. Whatever reservations one may make, however much the author may poke fun at his dénouement, the plain fact is that he is withdrawing—and withdrawing in a fashion that is oddly reminiscent of that other observer and writer, the young daguerreotypist: who, as we have seen, after weaving *his* spell out of a series of nicely edged comparisons between past and present, suddenly dissolves it, breaks the enchantment and releases Phoebe from his power. Abjuring his rough magic, the author of *The House of the Seven Gables* ends effectively as the author of 'Alice Pyncheon' does, by returning both himself and his audience to a more prosaic world where certain crudely specific and rather simple-minded choices are to be made.

Still, there is no point in dwelling upon this, Hawthorne's eventual reluctance either to reside amidst doubts or to resolve them. The final chapter may be a disappointment, there may be other weaknesses, but *The House of the Seven Gables* remains a remarkable and puzzling novel—and remarkable, perhaps in part, because it is so puzzling. Its incidental pleasures are numerous: the style, with its beautifully equivocal mixture of the colloquial and the elevated, the narrative easing itself backwards and forwards in time, and that peculiar blend of domestic detail and Gothic melodrama about which Hawthorne was, at times, so nervous. Then there are the greater achievements of the book: a narrator playing cunningly with different masks and creating a consistent identity out of them, the complicated series of figurative references which is

106

given coherence and a sense of meaning by the dominating presence of the house. And, above all perhaps, Hawthorne's agnosticism: his willingness to ask questions, and offer different sets of possibilities, in a way that is at once sportive and deeply serious. At his best, indeed, which means in this novel most of the time, Hawthorne makes a positive virtue out of what he sees as necessity and turns uncertainty itself into an art; suspecting that any human category is arbitrary and conjectural, he offers us a conflict between different categories, various idioms and systems, which is only resolved, if at all, by each reader. What it comes down to, in the end, is something very simple: if the book strikes us as a problem then, quite probably, it was meant to. If the old Pyncheon house seems at once intimate and mysterious, a home and a place of imprisonment, then that perhaps is because the man who built it, Nathaniel Hawthorne, saw the world in precisely that way.

NOTES

1. Julian Hawthorne, *Hawthorne and His Wife: A Biography* (Boston, 1884), p. 386.
2. Frederick C. Crews, *The Sins of the Fathers: Hawthorne's Psychological Themes* (New York, 1966), p. 12.
3. Henry James, *Hawthorne* (1879; London, 1967 edn.), p. 118. See Q. D. Leavis's dismissive comment on the novel, cited in Hugo McPherson, *Hawthorne as Myth-Maker* (Toronto, 1969), p. 132.
4. *The House of the Seven Gables* (1851; New York: Signet Classics, 1961 edn.), p. 155. All subsequent references will appear in the text, and refer to this easily available edition.
5. Arlin Turner, *Nathaniel Hawthorne: An Introduction and Interpretation* (New York, 1961), pp. 2-3; Randall Stewart, *Nathaniel Hawthorne: A Biography* (New Haven, 1948), p. 2; Daniel Hoffman, *Form and Fable in American Fiction* (New York, 1961), p. 193; Hubert Hoeltje, *Inward Sky: The Mind and Heart of Nathaniel Hawthorne* (Durham, N.C., 1962), pp. 14-21, 343-46.
6. Stewart, *op. cit.*, p. 89.
7. Hoeltje, *op. cit.*, p. 349. See also, Stewart, *op. cit.*, pp. 54, 62; J. Hawthorne, *op. cit.*, pp. 215-16, 238, 247.
8. See William Charvat's Introduction to William Charvat and Fredson Bowers (eds.), *The House of the Seven Gables*, Vol. vii in *The Centenary Edition of the Works of Nathaniel Hawthorne* (Columbus, Ohio, 1965), p. xxiii.
9. J. Donald Crowley (ed.), *Hawthorne: The Critical Heritage* (London, 1970), pp. 161-62. See also. pp. 21, 155-56.
10. Ibid., p. 204; Charvat, *op. cit.*, p. xxvii. See also, Crowley, *op. cit.*, pp. 7-8; Charvat, *op. cit.*, p. xviii.

11. Charvat, *op. cit.*, pp. xvii-xviii, xxii, xxvii.
12. Claude M. Simpson (ed.), *The American Notebooks*, Vol. viii in the *Centenary Edition* (Columbus, Ohio, 1972), p. 167.
13. F. O. Mattheissen, *American Renaissance: Art and Expression in the Age of Emerson and Whitman* (London, 1941), p. 251
14. See Charvat, *op. cit.*, pp. xx-xxi; Crowley, *op. cit.*, pp. 22-3.
15. Charvat, *op. cit.*, p. xxvii. For other parallels with *Barnaby Rudge*, see the descriptions of London in Chapter III and the Maypole Inn after the riots in Chapter LV.
16. See Maurice Beebe, 'The Fall of the House of Pyncheon', *Nineteenth-Century Fiction*, XI (1956), 1-17; Rita K. Gollin, *Nathaniel Hawthorne and the Truth of Dreams* (Baton Rouge, 1979), pp. 179ff.
17. Charvat, *op. cit.*, p. xviii.
18. Yvor Winters, *In Defense of Reason* (London, 1960), p. 170.
19. Charvat, *op. cit.*, p. xxin.
20. Edward Wagenknecht, *Nathaniel Hawthorne: Man and Writer* (New York, 1961), p. 21; Alfred H. Marks, 'Who Killed Judge Pyncheon? The Role of the Imagination in *The House of the Seven Gables*', *PMLA*, LXXI (1956), 368; Hoffman, *op. cit.*, p. 199; Richard H. Fogle, *Hawthorne's Fiction: The Light and the Dark* (Norman, Okla., 1952), p. 155; Charvat, *op. cit.*, p. xxin.
21. Rudolph Von Abele, *The Death of the Artist: A Study of Hawthorne's Disintegration* (The Hague, 1955), p. 61; Nina Baym, *The Shape of Hawthorne's Career* (Ithaca, N.Y., 1976), p. 155.
22. Charvat, *op. cit.*, p. xviii.
23. *American Notebooks*, p. 28.
24. Crowley, *op. cit.*, p. 193. See also Kenneth Dauber, *Rediscovering Hawthorne* (Princeton, 1977), p. 128; Edgar H. Dryden, *Nathaniel Hawthorne: The Poetics of Enchantment* (Ithaca, N.Y., 1977), pp. 151-52.
25. Fogle, *op. cit.*, pp. 162-67.
26. See R. W. B. Lewis, *The American Adam: Innocence, Tragedy, and Tradition in the Nineteenth Century* (Chicago, 1955), p. 114.
27. Charvat, *op. cit.*, p. 22.
28. Terence Martin, *Nathaniel Hawthorne* (New York, 1965), p. 27. For the house image, see, e.g., J. Hawthorne, *op. cit.*, pp. 222, 223, and the tales, 'Peter Goldthwaite's Treasure', 'Edward Randolph's Portrait', 'Old Esther Dudley'.
29. See, e.g., D. H. Lawrence, *Studies in Classic American Literature* (London, 1924), pp. 106-7; Hyatt H. Waggoner, *Hawthorne: A Critical Study* (Cambridge, Mass., 1955), p. 170; Newton Arvin, *Hawthorne* (New York, 1929), pp. 187, 194-95.
30. See Roy R. Male, *Hawthorne's Tragic Vision* (Austin, Texas, 1957), pp. 119ff.; Michael D. Bell, *Hawthorne and the Historical Romance in New England* (Princeton, 1971), pp. 214ff.
31. See, e.g., Randall Stewart (ed.), *The English Notebooks* (New York, 1941), pp. 28, 89.
32. *The Classic* (London, 1975), p. 107.
33. See Avrom Fleishman, *The English Historical Novel: Walter Scott to Virginia Woolf* (Baltimore, Md., 1971), pp. 25, 42.

34. Claude M. Simpson and Fredson Bowers (eds.), *Our Old Home*, Vol. v in the *Centenary Edition* (Columbus, Ohio, 1970), pp. 33. See also pp. 19, 59-60, 63, 277-78, 308-9, 449.
35. Claude M. Simpson, Edward H. Davidson, and L. Neal Smith (eds.), *The American Claimant Manuscripts*, Vol. xii in the *Centenary Edition* (Columbus, Ohio, 1977), p. 15. See also, pp. 77, 147, 161-63, 185, 445-46.
36. Ibid., p. 82.

6

'Bitter Honey': Miles Coverdale as Narrator in *The Blithedale Romance*

by KEITH CARABINE

1

It is perhaps not surprising that Miles Coverdale is so distrusted and maligned a figure in *The Blithedale Romance*, since Hawthorne, by making him constantly expose his own limitations, could almost be thought to be disowning him. Critics have settled on three main charges. First, Coverdale is a 'literary snoop', suffering from 'a merciless inquisitiveness', who treats the feelings of his friends as a game, and thus loses their 'confidence' and dehumanizes himself. Both Coverdale's own fear that 'the cold tendency . . . which made me pry with a speculative interest into people's passions and impulses, appeared to have gone far towards unhumanizing my heart', and Zenobia's forthright denunciation of 'your game, groping for human emotions in the dark corners of the heart' (214) are taken to confirm this charge. Second, Coverdale is not to be trusted. Philip Rahv's argument that Coverdale is lying when he confesses at the end 'I—I—myself—was in love—with—PRISCILLA!' (247), because 'it is evident on every page that the only genuine relationship is that of Coverdale to Zenobia', is the bluntest expression of this distrust. Third, Coverdale is treated ironically by Hawthorne throughout the narrative. Not only does Coverdale spend most of his time trying to catch up with his own narrative, but, more importantly, he is, ironically, unable to understand it; and is, therefore, incapable of either self-awareness or moral or artistic maturity. Thus for J. C. Stubbs it is evident 'real people capable of real suffering exist just beyond the comprehension of the witless narrator'; for James H. Justus, 'If there is a tragedy attendant upon Zenobia's fate it takes shape, outside and beyond the range of Coverdale's perception', and for Nina Baym, 'Art is passionate and it celebrates passion; rejecting this truth, Coverdale is incapable of mature artistry and must remain a childish man, an ineffectual "poetling".'[1]

Such readings are altogether too simple. Coverdale allows Hawthorne to dramatize his own troubled, ambivalent perceptions of the artist's role and function. Indeed *The Blithedale Romance* is organized so that the apparent subject matter (the love quartet, the Blithedale community experiment itself, the issue of possession) and the major metaphors (veils and masquerades, mesmerism and clairvoyancy) are all made to bear on this central concern. I will concentrate on the changing status of the narrative; on Coverdale's developing relation to the characters whose story he tells, and upon the paradox at the heart of his final accession to authority. Only through these approaches, in my judgement, can Coverdale properly receive the sympathetic hearing his problems demand.[2]

2

It is characteristic of Hawthorne's craft in *The Blithedale Romance* that the opening chapter hints how we are to read the narrative, and alerts us to the extraordinary relation of Coverdale to his own narrative, and why that relation is significant. Also, in retrospect, we see how Hawthorne has worked for suggestive analogies in 'The Veiled Lady', and in the association of both her exhibitor and his victim, with the exhibitor of the romance itself.

The wonderful exhibition of the veiled lady 'under such skilfully contrived circumstances of stage effect, . . . which at once mystified and illuminated' her 'remarkable performances' (5) is a triple image: of the very form of the story—a 'skilfully contrived' masquerade; of the reader's position—'mystified' and awaiting 'illumination'; and of a judgement upon the Blithedale experiment itself as another form of 'mock life' (227).

Westervelt as the 'exhibitor' (5) of Priscilla works both as an analogy with and a contrast to Coverdale who is himself an 'exhibitor' of 'three characters who figure so largely on my own private theatre' (70). Unlike Westervelt we are continually made aware that Coverdale is not in charge of affairs. He is obliged for much of his narrative, as with Moodie in the first chapter, to 'arrive' 'only through subsequent events', 'at a plausible conjecture as to what his business could have been' (8). In fact, his stance is extraordinary: writing twelve years after the events he describes he still 'conjectures' as to 'Zenobia's whole character and history;. . . . her later purposes towards Hollingsworth' (215). He confesses he is 'a secondary or tertiary personage' (70) in his own narrative, and, characteristically, he is either a distant observer of the action, or he stumbles upon an event, such as Zenobia's 'trial' (Chapter XXV), thirty minutes after it is over. Moreover, unlike Westervelt, the manager of 'the phenomenon in the mesmeric line' (5) who keeps Priscilla under a spell 'enshrouded with the misty drapery of the veil' insulated from 'the material world, from time and space' (6), Coverdale does not *possess* the 'subjects' of his theatre. In fact, it is precisely because Coverdale's characters are not puppets, and can, like Moodie, continually interrupt and surprise his bewildered speculations, that Coverdale avoids 'the cold tendency' which is truly embodied in the 'unhumanized' heart of Westervelt.

Coverdale's remarkable position in relation to his own narrative, and the consequences of that relation with regard to how his story will be told, are captured in his response to 'the Veiled Lady's' 'Sibylline' prophecy: he is left 'turning' a 'riddle in my mind, and trying to catch its slippery purport by the tail' (6). Unlike Westervelt who deals in spells, Coverdale is still, at the time of writing, probing a mystery. And we are invited to share both the process of his discoveries and his struggle to establish his authority over the 'slippery' meanings and the consequences of the tale he has to tell.

It is the analogy with Priscilla which establishes that, though Coverdale may not be the artist as mesmerist, he *is* the artist as clairvoyant or medium, flickeringly aware of the future, and responsive, like Priscilla to Westervelt, to the moods and demands, to the *influence* of his characters. Thus during his first night at Blithedale, Coverdale's 'half-waking dreams . . . anticipated several of the chief incidents of this narrative including a dim shadow of its catastrophe' (38). As Coverdale recognizes, he is, willy-nilly, 'something like a mesmerical clairvoyant' (47) who operates through 'a species of intuition' which renders him subject to being taken over, like Priscilla, by forces he cannot control. I take this to be the meaning of the curious moment when Coverdale, high in his hermitage, is visited by 'a mood of disbelief in moral beauty or heroism, and a conviction of the folly of attempting to benefit the world' (10). It is only when Westervelt hoves into view that Coverdale recognizes it was 'chiefly . . . this man's influence' that had sponsored the sceptical and sneering view which '. . . had filled my mental vision in regard to all life's better purposes' (101).

It is surely apt that Coverdale first meets the woman he loves under the 'management' (5) of a mesmerist. That it is his fate to love a woman who is always free to be someone else's possession, who is always a medium for others' designs, ironically mirrors the position of the artist in relation to his own creations, of man in relation to his fellows, and of his fellows in association with each other. These issues are illuminated in the sequel to the first chapter, namely Coverdale's second visit to see 'the Veiled Lady' in 'A Village Hall' (Chapter 23).

Coverdale's involuntary intuition in his 'hermitage' prepares us for his 'horror and disgust' as he realizes that if the mesmerist's claims 'of the miraculous power of one human being over the will and passions of another' are true, then 'the individual soul was annihilated . . . and . . . the idea of man's eternal responsibility was made ridiculous, and immortality rendered at once, impossible, and not worth acceptance' (198).[3] Furthermore that Westervelt imbues Coverdale with 'a sneering view' ensures that Coverdale can recognize 'the smell of corruption' in the latter's talk of 'a new era that . . . would link soul to soul, and the present life to what we call futurity' and 'finally convert both worlds into the great mutually conscious brotherhood' (200).

The implications of Coverdale's noble judgement are threefold. Firstly, as Coverdale is aware, for the artist to mimic the mesmerist is both to annihilate the individual soul of his creations, to deny his 'responsibility', and, therefore, to damn himself. The consequence is that his characters must be 'free' to decide their own fates; thus ensuring the writer's authority is provisional. Secondly, if the author as man responds similarly to the integrity of his fellows, and does not act (as Hollingsworth does in this scene when he takes Priscilla away from Westervelt) he must remain a perennial observer experiencing life, like Coverdale, as both alienation and loss. Coverdale suffers the mortification of watching Priscilla's rescue from Westervelt, 'her deadliest enemy', to land 'safe forever!' (203)—in the equally possessive arms of Hollingsworth. Thirdly, and even more importantly, Coverdale's recognition that Westervelt's aims express a 'cold and dead materialism' (200), masquerading as brotherhood, enables Hawthorne to establish the authority of his narrator. After all in losing Priscilla 'forever' he learns the hard way that Westervelt's ideal 'brotherhood' operates as a black parody of Blithedale's aims for a better world. Both systems indeed are not 'new sciences' but the revival of 'old humbugs' (5) which deny the possibility of new sympathetic forms of human relations.

3

Coverdale's responsiveness as medium, his perceptions as clairvoyant, and his doubts about both, are essential, initially, to an understanding of his function. Even his 'hermitage' which he ironically confesses 'was my one exclusive possession, while I counted myself a brother of the socialists', and which is commonly regarded as proof of his fundamental disaffection from the aims of Blithedale is less self-serving and defensive than it appears. His 'hermitage' is in fact at once an embodiment and an outcome of a series of devastating perceptions. Indeed, he only retreats to it after recognizing 'the presence of Zenobia caused our heroic enterprise to show like an illusion, a masquerade, a posture, a counterfeit Arcadia' (21); after he discerns that Hollingsworth 'had come among us, actuated by no real sympathy with our feelings and hopes' (54–5); after he grimly divines that 'for a girl like Priscilla and a woman like

Zenobia to jostle one another in their love of a man like Hollingsworth, was likely to be no child's play' (72); and still more importantly, after he recognizes 'my own part in these transactions was singularly subordinate. It resembled that of Chorus in a classic play' (97).

Coverdale's retreat is also a necessary step because unlike his fellow medium, Priscilla, he questions his 'species of intuition' and lives in terror that the source and consequences of his clairvoyance may be demonic—thus rendering him susceptible to confusing 'a spiritual lie' and 'a subtle recognition of a fact' (46). Coverdale's wise awareness of this danger saves him not only from Westervelt's demonism, but, too, from 'the spiritual lie' which Hollingsworth unwittingly lives. Thus, whereas the latter wastes 'all the warmth of his heart' on his 'philanthropic theory!' (55) which turns into 'a cold spectral monster which he had himself conjured up', Coverdale recognizes that too exclusive a devotion 'to the study of men and women' risks fashioning 'a monster' which 'after all . . . may be said to have been created mainly by ourselves' (69). Coverdale, therefore, withdraws from Hollingsworth not because of 'his reticence to commit himself humanly to others'[4] but because his friend's 'spiritual discipline' (53) masks egotistic designs like Westervelt's which violate the very spirit of Blithedale and enslave the wills of Priscilla and Zenobia. Hollingsworth in his treatment of Priscilla fails therefore the victim figure who, as he recognizes, will prove *a test case of Blithedale values:* 'as we do by this friendless girl so shall we prosper' (30).

As refractions of the artist's problems, then, Westervelt and Hollingsworth establish that it is to Coverdale's credit that he is aware of the risks of 'demonism' and of self-conjured 'spectral monsters'. It is however, Priscilla, who is oblivious to such dangers, who is the major key to Coverdale's authenticity as an artist and his limitations as a man. As Priscilla is not free of Westervelt when she is brought to Blithedale, and experiences only another form of possession (which she accepts unquestioningly), so Coverdale discovers that he cannot, either in his hermitage or in Boston, avoid the responsibilities of his 'sympathies' (157)—root meaning 'having a fellow feeling'— sponsored by his commitment, no matter how consciously ambivalent, towards the Blithedale experiment, or, more importantly, by his 'species of intuition', which ties him, irrevocably, in ways he had not anticipated, to his friends. Thus even though he leaves Blithedale for Boston after 'the tragic passage-at-arms' (137) with Hollingsworth, and after Zenobia's stagy rejection of his counsel ('It needs a wild steersman when we voyage through chaos! The anchor is up! Farewell!' (142)), 'they first' begin to 'encroach upon' his 'dreams' (153) and then, again, press back into his life as he looks out of the back window of his hotel only to see Priscilla, Westervelt and Zenobia together in 'a rather stylish boarding house' (150). In one of the central passages in the romance he reflects:

> There now needed only Hollingsworth and old Moodie to complete the knot of characters, whom a real intricacy of events, greatly assisted by my method of insulating them from other relations, had kept so long upon my mental stage, as actors in a drama. In itself, perhaps, it was no very remarkable event that they should thus come across me, at the moment when I imagined myself free. Nevertheless, there seemed something fatal in the coincidence that had borne me to this one spot . . . and transfixed me there, and compelled me again to waste my already wearied sympathies on affairs which were none of mine, and persons who cared little for me. . . . After the effort which it cost me to fling them off—after consummating my escape, as I thought, from these goblins of flesh and blood and pausing to revive myself with a breath or two of an atmosphere in which they should have no share—it was a positive despair, to find the same figures arraying themselves before me, and presenting their old problem in a shape that made it more insoluble than ever.
>
> I began to long for a catastrophe. If the noble temper of Hollingworth's soul were doomed to be utterly corrupted by the too powerful purpose, which had grown out of what was noblest in him; if the rich and generous qualities of Zenobia's woman-hood might not save her; if Priscilla must perish by her tenderness and faith, so simple and so devout;—then be it so! Let it all come! . . . I would look on, as it seemed my part to do, understandingly, if my intellect could fathom the meaning and the moral, and, at all events, reverently and sadly. The curtain fallen, I would pass onward with my poor individual life, which was now attenuated of much of its proper substance, and diffused among many alien interests. (156-57)

It is Priscilla's fate to be pursued by two figures she never recognizes as 'goblins of flesh and blood'. Westervelt exploits her for her clairvoyance and Hollingsworth for her money. Her 'faith, so simple and devout' ensures she does not realize at the end that the vindictive shadow' of Zenobia—another 'goblin of flesh and blood'—'dogs the side' of Hollingsworth 'where' she 'is not' (243). Yet as Coverdale ruefully acknowledges her 'fine heart' has found in the broken, 'child like' (242) Hollingsworth 'its proper substance', whereas his own 'life' is indeed 'attenuated'. His fate, as a human being, in contrast to Priscilla's, as he now courageously and honestly acknowledges, is to be an onlooker, wasting 'his weary sympathies on affairs which were none of mine and persons who cared little for me'. Coverdale's 'let it all come' is not, as Crews argues, 'a vengeful daydream',[5] nor is it merely fatalism; he is beginning to learn that he cannot change the role he must, ineluctably, play of 'Chorus in a classic play' (97). In fact *The Blithedale Romance* is, in part, about the education of Coverdale, into an acceptance of the role of the artist as sympathetic observer who misses out on life.

The 'goblins of flesh and blood' who will not be flung off and who present 'their old problem in a shape . . . more insoluble than ever' tempt him as an artist in ways Priscilla can never know. Zenobia, Hollingsworth and Priscilla are, to paraphrase Pirandello, 'three characters in search of an author'. Their search, as Coverdale recognizes, involves the artist in a paradox. An attempt to understand and solve 'their old problem' involves the artist both as medium and as diagnostician: and both functions involve the artist's recognition that his characters are 'goblins of flesh and blood'. They are 'goblins' in the precise meaning of the term: 'ugly and mischievous demons' who fly about the world deceiving folk. Their need to have their story told and their 'old problem' understood tempts Coverdale to commit the unpardonable Hawthorneian sin of violating their 'flesh and blood' by restricting them to his 'mental stage' and thus surrendering like Westervelt to 'the miraculous powers' of demonism. Furthermore the artist cannot refuse them because they are, too, 'of flesh and blood', they are his friends, able at once to 'encroach' upon his 'dreams' and to solicit his essentially unwearying sympathies. Yet, simultaneously, as goblins, eager to damn him, they unavoidably stimulate the arrogance resident even in sympathy and proceed to induce Coverdale and Hawthorne to produce yet another version of 'mock life' masquerading this time as sympathy and accordance.

The paradox heightens, because as the passage I have quoted illustrates, as Coverdale must distance himself to understand the problem of his characters, so Hawthorne must distance himself in order to use and to understand his chosen narrator, Coverdale. Hence both the coolness and the comedy in Hawthorne's relation to Coverdale. The latter's rather calculating remarks at the beginning of the passage reflect Hawthorne's typical self-referentiality: the 'method', the use of 'the knot of characters' is *his* way of ensuring that the inherent duplicity of his romance works. Hawthorne's 'theatre', his masquerade, is not as much of 'a fancy-sketch' as he would have us believe in his Preface. Nor clearly is his 'whole treatment of the affair' of Brook Farm 'incidental to the main purpose of the romance' (1).[6] The 'old problem' which Coverdale accepts as his business to solve involves an estimation of why the oldest story of all—unrequited love—seems to embody the reasons for the failure of the Blithedale experiment. Coverdale's analysis reveals that 'their old problem' like the Blithedale community's efforts to change the relation between the sexes, to strive for brotherhood and to escape from individualism and ego, stumble inexorably against the stubborn fact of 'the self' (218).

That Hawthorne distances himself from Coverdale who feels estranged from his own narrative is entirely unsurprising. As Mark Kinkead-Weekes remarks in this volume, we confront, even in *The Scarlet Letter*, 'an authorial *persona*, persistently interposing a highly artificial style between us and what we see'—and, one might add, receive.[7] Of course Hawthorne treats Coverdale on occasion as a comic figure. Coverdale's earnest protestations that he thought he had escaped these 'goblins of flesh and blood' involves a ludicrous, even surrealistic aspect (never entirely missing in Hawthorne's fiction) which will wax larger when Coverdale is chased by 'chimeras' (211). Further, Coverdale's sober projection of an anticipated stance ('The curtain fallen, I would pass onward, with my poor, individual life') is slightly in excess of its

occasion, and thus again works ironically at his expense. Again
Hawthorne is quite capable of burlesquing his narrator's
'curiosity' (and incidentally the conventions of the first person
novel) when he places his narrator in his hermitage straining to
hear what Westervelt and Zenobia have to say. Coverdale is
obliged to confess mournfully (and therefore comically), 'I
could hardly make out an intelligible sentence on either side'
(104).

I think it is a mistake, however, to think that, because
Coverdale is treated in part as a comic figure, who is reluctant
even to tell the story, and who doubts his fitness for the task,
that therefore he is not to be taken seriously. Rather I would
stress that Hawthorne has also invested in Coverdale (in his
only novel which grew out of a shared experience with friends
and associates) his deepest feelings and perceptions concerning
the place and responsibility of the artist in relation to his fellow
men and to society at large. Through Coverdale he ponders the
right of the artist to treat and remould communal human
experiences.

Coverdale's position is even more treacherous than
Holgrave's in *The House of the Seven Gables*, another
Hawthorneian artist and analytical observer. Holgrave, the
descendant of a wizard, recognizes (like Coverdale) that 'A
mere observer like myself . . . is pretty certain to go astray.'[8]
After seeing Judge Pyncheon's corpse, however, he can turn to
Phoebe, the woman he loves, and confess his bewilderment: 'I
am all astray, and need your counsel' (302). Priscilla, in
contrast to Phoebe, is perpetually beyond Coverdale's reach
and he, unlike Holgrave, is pursued by 'goblins of flesh and
blood'. Yet, it is his unrequited love for her, his recognition of
the essential value of her 'true heart', which ensures he is not
possessed and destroyed as both man and artist by the 'goblins'
who seek him out. We may grin at his putative stance but it
reveals he possesses a complex sense of both the issues and the
costs of authorship. His awareness of the risks confirms that he
is ready to play his part 'reverently and sadly', and with
increasing authority, as events move steadily towards the
'catastrophe' he increasingly envisages.

4

The last third of the romance confirms that Coverdale's quest for artistic authority involves him in a continual struggle to balance the competing claims and dangers of both his analytic detachment and his sympathetic involvement.

Early in Chapter 19 Coverdale honestly and painfully acknowledges his 'keen, revengeful sense of the insult inflicted by Zenobia's scornful recognition, and more particularly by her letting down the curtain' but he asserts nonetheless his fitness as 'chorus'.

> She should have been able to appreciate that quality of the intellect and the heart, which impelled me (often against my own will, and to the detriment of my own comfort) to live in other lives, and to endeavour—by generous sympathies . . . and by bringing my human spirit into manifold accordance with the companions whom God assigned me—to learn the secret which was hidden even from themselves. (160)

Hawthorne is dramatizing here his own, as well as Coverdale's, sense of the arrogance of the artist who wishes 'to learn the secrets . . . hidden even from themselves'. Both author and narrator escape demonism on the one hand and loss of self on the other, because they struggle to bring their 'human spirit into manifold accordance' (root meaning 'to bring heart to heart') 'with the companions . . . God assigned' them.[9] *They both strive in their art to fulfil the aims of Blithedale.* The quest for 'accordance' is in diametrical opposition to Westervelt's 'cold and dead materialism', to Hollingsworth's divisive, self-deceiving philanthropic system, and to Zenobia's display of self. Even more crucially Coverdale's 'accordance', though stimulated by Priscilla's 'tender faith', involves an effort to understand (with all the risks involved) which 'a character so simply constituted as hers', and which 'has room only for a single predominant affection' (241), can never face. Priscilla's love then is, paradoxically, the opposite of the Hawthorneian artist's understanding.

Once Hawthorne has established that an effort to bring about a 'manifold accordance' sustains both Coverdale's authority—and his own—it is not surprising that the following sequence clarifies both Coverdale's awakening sense of the

shape his narrative will take and the kind of response he expects
to develop in his reader. Confident now of his fitness for 'the
office' of 'observer' he continues in Chapter XIX:

> True; I might have condemned them. Had I been judge, as well
> as witness, my sentence might have been stern as that of Destiny
> itself. But still, no trait of original nobility of character; no
> struggle against temptation; no iron necessity of will, on the one
> hand, nor extenuating circumstance to be derived from passion
> and despair, on the other; no remorse that might co-exist with
> error, even if powerless to prevent it; no proud repentance that
> should claim retribution as a meed—would go unappreciated.
> True, again, I might give my full assent to the punishment which
> was sure to follow. But it would be given mournfully, and with
> undiminished love. And, after all was finished, I would come, as
> if to gather up the white ashes of those who had perished at the
> stake, and to tell the world—the wrong being now atoned for—
> how much had perished there, which it had never yet known how
> to praise. (161)

Leo B. Levy detects in such passages 'the sterness of the
Puritan age . . . [persisting] in Coverdale's fantasy of con-
demning to the stake those who have failed to confide in him.'[10]
He fails to recognize that at such moments Coverdale is less
concerned with judgement than with appreciation and with
tragic waste. Coverdale's terms may serve as a summary of the
great themes and attitudes of Shakespearean tragedy.
Hawthorne's aim, no less, is to write a tragic romance which
will mould and measure the human loss, the tragic waste, at the
heart of the love quartet and of the Blithedale experiment in
'accordance'.

We miss both the distinction and the oddity of *The Blithedale
Romance* if we do not realize that Hawthorne deliberately trusts
such solemn business to a narrator who 'exaggerates' his 'own
defects' (247), who is, as we have seen, both bewildered and
clairvoyant, both eagerly curious and painfully shy, both
intuitive and distrustful of his intuitions. In the world of
Hawthorne's fictions such opposing responses are just. As
Coverdale brilliantly realises, 'a man cannot always decide for
himself whether his own heart is cold or warm' (154). In
Hawthorne the human heart never knows itself well enough to
set up the kingdom of heaven on earth (as the Blithedalians

wish)—let alone to securely anticipate the kingdom of heaven itself, as his 'good . . . just and sage' Puritans do.[11]

That Hawthorne trusts his narrative to a narrator who 'exaggerates' his 'own defects' as surely as Hawthorne reveals them and that he so remorselessly pressurizes his narrator and ensures he is accused of every failing and every danger the Hawthorneian artist is prone to, means inevitably that Coverdale struggles to establish his authority. As readers, we are obliged to share Coverdale's ambivalent responses to 'the goblins of flesh and blood' who haunt, oppose, and finally in the figure of Zenobia, solicit him 'to turn the affair into a ballad' (223). In the closing chapters it is not Coverdale who is 'witless'. Rather his and our pain is that we watch his friends, witless of their fate, accuse him of meddling. Thus in Chapter XX Zenobia anticipates Coverdale's desire to rescue Priscilla from Westervelt: 'With all your fancied acuteness, you step blindfold into these affairs. For any mischief that may follow your interference, I hold you responsible!' (171). Zenobia's blind outrage at the only person who is aware of the impending 'mischief' is outrageous. She knows better at the close.

Priscilla confesses to Coverdale that 'I am blown about like a leaf. . . . I never have any free will' (171) and Coverdale too, discovers—try as he might—that he, too, cannot 'resume an exclusive sway over' himself (194). He confesses: 'Hollingsworth, Zenobia, Priscilla! These three had absorbed my life into themselves. Together with an inexpressible longing to know their fortunes, there was likewise a morbid resentment of my own pain, and a stubborn reluctance to come again within their sphere' (194). Coverdale, however, is inextricably bound to them; apart from them his life is 'a restless activity to no purpose' (195). Both his sympathy as a medium and his analytic desire to understand their 'old problem' ensure that he cannot escape 'the goblins of flesh and blood' who want their story told.

'Two nights' after accidentally seeing Hollingsworth rescue Priscilla from Westervelt in 'A Village Hall' he returns to Blithedale 'with a yearning interest to learn the upshot of all my story' (205). As usual, he fears that his 'sickness of spirits' alone, has engendered 'the spectral throng so apt to steal out of an unquiet heart' (206), and thus render him vulnerable to 'a spiritual lie'; but his intuition that 'some evil thing had befallen us or was ready to befall' (207) is confirmed by the 'fantastic rabble' (211) of 'the Masqueraders'. The masqueraders, like Zenobia, confirm 'our heroic enterprise' to be 'an illusion, a masquerade, a counterfeit Arcadia' (21)—a kind of extended 'Maypole of Merrymount'—and when they pursue him he is indeed 'a mad poet haunted by chimeras' (211). The fate he has tried to avoid suddenly overtakes him. The moment is surreal. Coverdale is here intensely comic; yet the cry of the masquerader dressed like the devil—'he is always ready to dance to the devil's tune' (211)—expresses both his deepest fear and that of his creator, of the artist's potential doom. 'Quite lost in reverie' (212) he stumbles on (note he does not seek out) 'the goblins of flesh and blood' who have absorbed him into themselves and will not let him rest. Respectful of their passion, awed and fearful, Coverdale says:

> 'I will retire'.
> 'This place is free to you', answered Hollingsworth.
> 'As free as to ourselves', added Zenobia. 'This long while past, you have been following up your game, groping for human emotions in the dark corners of the heart. Had you been here a little sooner, you might have seen them dragged into the daylight. I could even wish to have my trial over again, with you standing by, to see fair-play! Do you know, Mr. Coverdale, I have been on trial for my life'.
> She laughed while speaking thus. But, in truth, as my eyes wandered from one of the group to another, I saw in Hollingsworth all that an artist could desire for the grim portrait of a Puritan magistrate, holding inquest of life and death in a case of witchcraft;—in Zenobia, the sorceress herself, not aged, wrinkled, and decrepit, but fair enough to tempt Satan with a force reciprocal to his own;—and in Priscilla, the pale victim, whose soul and body had been wasted by her spells. Had a pile of faggots been heaped against the rock, this hint of impending doom would have completed the suggestive picture.
> 'It was too hard upon me', continued Zenobia, addressing Hollingsworth, 'that judge, jury, and accuser should all be comprehended in one man!' (214)

On trial here is not merely Zenobia before Hollingsworth, or Coverdale before Zenobia, but the Hawthorneian artist before

NATHANIEL HAWTHORNE: NEW CRITICAL ESSAYS

his characters: which is to say Hawthorne before his conscience or what James calls his 'morality'.[12] Hollingsworth 'as puritan magistrate' is a reincarnation of iron Puritans such as Endicott and Governor Bellingham and Hawthorne's own great, great grandfather John Hathorne, who, as Hawthorne wrote in 'The Custom-House Sketch', 'made himself so conspicuous in the martyrdom of the witches that their blood may fairly be said to have left a stain upon him.'[9] Hollingsworth is the very representative of 'a goblin of flesh and blood' piping the devil's tune, holding like the puritan magistrates, the power of life and death over helpless so-called sorceresses like Zenobia or innocent victims such as Priscilla. The magistrates in *The Scarlet Letter* are self-righteously certain that they can use the letter A as 'a living sermon against sin, until the ignominious letter be engraved upon her tombstone' (63), but the omniscient narrator states 'out of the whole human family, it would not have been easy to select the same number of wise and virtuous persons who should be less capable of . . . judgement on an erring woman's heart' (64). In contrast to the certainty of judgement embodied in Hollingsworth and the long line of Puritans behind him, we have the Hawthorneian artist desperate once again to emphasize the secretiveness, the mystery and the freedom of his characters: they have not faced 'judge, jury and accuser comprehended in the *one man of the artist*'! Rather the counter-movement, as we have seen, is that the characters *demand* their story be told.

Zenobia is crucial to this thrust. As early as Chapter 5 she teases Coverdale about his fascination for Priscilla: 'Since you see the young woman in so poetical a light . . . you'd better turn the affair into a ballad. It is a grand subject and worthy of supernatural machinery' (33). The culminating moment of this theme occurs after the trial scene when Zenobia and Coverdale are left alone in perhaps the most moving and powerful moment in the whole of Hawthorne's fiction:

> Zenobia had entirely forgotten me. She fancied herself alone with her great grief. And had it been only a common pity that I felt for her . . . the sacredness and awfulness of the crisis might have impelled me to steal away silently . . . But . . . I never once dreamed of questioning my right to be there, now, as I had questioned it just before, when I came so suddenly upon

Hollingsworth and herself . . . It suits me not to explain what was the analogy that I saw, or imagined, between Zenobia's situation and mine; nor, I believe, will the reader detect this one secret, hidden beneath many a revelation which perhaps concerned me less. In simple truth, however, as Zenobia leaned her forehead against the rock . . . it seemed to me that the self-same pang, with hardly mitigated torment, leaped thrilling from her heart-strings to my own. Was it wrong, therefore, if I felt myself consecrated to the priesthood by sympathy like this, and called upon to minister to this woman's affliction, so far as mortal could?

'But, indeed, what could mortal do for her? Nothing! The attempt would be a mockery and an anguish . . .'

'Is it you, Miles Coverdale?' said she, smiling. 'Ah, I perceive what you are about! You are turning this whole affair into a ballad. Pray let me hear as many stanzas as you happen to have ready!'

'Oh, hush, Zenobia!' I answered. 'Heaven knows what an ache is in my soul!'

'It is genuine tragedy, is it not?' rejoined Zenobia, with a sharp, light laugh. 'And you are willing to allow, perhaps that I have had hard measure. But it is a woman's doom . . . But, Mr. Coverdale, by all means write this ballad, and put your soul's ache into it, and turn your sympathy to good account as other poets do, and as poets must, unless they choose to give us glittering icicles instead of lines of fire. As for the moral, it shall be distilled into the final stanza, in a drop of bitter honey'. (222-24)

Coverdale does not question his 'right to be there, now', as he shares with Zenobia the finest moment of accordance in the romance. The secret analogy with Zenobia contains a deeply felt paradox: Coverdale with Priscilla, and Zenobia with Hollingsworth, experience the torment of loss of self to the other without hope of togetherness; but because their hearts have been touched they are both at this moment 'beings of reality', united in their anguish and grief.

Zenobia the self-appointed 'tragedy queen' (142) of the story thinks 'It is a genuine tragedy' because it tells of 'a woman's doom'. But though Coverdale, after her suicide, accepts her judgement ('the world should throw open all its avenues to the passport of a woman's bleeding heart' (241)) the tragedy has wider implications. These are embodied in Coverdale's final

reflections on Hollingworth's 'perilous', 'exclusive' philan-
thropy: 'I see in Hollingsworth an exemplification of the most
awful truth in Bunyan's book of such;—from the very gate of
Heaven, there is a by-way to the pit!' (243). That 'by-way' is a
broad path in the actual slough of this world, in which the road
to hell is paved with good intentions—the good intentions of the
original pilgrims to whom Coverdale compares the Blithe
dalians; of the latter in their effort 'to establish the one true
system' (227); of Hollingsworth for prison reform; of Zenobia
for women's rights; of Coverdale for a better world. All prove in
Zenobia's words 'varieties of mock life' (227).

Hawthorne's vision of mankind anticipates Conrad's and
T. S. Eliot's. The Congo to Marlow like the Blithedale world to
Hawthorne is 'a dream sensation' and 'what redeems' both
ventures 'is the idea only'.[13] But in Eliot's words in 'The Hollow
Men':

> Between the idea
> And the reality
> Between the motion
> And the act
> Falls the Shadow

'The shadow' in Hawthorne, as Zenobia tells Hollingsworth,
is 'Self, self, self!' (218), which is inexorably embodied in any
project, and which threatens to turn all human plans and
ambitions into masquerades. Not least the writing of tales. As
Coverdale realizes Zenobia's version of her 'genuine tragedy' is
the *romantic tragedy*, of the ballad of 'village maidens . . . wronged
in their first love . . . seeking peace in the bosom of the old,
familiar stream' (236). The 'drop of bitter honey' 'distilled into
the final stanza' of her version, and of her life, is the old story of
the woman who dies for love. It is a grim irony that in com-
pleting *that* pattern Zenobia confirms that the shadow of 'the
self' was with her until the very end, because her postured
romantic death embodies, as Coverdale gloomily realizes,
'some tint of the Arcadian affectation' (237).[14]

Whereas Zenobia takes her 'soul's ache' to a watery grave
which hideously rigidifies her, the shy, frail, self-mocking
Coverdale puts 'his soul's ache' into a *tragic romance* which truly
ends with a 'moral' and 'a drop of bitter honey'. Thus

Coverdale's final disclosure confirms that the projected 'life of love and free-heartedness' (29) which Zenobia has looked to as the goal of Blithedale is an impossibility. 'Love and free-heartedness', as the romance demonstrates, are at odds. And that bitter-sweet recognition has profound implications for Coverdale. Early in the romance the minor poetaster has enthusiastically explained to Zenobia that he means 'to produce . . . poetry—true, strong, natural and sweet, as is the life we are going to lead' (14). By the close he knows better: 'As for poetry, I have given it up' (246). But, most importantly, Coverdale's last revelation, which in turn reveals that Hawthorne has deliberately thrown a 'veil' over his narrative, draws our attention to the novel as 'a masquerade', one that has deliberately mystified and deceived us so that we *realize* the consecrating power of the artist, the fakes and ploys of whose masquerade serve to ensure that Coverdale truly fulfils his role:

> It resembled that of the Chorus in a classic play, which seems to be set aloof from the possibility of personal concernment, and bestows the whole measure of its hope or fear, its exultation or sorrow, on the fortunes of others, between whom and itself this sympathy is the only bond. Destiny . . . chooses . . . the presence of at least one calm observer. It is his office . . . to detect the final fitness of incident to character, and distil, in his long-brooding thought, the whole morality of the performance. (97)

One of the great distinctions of *The Blithedale Romance* is that it captures what it costs in human terms for an author to be 'a calm observer'. It is at once to live off and in 'the fortunes of others'. As both Coverdale and his creator know, keen perceptive and analytic powers lead to a deficiency in feeling and the risk of the artist's estrangement from his fellows. On the other hand, the romance captures the consecrating powers of the artist. The artist is 'sacra-re' that is 'made sacred' because he is 'set apart' (*O.E.D.*); but he works also for accordance (con = together.) The Hawthorneian artist strives to give us 'the whole morality' and the whole cost.

Thus 'the final passage' is indeed 'bitter honey'. The oxymoron is precise. Coverdale's life has been *bitter* honey. He cannot understand why Zenobia and Priscilla should be under the sway of such a monster of selfishness as Westervelt and such a distinctively egoistic spirit as Hollingsworth. We come to realize, however, that the very ego and purpose of these figures have seemingly conferred meaning upon the lives of the women who surround them. '*Bitter* honey', too, because Coverdale's analytic curiosity ensures his divorce from the woman he loves. The artist as man pays a high price for his scepticism. Like Theodore in Zenobia's legend he is left to pine 'for ever and ever for another sight of that dim mournful face—which might have been his life—long, household, fireside joy—to desire, and waste life in a feversih quest, and never meet it more' (114).

Yet, too, both as a man and an artist he has experienced 'bitter *honey*'; he has been haunted by three characters in search of him who, though they have sought definition from him, they have provided, too, the only definition and 'proper substance' he himself is ever to know in life. Hence his attenuation whenever he is apart from them, and Blithedale is over. But truly 'bitter honey' because, as an artist Coverdale gives shape and purpose to their lives in the tragic romance he has written. It is surely satisfying to the reader to know that at least one person has loved that test case of Blithedale values, Priscilla. Moreover, because Coverdale's heart is and was touched; because he once did have hopes for Blithedale which he still remembers as 'our beautiful scheme of a noble and unselfish life' (245); because he can attest even at the end 'I feel we had struck upon what ought to have been a truth' (245-46) he has *earned* the 'consecrated' right to turn 'his sympathy to good account' and to write if not Zenobia's romantic tragedy, his own tragic romance. That is *The Blithedale Romance* in which, for once in his artistic career, he is able 'to detect the final fitness of incident to character, and distil, in his long-brooding thought, the whole morality of the performance' (97).

NOTES

1. These quotations are taken from the following:
    Frederick C. Crews, *The Sins of the Fathers: Hawthorne's Psychological Themes* (New York: Oxford University Press, 1966), p. 200; Arlin Turner, Introduction to *The Blithedale Romance* (New York: The Norton Library, 1958), pp. 20, 23; Millicent Bell, *Hawthorne's View of the Artist* (State University of New York, 1962), p. 155; *The Blithedale Romance and Fanshawe*, The Centenary Edition, Volume III (Ohio State University Press, 1964), p. 154 (hereafter all page references in the text are to this

edition); Philip Rahv, 'The Dark Lady of Salem', *Partisan Review*, 8
(1941), 377; J. C. Stubbs, *The Pursuit of Form: a Study of Hawthorne and the
Romance* (Chicago: University of Illinois Press, 1970), p. 122; James A.
Justus, 'Hawthorne's Coverdale: Character and Art in *The Blithedale
Romance*', *American Literature*, 47 (1975), 30; Nina Baym, '*The Blithedale
Romance:* A Radical Reading', *Journal of English and Germanic Philology*, 67
(1968), 555. (Ms. Baym's point of view is the opposite of my own. She
argues, ingeniously 'that Coverdale is not considered, either by
Hawthorne or himself to be an artist. He is an amateur, a dilettante, a
minor—because uncommitted poetaster' (p. 549).) The Norton Critical
Edition, edited by Seymour Gross and Rosalie Murphy (New York: 1978)
reprints the Centenary Text and includes excerpts from several critics I
allude to: they are Crews, Rahv, Stubbs, Justus, Baym and Leo B. Levy.
2. William L. Hedges, 'Hawthorne's *Blithedale*: The Function of the
Narrator', *Nineteenth Century Fiction*, 14 (1960), 303-16, is the most
sympathetic treatment of Coverdale I have read. He argues that
'Coverdale . . . achieves a tragic realization, which to an appreciable
extent humanizes him' (305); and 'his tensions make him an interesting
person' (308). Hedges's fine essay concentrates on Coverdale as narrator
whereas I dwell more on Coverdale as artist and on his relationship to his
friends/characters. My own account is, too, more positively pro-
Coverdale.
3. We know Hawthorne shared Coverdale's strong sentiments. Compare his
letter from Brook Farm (18 October, 1841) to his fiancée, Sophia
Peabody, where he beseeches her to take no part in 'these magnetic
miracles'—*Love Letters of Nathaniel Hawthorne* (Chicago: The Dofobs
Society, 1907). The letter is reprinted in the Norton Critical Edition of *The
Blithedale Romance*, pp. 242-44.
4. James H. Justus, p. 31.
5. Crews, p. 200.
6. A. N. Kaul, *The American Vision: Actual and Ideal Society in Nineteenth-Century
Fiction* (New Haven, Yale University Press, 1963) pp. 196-213, contains a
fine discussion of this aspect.
7. p. 69. I would like to take this occasion to thank Professor Kinkead-
Weekes for his rigorous, sympathetic appraisal of the first draft of my
essay.
8. *The House of the Seven Gables*, The Centenary Edition, Volume II (Ohio
State University Press, 1965), p. 179. Hereafter all page references in the
text are to this edition.
9. In a remarkable letter (4 October, 1840) Hawthorne records this
movement from arrogance to 'accordance': 'I used to think I could
imagine all passions, all feelings, and states of the heart and mind; but
how little did I know! . . . Indeed, we are but shadows; we are not endowed
with real life . . . until the heart be touched. That touch creates us,—then
we begin to be,—thereby, we are beings of reality and inheritors of
eternity'—*Passages from the American Notebooks* (Boston and New York:
Houghton, Mifflin and Co., 1883), p. 223.
10. Leo B. Levy, '*The Blithedale Romance*: Hawthorne's "Voyage Through

Chaos",' *Studies in Romanticism*, 8 (1968), 3.

11. *The Scarlet Letter*, The Centenary Edition, Volume I (Ohio State University Press, 1965), p. 64. Hereafter all page references in the text are to this edition.

12. Talking of Hawthorne's 'sense' of 'that . . . spell of the continuity of his life with that of his predecessors' James remarks: 'There is a very American quality . . . It is only in a country where newness and change and brevity of tenure are the common substance of life that the fact of one's ancestors having lived for a hundred and seventy years in a single spot would become an element of one's morality'—Henry James, *Hawthorne* (London: Macmillan and Co., 3rd Edition, 1887), p. 14.

13. Joseph Conrad, *Youth, Heart of Darkness,* and *The End of the Tether* (London: J. M. Dent and Sons, Collected Edition, 1946), p. 82, p. 51.

14. My reading contradicts James H. Justus's view that 'Coverdale's "romance" is one of the thinner kinds' because he 'diverts the tragedy of Zenobia into nineteenth century melodrama', pp. 30-1.

7

To Transform and Transfigure: The Aesthetic Play of Hawthorne's *The Marble Faun*

by GRAHAM CLARKE

The great difference between Italian scenery, and all other, with which he was acquainted, lay, with Cole, less in its material, than in its moral and historical elements. Hitherto he had walked with nature in her maidenhood, her fair proportions veiled in virgin robes, affianced indeed to human associations, but unpolluted, unwasted by human passion. But now he was in converse with her, after long centuries of marriage with man. As the word and worship of God carry forth into the events of the great future, so the very verdure of solitudes and the solemnity of voiceless evening skies swept his spirit back to mingle with the doings of past ages. Everywhere was the repetition of one, awful, grand expression:—mortal triumph and defeat—mortal strength and weakness—mortal pride and degradation—man's rise and fall—man's wrestling with his fellow—his feeble strife with time, and childish struggles on the bosom of the mother earth.

—*The Life and Works of Thomas Cole.*[1]

1

Thomas Cole, principal figure of the Hudson River School of landscape painting, embarked on a two-year visit to Europe in

1829, some twenty-nine years before Hawthorne's own European experience. On one level, of course, Cole's response as given above falls into the tradition of American writers and artists who have weighed the Old Home against the seemingly fresher, younger habitat of their own continent. His reaction, however, has a special significance for us in relation to *The Marble Faun* and in relation to Hawthorne's own response to the Italy which feeds into his romance. Part of that significance is that to Cole, as painter, the Italian landscape offered not only a different symbolic meaning, it compromised his sense of art, forcing upon him an iconography which questioned the whole imagery of innocence in American culture. His picturing of America was transformed by Italy and the human experience to which it spoke; man falls from grace confronted by a living text of history and time rather than by America's virgin terrain. If in Cole's 'Essay on American Scenery',[2] the continent is a living emblem of a green world, what James Jackson Jarves called 'God's sensuous image of revelation' where Americans are 'still in Eden', in Italy the ideal picturing gives way to a flawed and disfigured, a more complex imagery of human existence, which is essentially that of *The Marble Faun*.

I am, of course, being unfair to Cole's *oeuvre* and his position within an American landscape tradition, but the two poles of his experience, the two sets of imagery by which he reads and pictures landscape helps us place the particular nature of *The Marble Faun* in a more accessible angle of vision than it has usually been granted. To put it at its most obvious the book is almost wholly concerned with the nature of art and the art-making process; with the relative methods by which man, and especially American man, seeks to interpret life and nature; and with the incipient urge to create form out of a defiant, entangling, elusively historic, complex reality and human psychology. Its overriding concern with art and aesthetics pulls us into a marvellously realised debate about the nature of art and, in turn, the fate of an American art which seeks (and sees) only an ideal imagery. Against the 'massiveness of Rome' Hawthorne creates a perspective which gives to the creative process the force of myth and, once again, places the declared intentions of nineteenth-century American idealism, and the outlook of his American protagonists, in a more ambivalent and complicating *picture* of life's meanings.

Bryant wanted Cole to retain the 'bright' image of American mission and revelation—a typology of light and knowledge set within the frame of an imagined ideal scene.[3] But Hawthorne's image, his light, offers a different play within his verbal framework, his picture of human and American experience. Hawthorne's artist would so manage 'his atmospherical medium as to bring out or mellow the lights, and deepen and enrich the shadow, of the picture'.[4] Brightness would be too obvious, too crude, lacking in subtlety, knowingness, and mystery. Hawthorne seeks the deep tones of shadow, a *chiaroscuro* effect of play and energy intent on a verbal picture the effect of which is to deny a fixed and projected patterning onto the canvas. Rather, his art pulls us into a constant awareness of artistic process so that the *act* of picturing rather than the picture becomes dominant. Much of Hawthorne's work is concerned with this sense of art, its limits and possibilities. But in *The Marble Faun* the entire texture of the work is bound up *within* this awareness, this concern, with the relationship between art and life, life and art. Constantly it speaks to the energies at work behind (and in) the making, shaping, moulding, and carving of artistic material (stone, paint, language) into an adequate image of the relationship between the 'Actual and the Imaginary'. In so doing, I believe, Hawthorne's consistent concern with the nature of art achieves its most fully developed and realized form.

If *The Marble Faun* embodies many of the essential elements of the 'international theme'—America and Europe, Catholicism and Protestantism, past and present, innocence and experience, the ideal and the real—it does so within this play of artistic and aesthetic possibilities. The clash of cultures and sensibilities, so central to the work's meaning, bears directly upon the state of man amidst his artistic perspectives, constantly weighing the claims of an ideal art, an ideal reading of the world, within the realized texturing of a 'flawed humanity'. Thus, when Kenyon declares, near the close of the work, that it is the 'story of the fall of man!' and asks 'Is it not repeated in our romance of Monti Berni?' he points up *The Marble Faun*'s mythical intention and its allegorical functioning in relation to art. Like Cole, Hawthorne's American characters

133

'fall' into the darker claims of a European past and come to a moral awareness of guilt and sin. Hilda as 'faithful protestant' and 'daughter of the puritans' is enmeshed in the dark secret of the murder just as much as Miriam, the dark European spirit, is isolated and plagued by the shadow of her own history. But Hilda is also a copyist, just as Miriam is a painter, and the experience of the two women cannot be understood properly unless we recognize their status as representatives of their particular arts. Hilda's view of art—like that of Kenyon, the sculptor, like that of Miriam—mirrors her view of life and vice versa. When Hilda witnesses the murder, by Donatello, of Miriam's 'shadow', she is not only initiated into a knowledge of sin, she is forced to acknowledge its existence as a primary element in the aesthetic and artistic process. Before this Hilda can only copy the works of the old masters, seeing in them a purity of intention and achievement which lifts them out of a human world and life and puts them on isolated display in the galleries and museums of Rome. Just as much of *The Marble Faun* is conceived of in terms of set scenes, of framed pictures, so Hilda witnesses the murder as a painting, no longer as spectator or copyist, but as a participant in its dark message: the mythical scene of the fall, played out in endless paintings, repeated to her as art transformed into a living tableau. It is only after this, and her subsequent acceptance of struggle and guilt at the basis of human life, that Hilda can return to art, meeting and relating its message to a battered humanity. As the early ideal landscapes of the work, often reminiscent of Claude's Arcadian scenes, give way to an increasing sense of Rome's weight as a receptacle of human life and tragedy, so Hilda's experience is seen as necessary to any measured view of the meaning of 'true' art and creativity. As the image of an American Eden was displaced by Europe for Cole, so Arcadia and Eden leave Donatello and the work's early 'bright' scenes for a more mellowed and weightier sense of human mystery amidst the conundrum of artistic process containing, enveloping itself, in the opacity of ultimate meaning. Hilda's (and Kenyon's) transformation speaks against the fixed image, the ideal picturing of life: their knowledge brings them into a corrected sense of the processes of art and the struggle to achieve form and image adequate to a 'true' (*sic*) realization of man's estate.

134

And equally with Donatello's own transformation. Before his fall he is a 'child' and a 'simpleton' who knows nothing 'about the intertwining light and shadow of human life'. Expelled from this state after his act of murder he 'becomes' human. As Kenyon states:

> 'Here comes my perplexity,' continued Kenyon. 'Sin has educated Donatello, and elevated him. Is sin, then—which we deem such a dreadful blackness in the universe—is it, like sorrow, merely an element of human education, through which we struggle to a higher and purer state than we could otherwise have attained? Did Adam fall, that we might ultimately rise to a far loftier paradise than his?[5]

The question, of course, cannot be answered, for Hawthorne's text does not offer explicit answers. What it does, rather, is to achieve a realized texture and patterning within which Kenyon's question cannot only be properly posed but *felt* within the context of man's urge to make art. If it takes as its basis the myth of man's fall, *The Marble Faun* fulfils its intention through the myth of art: the endless cycle by which we define, project, and encompass our sense of ourselves and the world; once again the constant interplay between art and life. The force of Hawthorne's text is the fate of art within the alembic of continuous creative process. Art, like man's attempts to read and picture the world of his experience, is seen as a necessary struggle towards an achieved clarity and knowledge, both false and true. But Hawthorne's 'truth' is not to be equated with a Keatsian 'beauty'. Rather, it is to be glimpsed within a 'negative capability' wherein we perceive the process at work, deep within the recesses, the shadows, of human existence.

Ultimately, then, Hawthorne is intent on judging the veracity of creative process in relation to an ambivalent and mysterious reality; why it is we should not forget that Donatello *is* the object of the book: the marble Faun of Praxiteles come to life. His fate is that of art in life. The ideal state of the faun as artifact is forced to exist within a human theatre of time and history rather than the coveted stillness of the rarefied museum and gallery. Like the wider rhythms of the work, Donatello is art in life, and life in art: the reciprocal interaction of the book's essential states of being, its ambiguity and suggestiveness. At its most intense *The Marble Faun* works through these opposing forces and energies within created form; the interaction and play of opposites so characteristically Hawthorneian, light and dark, flux and stasis, the spiritual and material, opacity and clarity, the sculptural and the pictorial. The constant sense of metamorphosis is basic to its dialectic, of man making, shaping, and picturing the world in an attempt to know the answer to Kenyon's fundamental perplexity. Indeed, the awareness of making art becomes the central axis around which the text turns speaking consciously to the active relationship between art and life, life and art, artist and art, artist and life. The resulting effect, for all its defects as a romance, is a sense of the deeper shadows of a work's being; the fixed and the static giving way to the ineffable and immutable presence of verbal play amidst the ultimate riddle—how and why art?

Indeed, Hawthorne's problem with finding a suitable title for the work testifies to precisely this process. In England it was published as *Transformation*, a title Hawthorne called 'very flat and inexpressive'.[6] And yet the book is full of transformations—of characters, life, and art moving between and through different states and forms, so why should Hawthorne not feel that it captured the central aspect of the work? Part of the answer might lie in an alternative title which Hawthorne discarded: *Marble and Life; a Romance*. This points more directly to the sense of the work that I am concerned to suggest; the reciprocal claims of art and life. But this too fails to evoke the deeper tensions and play within it, relying, as it does, on a too obviously declared labelling of the work's intention. What we can turn to in its place is a term (and a work of art) which does indeed make 'transformation' flat and inexpressive: 'Transfiguration'. On the level of transformation the work extols the obvious characteristics of its surface texture: allegory, story, and character. On the level of transfiguration it invokes and seeks its dominant energy—the play of form and meaning to which there is no fixed resolution. Transformation is static, one dimensional, reducible and discernible; a literal movement of one state to another. Transfiguration is much less substantial: more suggestive, more spiritual and immaterial in its religious and Christ-like associations. It suggests the text at its most mysterious, not only between states, but between figures of the

136

imagination in which are held the creative energies of man's attempt at truth—the figural and figurative—the making, casting, moulding, and drawing of shapes, of forms and figures. To transform is to complete, to carry over into a closed statement. To transfigure is to become shifting and ineffable, a symbiotic rather than osmotic process between and in *states* of being. It is, so to speak, the sub-surface of Hawthorne's own art, the 'neutral territory' of the romance; the interplay of opposed states in a shifting but ever present metamorphosis.

Hawthorne's experience of Raphael's *Transfiguration* is particularly significant here. On confronting it in Rome he noted (in the *Italian Notebook*) that it was the 'one glorious picture' he had seen. On another occasion, he noted that 'no copy could ever produce all the life and expression' he saw in it. It suggests for him, then, something of the spirit of his own art and although it fails to emerge as one of the set-pieces in *The Marble Faun* its presence is more than implied. If Donatello is 'transformed', Hilda, after her benediction, is in a state of 'transfiguration' and in 'The Emptiness of Picture Galleries' when he comes to it as an example of Renaissance art, he belies his criticism of 'dead' art and declares that he will 'withdraw all that we have said'. And yet Hawthorne is not entirely uncritical of it:

> I am not convinced of the propriety of its being in two so distinctly separate parts; the upper portion not thinking of the lower, and the lower portion not being aware of the higher. It symbolises, however, the shortsightedness of mankind that, amid the trouble and grief of the lower picture, not a single individual . . . lifts his eyes to that region one glimpse of which would set everything right.[7]

What Hawthorne finds at fault in Raphael's painting he seeks to avoid in his parallel picturing of man's state, for the iconography of the painting is basic to *The Marble Faun* in its play of opposites and the attempts of man's own art to figure his own resurrection. But whereas the Raphael, for Hawthorne, falls into two halves, so Hawthorne's work interacts in an active process of aspiration and ultimate suspension between the ideal and the real, art and life, as they relate to and are dependent upon each other. The verbal play, the shadows of the struggle toward definition, the varying claims of art and life, again must remain active and immutable. Once art loses this 'life' so it solidifies into either dead copying and statement or single mass and weight.

This is, in one sense, why Rome is central to the work's message and why to see it as mere setting, culled from Hawthorne's own comments from the *Italian Notebook*,[8] is to misread its place within the whole. Rome is neither wholly rejected nor wholly embraced. Rather, it exists as an holistic symbol, a perceived reality, of man's (and the artist's) attempts towards truth and salvation. Its historical, religious, and artistic elements create the ultimate text of the perplexity of man's existence. Its rich texture, 'Etruscan, Roman, Christian, venerable with a threefold antiquity' eludes direct treatment. It is a 'dreary city' with a 'contagious element, rising foglike from the ancient depravity of Rome, and brooding over the dead and half-rotten city, as nowhere else on earth'. The 'massiveness' of its past lingers 'like a long-decaying corpse', the spiritual and material efforts of the past 'piled up' in its buildings. And yet this is also the Eternal city where, if there is the 'pretence of holiness and the reality of nastiness, each equally omnipresent' there is also the 'world's cathedral' which dazzles with its 'visionary splendour and magnificence'. Its largesse comes from the interminable sense and evidence of the struggle of a 'battered' humanity to achieve grace: the mix, and the resulting ambiguity of the real and the ideal. Rome is equally the repository of living and dead art: church and cathedral, museum and gallery, ruin and monument make it a living hieroglyph littered with the high points of Western art. Within it are such luminous moments of artistic achievement as Guido's 'Archangel' and 'Beatrice Cenci'. Its constant pull for artists forces them to exist in a single complex of art and life: the final text towards which all their efforts move and against which they are to be judged. It is the ultimate museum of their aesthetic habitat: architecture, painting, sculpture, stained-glass, frescoes, and sketches mingle together with the constantly changing life which surrounds them. Indeed, the extent to which Hawthorne's romance is both concerned with and addresses itself to art should alert us to the very particular nature of Rome as the setting of the work. The aesthetic and artistic attempts of its characters are placed within a marvellously perceived sense of the detail of the city, a thickness of texture and interlocking observation which creates Rome as the ultimate art object: a brilliant text of all art and life; a proper *exemplum* of man's efforts to escape from his fallen state and achieve the 'truth' of the world in the made image.

It is against this background that the specific debate on the relative forms of art must be placed. The book's 'aesthetic company' and their related arts are judged on their ability to embrace the city, in both its positive and negative states. In the characters, for example, of Kenyon, as sculptor, Hilda, as copyist, and Miriam, as painter, Hawthorne invokes the relative claims and merits of the two central arts within the work: painting and sculpture. In turn, he relates them to the development of the two Americans as, like Cole, Hilda and Kenyon are made to evaluate their sense of art and life in the face of the 'dark secret' that Rome throws upon them. But, as with so much of the text (and Hawthorne's own art) there is no single viewpoint by which we are allowed to judge one against the other. The values of painting and sculpture, and their meaning to Hawthorne, lies in the interaction of the two. If Kenyon and Hilda, in their respective arts, posit cold against warmth, intellect against imagination, it is the union of the two within his own text—his celebrated 'neutral territory'—that Hawthorne most seeks. On their own they personify extreme forms of artistic principles. Indeed, as a copyist Hilda lacks that sense of light and play, that sense of active engagement to which the 'magic realm of picture' of Hawthorne's own art speaks. Both characters must come together; their combined knowledge a synthesis of a more appropriate artistic outlook on the life which surrounds them.

In its 'dead' form, for example, Kenyon's art is seen as 'cold' and 'hard'. In his search for ideal grace and beauty his sculpture breaks away from a necessary contact with life into a timeless fixity; what Miriam calls a 'fossilizing process', a 'frozen art' which has 'nothing like the scope and freedom of painting'. It is, says Hilda,

> because you are a sculptor that you think nothing can be finally wrought except in the cold and hard, like the marble in which your ideas take shape. I am a painter, and know that the most delicate beauty may be softened and warmed throughout. (105)

Kenyon's is a 'cold pastoral', offering only a static image of life. His dependence on fixed ideas makes of his art mere mannerism, a plagiarized form which has 'no place among the living arts'. It is, indeed, precisely this state that Kenyon comes to recognize when he seeks for his ideal not in stone, but in the living presence of Hilda:

> he had suspected that it was a very cold art to which he had devoted himself. He questioned, at that moment, whether sculpture really ever softens and warms the material which it handles; whether carved marble is anything but limestone, after all, and whether the Apollo Belvedere itself possesses any merit above its physical beauty, or is beyond criticism even in that greatly acknowledged excellence. (391)

The *beau ideal* speaks to an abstracted purity, an absolute meaning and image which has little efficacy in the light of human experience. Thus Kenyon's own fall into coldness, cutting out the human as he cuts into stone. In such an extreme state the art speaks simply to its own mass: pure weight and substance. Kenyon's realization is that he had 'cut his life in marble' and, in so doing, had killed 'imagination and the love of art'.

But against Kenyon's sense of failure rises an alternative form of sculptured art where, rather than seeing the material of stone imprisoning life, Hawthorne imagines it as allowing life to struggle out of the raw material. The artist here, as he encounters the basic material of his art, grapples with his ideal in the active and kinetic relationship of making art. The stone becomes a perfect material, 'a pure, white, undecaying substance'. It has an 'incorruptible fidelity' but only when handled with a necessary reverence:

> Under this aspect, marble assumes a sacred character; and no man should dare to touch it unless he feels within himself a certain consecration and a priesthood, the only evidence of which, for the public eye, will be the high treatment of heroic subjects, or the delicate evocation of spiritual, through material beauty. (136)

This is the mystery of both form and material. For if the sculptor comes to it with a recognized sense of that necessary struggle between art and life, so he may sense, but not necessarily achieve, 'the possibility of ideal grace.' But, like the unfinished bust of Donatello, it is art which is active, with the features 'struggling' out of the stone. Such an interpenetration, between the spiritual and material, between life and art, will achieve its own immutability, suggestive of particular states without simply being cold imitation. The sculpture will take upon it a 'marvellous repose' as an incarnation, a transfiguration, of that struggle towards perfect form. Just as Kenyon's statue of Cleopatra is 'fierce, voluptuous, passionate, tender, wicked, terrible, and full of poisonous and rapturous enchantment' but caught within the sacred presence of its solid material. At such a moment there is an apotheosis of matter and spirit which retains, achieves, a caught moment of transfiguration; of life into art and art in life. Thus the use of Thorvalden's 'three-fold analogy—the clay model, the life; the plaster cast, the death, and the sculptured marble, the resurrection'. Raphael's play of opposing states between the material and the spiritual remains a 'perplexity', a riddle, in its force of truth to the life around it.

There is, then, no single viewpoint expressed on sculpture. Kenyon's art revives because he can lay claim to a human sympathy which, at the beginning of the work, he lacked in his stern and austere identification with a cold art. He moves from a fixed and static view of art and life to an active sense of necessary struggle between states, more complete in an acknowledged complexity to both the work's and life's meanings.

And just as Kenyon and the art he represents is transferred and transfigured, so is Hilda and her sense of painting. She too undergoes a crisis in her sense of painting's message, seeing in it, before her initiation, a purity of intention which lifts it from a human context. As a copyist rather than an original artist she feels 'through and through a picture' a sympathy which exists on the level of unstained artistic endeavour:

> She went straight to the central point, in which the Master had conceived his work. Thus, she viewed it, as it were, with his own eyes, and hence her comprehension of any picture that interested her was perfect. (57)

But her faithfulness is one-sided, too, as Miriam charges her, innocent in its reverence for the high ideal of art. Like Kenyon, she seeks a 'timeless repose' in a finished state, the transference of life to a caught and completed image on the canvas. It is precisely this of which Miriam, the *painter*, is so critical. Looking at Guido's 'Archangel', for example, she speaks to Hilda's one-sidedness, her incompleteness in that 'if her soul were less white and pure, she could be a more competent critic of this picture, and would estimate it not half so high.' What Miriam sees in it is the 'death-struggle with Evil' but for Hilda it is the 'most beautiful and the divinist figure that mortal painter ever drew'.

Yet after Hilda's fall into a moral awareness of sin and guilt, her sense of high art to which she had once so faithfully given herself, is lost in her changed sense of the world. In 'The Emptiness of Picture Galleries' the Old Masters cease to have meaning for her, no longer 'warming' her with their influence. Her painterly eye 'grows dim' with the 'shadow' of her experience. Hilda's response is rather to find an 'incontestable corruption' in them which, in its extreme inability to conceive of their human elements, renders them false. What strikes her now is a different kind of truth, the cold formality of the Dutch school as against the human involvement of Renaissance art. Her inability to acknowledge sin, evil and struggle, at this point, allows the 'Mephistopheles' of artistic spirit to guide her back towards pictures of objects which lie closer to mere imitation and copying:

> He annihilates color, warmth, and, more especially, sentiment and passion, at a touch. If he spare anything, it will be some such matter as an earthern pipkin, or a bunch of herrings by Teniers; or brass kettle, in which you can see your face by Gerard Douw; a furred robe, or the silken texture of a mantle, or a straw hat, by Van Mieris; or a long-stalked wine-glass, transparent and full of shifting reflection, or a bit of bread and cheese, or an over-ripe peach, with a fly upon it, truer than reality itself, by the school of Dutch conjurors. These men, and a few Flemings, whispers the wicked demon, were the only painters. The mighty Italian masters, if you deem them, were not human, nor addressed their work to human sympathies, but to a false intellectual taste, which they themselves were the first to create. Well might they call their doings 'art', for they substituted art instead of nature. Their fashion is past, and ought, indeed, to have died and been buried along with them. (336)

Although Hawthorne is often critical of Renaissance art for its 'lack of variety', his attack on the Dutch, and the depiction of Hilda's deceptive move to them as against her Old Masters, is offered as an equivalent low point to Kenyon's own development. For Hilda art has 'lost its consecration', but the Dutch school offers no alternative. Its 'picturing' is a cold art of imitation, of copying in a mechanical and one-sided relationship between art and life. It is a dead art, its realistic impulse denying the poetry, the spiritual element of Raphael or Guido. It takes nature as given without mystery or complexity but, above all, it refutes the sense of struggle to which, once again, Hilda, like Hawthorne's own art, must come, if a right balance is to be achieved. In the face of her knowledge, Hilda's 'pictorial imagination brought up vivid scenes of her native village' amidst the 'crumbly magnificence' of Rome. She seeks a 'native homeliness' which, as for Cole, has been expunged from her picture of human experience. What she is moved to confront, as is *The Marble Faun* itself, is, once again, the play of opposites, the transformation and transfiguration of states and energies caught within the artistic frame. Thus, against the mirroring of reality by the Dutch, Sadoma's 'Christ bound to a pillar' becomes a 'visible prayer' because, like *The Marble Faun*, we identify with it the attempt at 'reconciling the incongruity of Divine omnipotence with outraged suffering humanity'. The active substantiation of Raphael's *Transfiguration*:

> This hallowed work of genius shows what pictorial art, devoutly exercised, might effect on behalf of religious truth; involving, as it does, deeper mysteries of revelation, and bringing them closer to man's heart, and making him tenderer to be impressed by them, than the most eloquent words of preacher or prophet. (340)

Here, then, lies a central clue to the ultimate spirit of *The Marble Faun*, as it too seeks the 'deeper mysteries of revelation' of art's cause. The realisation of achieved image is that of Hawthorne's own artistic process. Like its title, *Christ Bound to a Pillar*, the work evokes art *bound* to life, of the spiritual *bound* to the material in a verbal dialectic of play and energy. The resolution of the work, like Hilda's and Kenyon's, is not towards an explained closure but to a coming together of opposites in the attempt at endless transfiguration. Painting and sculpture, in the end,

143

come together in a synthesis of opposed arts which evokes Hawthorne's own sense of artistic process. Hilda and Kenyon's 'fall', like Cole's, opens to them the capacity to sense a rightful complexity and mystery at the centre of both art and life.

This, surely, is the process towards which *The Marble Faun* moves. It seeks an art which retains the play of light and energy, the play of opposites, as central to its substance, its very being. Yet for all of Hawthorne's insistence on the pictorial, the shadow and magic of picture as a metaphor for the written text, it is characteristic of *The Marble Faun* that it seeks a balance between the sculptured and the pictorial. Art must retain 'life' without being a mere copy: a 'life' fixed in its *constant* capacity to move in and between states. If it finally reveals itself, its meaning, it becomes, like the butterfly impaled by the pin, static and dead.

Hawthorne's response to frescoes—what we might see as painting on stone—indicates his interest in a limited form of the mingling of the two states. The *Italian Notebook* is full of references to frescoes and Hawthorne's reaction, more often than not, is to see them as examples of an altogether too modest artistic achievement. Certainly, on one level, Hawthorne's response is worryingly pedestrian (even provincial) as is so much of his sense of the art he sees in Italy. But as a metaphor for the art-making process, for the 'truth' art can suggest to us, they offer useful pointers for an understanding of his work. His negative sense of them comes from their deterioration through time. They make him 'desperately miserable' and are 'poor, dim ghosts' of what they were so that 'scarcely a hint of design or expression can glimmer through the dusk'. Once they 'glowed' with 'the living spirit of catholicism'. But now

> that the colours are so wretchedly bedimmed—now that blotches of plastered wall dot the frescoes all over, like a mean reality thrusting itself through life's brightest illusions—the next best artist to Cimabue or Giotto or Ghirlandajo or Pinturicchio will be he that should reverently cover their ruined masterpieces with white-wash! (303)

These, then, bespeak a dimmed and begrimed art which reality and time break down. Their supposed glory is a transient and illusory casting of images within a process which is both limited

144

and, finally, static.

But, typically, Hawthorne offers an art form which, I suggest, approaches that 'resolution', that balance of opposites which his art and *The Marble Faun* seeks. This is an art which is both spiritual and material, which has energy and life while being cast in a solid and static form. It retains an inner mystery and suggestiveness which refutes any attempt to break it down:

> These were the painted windows; and as often as he gazed at them, the sculptor blessed the medieval time, and its gorgeous contrivances of splendour; for surely the skill of man has never accomplished, nor in his mind imagined, any other beauty or glory worthy to be compared to these.
>
> It is the special excellence of pictured glass that the light, which falls merely on the outside of other pictures, is here interfused throughout the work; it illuminates the design, and invests it with a living radiance; and, in requital, the unfading colours transmute the common daylight into a miracle of richness and glory in its passage through the heavenly substance of the blessed and angelic shapes which throng the high-arched window. (304)

Surely this is one of Hawthorne's high points in his search for a metaphor adequate to his sense of art. The window, like the word, becomes its own hermetic text, a riddle which, while aware of its own artistry, achieves the presence of mystery. Indeed, we should not forget that this is a *stained* glass so that the images are not painted *or* cut but fixed *in* the material— transmuted, transformed and transfigured. The window becomes a point of balance, of interaction to which *The Marble Faun* moves, just as from the outside of a church, we see in the window only a black, almost non-existent pattern and colour; but from inside we can see the radiance of the light *from* the life outside. Thus again, the immutable play of opposites and energies confounds our attempt to seek a single viewpoint. The window is the ultimate medium between life and art's 'inner' message.

But to leave us with the 'pictured-windows' as the final image of the art process would do damage to the true nature of *The Marble Faun*. It has to be taken in relation to the life which surrounds it, the reality which spreads away from the church in which they are placed.

145

Without a firm sense of this context, this broader perspective, one could distort the work's declared commitment to art and life, the balance between its symbolism and its detailed observation of Roman life. The 'oneness' of the glass must be seen in relation to the human, that mutual balance which the characters perceive in the sketches of Renaissance art. These give the sense of 'power' rather than 'the final flow and perfected art' of the finished picture so that there is a 'charm' in their *imperfection*. They retain the reek of the human in their closeness to the original energy of artistic process and life—once again, the effort towards transfigurations, the mystery of art in the making, the balance between the ideal and the real—the declared struggle and awareness of idea into form, of image and figure.

And thus the concluding carnival in the work: for this is both Kenyon's and Hilda's rightful immersion into art *as* life. Whereas the earlier festival in the text was seen in terms of sculpture and ideal pictorial scenes, a Claudian Arcadia, the carnival at the end creates 'art' as a continuing effort and mystery. It is both an active sculpturing and painting, the play of shape and image, just as the figures are the re-incarnation of myth and fantasy. Kenyon moves into a street 'thronged with festive figures' and 'peopled with hundreds of fantastic shapes'. He is forced into 'the midst of the mad, merry stream of human life' which becomes Hawthorne's living painting—a mythical picturing not of Arcadia, but of a human world which refuses to 'solidify' into dead art. Just as the form is judged and 'made' by its immersion into time and human contact, so the work, in the final carnival scene, reverts Keats's ideal in the 'Grecian Urn'. The experience, like *The Marble Faun* as a whole, speaks to both a celebration and a tragic sense of life's mystery and the capacity of art to plumb and define it. In the end art and life come together as Hawthorne, like Cole, seeks the ultimate 'picture' in art and life as they cohere in 'one, awful, grand expression' of our condition—the incessant urge to transform and transfigure in an endless cycle of symbolic repetition.

NOTES

1. Louis Legrand Noble, *The Life and Works of Thomas Cole* (Cambridge, Massachusetts, 1964), p. 110.

2. See Cole's 'Essay on American Scenery' in J. W. McCourbrey (ed.), *American Art 1700–1960 Sources and Documents* (Englewood Cliffs, New Jersey, 1965), pp. 98–110.
3. In his poem 'To Cole, The Painter Departing for Europe' Bryant speaks of a Europe with 'everywhere the trace of men' and asks Cole to keep 'that earlier, wilder image' of his American scenes 'bright'.
4. Hawthorne, of course, says this in his 'Preface' to *The House of the Seven Gables*.
5. *The Marble Faun or the Romance of the Monti Berni*, Centenary Edition, Volume IV (Ohio State University Press, 1968), p. 460. All subsequent references are to this edition with the page numbers following in brackets.
6. See the introduction to the Centenary Edition of *The Marble Faun*.
7. See pp. 186-87 of *The French and Italian Notebooks*, Centenary Edition, Volume XIV (Ohio State University Press, 1980).
8. The extent to which Hawthorne made use of the *Italian Notebook* in *The Marble Faun* hardly needs commenting upon. For a specific analysis of the relationship between the two see the 'Appendix' to the Centenary Edition of *The French and Italian Notebooks*, pp. 993-1009.

8

Hawthorne's Old Home

by ARNOLD GOLDMAN

> Every phrase and every sentence is an end and a beginning,
> Every poem an epitaph. And any action
> Is a step to the block, to the fire, down the sea's throat
> Or to an illegible stone: and that is where we start.
> We die with the dying:
> See, they depart, and we go with them.
> We are born with the dead:
> See, they return, and bring us with them.
> The moment of the rose and the moment of the yew-tree
> Are of equal duration. A people without history
> Is not redeemed from time . . . .
> History is now and England.
>
> —T. S. Eliot, 'Little Gidding'.

When Hawthorne assumed a public appointment for the third time in his life, it seemed a mixed blessing. What the Liverpool (and Manchester) Consulship appeared most to offer was financial security, provision for his young family. The actual remuneration proved a disappointment—Congress soon cut the salary part—and while Hawthorne did finally manage to pay off his debts, the Liverpool years furnished him with little more than enough for the sojourn in Italy, time to complete *The Marble Faun* in Redcar and Leamington, and repairs to the Wayside in Concord. He would later reflect with distaste on the Liverpool Consulate and 'the dusky and stifled [*sic*] chamber in which I spent wearily a considerable portion of more than four good years of my existence'.[1] Being Consul would afterwards appear to him as a dissociation of self; he had, he wrote in

148

'Consular Experiences', 'an odd idea of having somehow lost the property of my own person' (11). Looking back, 'I could scarcely believe that it was I, that figure whom they called a Consul, but a sort of Double Ganger, who had been permitted to assume my aspect . . . while my real self had lain, as regarded my proper mode of being and acting, in a state of suspended animation' (38).

The drama of this loss of substance had occured before, when as a public servant in Salem he had also found his imaginative capacities stifled:

> I had ceased to be a writer of tolerably poor tales and essays, and had become a tolerably good Surveyor of the Customs. That was all. But, nevertheless, it is any thing but agreeable to be haunted by a suspicion that one's intellect is dwindling away; or exhaling, without your consciousness, like ether out of a phial; so that, at every glance, you find a smaller and less volatile residuum. Of the fact, there could be no doubt; and, examining myself and others, I was led to conclusions in reference to the effect of public office on the character, not very favorable to the mode of life in question. In some other form, perhaps, I may hereafter develop these effects.[2]

Whatever the effects 'on the character', the effects on 'the imaginative faculty' (30) were such that even under the most favourable of circumstances, 'in the chamber which I most absurdly termed my study . . . [or] when, late at night, I sat in the deserted parlour, lighted only by the glimmering coal-fire and the moon', *The Scarlet Letter* simply would not come alive. He feared it 'a hopeless case'.

True, during his Liverpool Consulship Hawthorne had returned to diurnal journal-keeping, to keep his hand in (as a puzzled Henry James, who could not in 1897 otherwise fathom Hawthorne's devotion to such *minutiae*, would grudgingly admit) and to provide material for 'an English Romance'. But the journals' development of the skeleton of that romance was confined to but a few speculations and the draft published posthumously as 'The Ancestral Footstep' stalled in Italy. There the production of *The Marble Faun*, under the trying circumstances of Una's illness, and its completion in Redcar and in Leamington, may have appeared to signal a blessed return of imaginative powers, but the novel's sales in America

149

and England, while respectable, failed to create the financial assurances for his family that his mind still dwelt upon. The matter of England was still unfinished business. Ensconced in the newly-constructed 'tower' room of his Concord house, Hawthorne returned to the matter of the English romance. But even in this 'ideal' physical environment specifically created to elicit the romantic genius, his 'imaginative faculty' remained torpid and flat, perhaps that 'hopeless case' he had long ago feared. The 'Etherege' and 'Grimshawe' manuscripts (as titled by their most recent editors) testify at terrible length to Hawthorne's inability to work out the basis of an English story and a texture of prose which could complete itself without internal self-contradiction or a collapse into feeble melodrama.[3] Nineteenth-century posthumous publication disguised the extent to which Hawthorne agonized over his inability, by suppressing those passages where he had recognized most clearly that his drafting was unsatisfactory: 'Try back again', 'It won't do', 'I can't possibly make this out', 'This is not the right tack', 'Here I come to a standstill!'[4]

When therefore Hawthorne set seriously to work to use the English journals for a series of travel sketches, he did so with a sense of failure, human and artistic. He needed money badly. He had not provided sufficiently for his family and he knew he would not now complete his English Romance. He wrote J. T. Fields, his publisher and the owner of the *Atlantic Monthly*—and later its editor—'I always feel a singular despondency and heaviness of heart in re-opening these old journals now' (*C*5, xvii). Fields, of course, could not be expected to show the same enthusiasm which he had displayed on first reading the manuscript of *The Scarlet Letter* a dozen years before. In fact, he was supportive of Hawthorne throughout, so much so that Hawthorne noted, 'you mollify me with a good deal of soft soap, but it is skilfully applied and effects all that you intend it should' (*C*5, xix). That is, it helped him simply to press on.

In the dedicatory preface to the book-publication of the English sketches as *Our Old Home* in 1863, Hawthorne noted that the material had been 'intended for the side-scenes, and back-grounds, and exterior adornment, of a work of fiction' which he now knows is an 'abortive project, . . . utterly thrown aside, and [which] will never now be accomplished' (3–4). What he then offers as the reason for his failure is the pressure on him of 'The Present, the Immediate, the Actual', by which he means specifically the 'catastrophe' of the Civil War. It is as if the state of war recalls or has recreated for him the conditions of public service, his imagination as 'stifled' as previously in Salem or his Liverpool chamber. But there may be a way out: however second-best, an alternative use of materials still seems possible. He is desperate for the money it will bring,[5] but he needs to accomplish something as well, for the sake of his artistic and human soul. The passage in the dedication to ex-President Pierce, a dedication insisted on by Hawthorne in the teeth of opposition, recalls those words in 'The Custom-House' introduction to *The Scarlet Letter* which just precede Hawthorne's reflections on the 'effect of public office' on authorship and character. There, unable to create his Romance, Hawthorne had considered what he might better have been about:

> The wiser efforts would have been, to diffuse thought and imagination through the opaque substance of to-day, and thus to make it a bright transparency; to spiritualize the burden that began to weigh so heavily; to seek, resolutely, the true and indestructible value that lay hidden in the petty and wearisome incidents, and ordinary characters, with which I was now conversant. The fault was mine. The page of life that was spread out before me seemed dull and commonplace, only because I had not fathomed its deeper import. A better book than I shall ever write was there; leaf after leaf presenting itself to me, just as it was written out by the reality of the flitting hour, and vanishing as fast as written, only because my brain wanted the insight and my hand the cunning to transcribe it. (32)

Here is projected the fruit of an active participation in 'the Present, the Immediate, the Actual'. When his creativity did then return—after his 'decapitation' as Surveyor of the Revenue—it gave Hawthorne the hitherto stalled *The Scarlet Letter*, but the 'effect of public office' might yet be related to a 'spiritualiz[ation]' of 'the opaque substance of today', 'the petty and wearisome incidents and ordinary characters' with which that office so signally put Hawthorne in touch. That a 'bright transparency' would have to be sought for and found is equally clear: failure to discover a 'deeper import' would leave the writer mired in that 'dull and commonplace' life.

Whether, when the English Romance had to be abandoned, 'these poor sketches' could take on the burden of the Actual and find the needed transformation is a question we may then ask—and whether *Our Old Home* is less a romance-substitute than that 'wiser effort' and resolute search for an understanding of a previously unwritten common humanity and Hawthorne's relation to it. Perhaps Hawthorne also felt that his own time was drawing short. He may have suspected by 1863 that the ill-health which had plagued him since his stay in Italy— prolonged colds, nosebleeds, fever, and general debility— boded worse to come. It might seem that he began to feel his physical condition the spur for more general reflections on humanity, mortality (including his own), and even salvation. As he pored over the verbal evidence of his life in England, and worked his way into his sketches, these matters come more and more to the foreground, absorbing if not displacing the ever-present themes of national character and the Anglo-American comparison.

It is in the matter of the 'American claimant' theme that we can clearly perceive the change that comes over Hawthorne's consideration of the Anglo-American relation. While the Romance could never clarify itself on the status, psychological and ethical, of the claimant, *Our Old Home*, even in its ambivalence, does. Placing 'Consular Experiences' first allows Hawthorne to begin *Our Old Home* with an explicit rejection of the American who imagines himself the heir to an English patrimony. Recollecting a 'ridiculous' episode of his Consulship, Hawthorne nevertheless notes 'a foolish kind of pathos entangled in it, which impresses me now more forcibly than it did at the moment' (15). An American country shopkeeper 'had left a flourishing business, and come over to England purposely and solely to have an interview with the Queen': 'Now the shopkeeper, like a great many other Americans, had long cherished a fantastic notion that he was one of the rightful heirs to a rich English estate; and . . . he had shut up his little country-store and come over to claim his inheritance' (16). Though robbed of his money on ship-board and a sorry sight to the Consul, the ·American claimant perseveres. To Hawthorne he was 'a complete booby' and as the representative of Government he 'laid his absurdity before him in the very plainest terms . . .' (17). To no avail. As he incorporates this episode in an essay, Hawthorne knows he has himself failed to bring to a conclusion a novel in which the sanity of the protagonist is not questioned, but is rather collusively promoted by the author. Suppressing his doubts as inconsistent with a romance, Hawthorne had attempted, unsuccessfully, to negotiate a claim which he knew to be fraught with psychological and cultural peculiarity. But in his public role he has gone, he realizes, to the other extreme. Lecturing his shopkeeper, the Consul, 'like many men who have been in the habit of making playthings or tools of their imagination and sensibility, . . . was too rigidly tenacious of what was reasonable in the affairs of real life' (17). The too-reasonable Consul attempts to starve the claimant into submission, refusing requests for money to put him on the road to Buckingham Palace. 'Finally, he disappeared altogether . . .' (18). Writing his sketch, restored to his 'real self', Hawthorne can not only examine his own behaviour and sentiments when a public servant, he can generalize on the matter of American claimancy, and arrive at a position which, as a romance-writer he had not been able to attain; having begun with *more* detachment he can now afford less:

> One circumstance in the foregoing incident—I mean the unhappy storekeeper's notion of establishing his claim to an English estate—was common to a great many other applications, personal or by letter, with which I was favored by my countrymen. The cause of this peculiar insanity lies deep in the Anglo-American heart. After all these bloody wars and vindictive animosities, we have still an unspeakable yearning towards England. When our forefathers left the old home, they pulled up many of their roots, but trailed along with them others . . . .
>
> . . . as an individual, the American is often conscious of the deep-rooted sympathies that belong more fitly to times gone by, and feels a blind, pathetic tendency to wander back again, which makes itself evident in such wild dreams as I have alluded to above, about English inheritances. . . . (18–19)

153

It is a 'diseased American appetite for English soil' (20) that Hawthorne first must exorcise, deflecting Americans from association with 'the massive materiality of the English character' (19). As he continues, however, there will be created a new conception of the meaning of 'English soil' and of the reasons why an American could, indeed should, retain his links with the 'Old Home'. The meaning of that Old Home had first to be altered, to be seen as an 'Actuality'.

The example of Emerson's *English Traits*, published in 1856, shows what reflections upon the 'actuality' and 'materiality' of England were to hand. What Emerson saw in the English was their 'tough, acrid, animal nature', a 'vigor of body and endurance' so great as to verge on 'brutality'. The brutes had 'stout and powerful frames'. The English are 'substantial', and even characterization as 'stunted and thickset' leaves them larger than Americans. Emerson's characteristic phrases for English character and manners are analogized from physical presence: stoutness, stolidity, gravity, stability.[6] So impressed is Emerson that he is compelled to alter his description of humanity when faced by such specimens of 'broad-fronted, broad-bottomed'[7] auditors:

> It was an odd proof of this impressive energy that in my lectures I hesitated to read and threw out for its impertinence many a disparaging phrase which I had been accustomed to spin, about poor, thin, unable mortals;—so much has the fine physique and the personal vigor of this robust race worked on my imagination. (106)

As Emerson's review of English 'race' and 'abilities' gathers force his admiration for the blend of such 'coarse strength' with qualities of imagination—as in his appreciation of Francis Bacon—begins to give way to a more ominous thesis: so great has been the 'mental materialism' of latter-day England that it has carried all before it. The old creative balance which had been the English genius, was lost. First, 'There is a prose in certain Englishmen which exceeds in wooden deadness all rivalry with other countrymen. There is a knell in the conceit and externality of their voice, which seems to say, *Leave all hope behind.* In this Gibraltar of propriety, mediocrity gets intrenched and consolidated and founded in adamant.' But when Emerson reaches 'Literature'—by which he means the civilization of the country—that which was merely 'torpidity on the side of religion' takes on its most ominous character. With John Locke, Emerson's prime villain, the balance tips disastrously—'Locke, to whom the meaning of ideas was unknown'. What he brings, fatally, is 'the influx of decomposition'.[8]

Emerson's theory of British culture is that it has suffered a dissociation of sensibility, and that materialism has carried the day. The baton has passed to Macaulay, a representative man:

> The brilliant Macaulay, who expresses the tone of the English governing classes of the day, explicitly teaches that *good* means good to eat, good to wear, material commodity; that the glory of modern philosophy is its direction on 'fruit'; . . . that, 'solid advantage', as he calls it, meaning always sensual benefit, is the only good. (247)

A review of current thinkers and literary figures produces no alleviation. Even Carlyle, Emerson's hero, has become embittered by the process and offers no hope:

> In the decomposition and asphyxia that followed all this materialism, Carlyle was driven by his disgust at the pettiness and the cant, into the preaching of Fate. In comparison with all this rottenness, any check, any cleansing, though by fire, seemed desirable and beautiful. . . . [H]is imagination, finding no nutrient in any creation, avenged itself by celebrating the majestic beauty of the laws of decay. (249-50)

Thus is 'England, an old and exhausted island' (he tells Carlyle), lost to 'the priapism of the senses and the understanding'. Its 'corporeality', which once seemed so promising to the American transcendentalist in search of a dialectic or a polarity in both of whose poles, ideal and material, he might believe, is now a 'drag of inertia' and all appearances are seen in hard, material terms. English 'Pauperism', for instance, 'incrusts and clogs the state, and in hard times becomes hideous.' Emerson's vision, however he wishes he could imagine it away, colours all that he sees—but only all that he sees in England. America is other: 'The capes of Massachusetts

155

and my own Indian stream . . . [and] the Alleghany ranges' remain pure and undefiled.[9]

Hawthorne had rather anticipated Emerson in recording such English earthiness and substance. We recall from *The Scarlet Letter* the 'coarser fibre in those wives and maidens of old English birth and breeding', who 'wedging their not unsubstantial persons . . . into the throng' even at public executions, speak their rough minds about Hester Prynne in the Market-Place. 'They were [Elizabeth's] countrywomen; and the beef and ale of their native land, with a moral diet not a whit more refined, entered largely into their composition. The bright morning sun, therefore, shone on broad shoulders and well-developed busts, and on round and ruddy cheeks . . .' (40). And in *The House of the Seven Gables*, even the 'somewhat massive accumulation of animal substance about the lower region of his face'[10] does not quite make 'The Pyncheon of To-day' the man his more English ancestor was:

> The long lapse of intervening years, in a climate so unlike that which had fostered the ancestral Englishman, must inevitably have wrought important changes in the physical system of his descendent. The Judge's volume of muscle could hardly be the same as the Colonel's; there was undoubtedly less beef in him. Though looked upon as a weighty man among his contemporaries, in respect of animal substance; and as favored with a remarkable degree of fundamental development, well adapting him for the judicial bench, we conceive that the modern Judge Pyncheon, if weighed in the same balance with his ancestor, would have required at least an old-fashioned fifty-six, to keep the scale *in equilibrio*. Then the Judge's face had lost the ruddy English hue . . . . (120-1)

(Well might we wonder how 'fundamental development' ever got by the vigilance of Sophia Hawthorne.)

By *Our Old Home*, however, going Emerson's Englishman ('of the earth, earthy . . . full of coarse strength, rude exercise, butcher's meat and sound sleep'[11]) one better, Hawthorne gives his notorious full-dress (or undress) picture of female British humanity as the only image which presents itself to him as he attempts to recall his days in Leamington Spa:

To say the truth, I have been holding the pen over my paper, purposing to write a descriptive paragraph or two about the throng on the principal Parade of Leamington, so arranging it as to present a sketch of the British out-of-door aspect on a morning walk of gentility. . . . Oddly enough, the only figure that comes fairly forth to my mind's eye, is that of a dowager, one of hundreds whom I used to marvel at, all over England.

. . . an English lady of fifty . . . has an awful ponderosity of frame, not pulpy, like the looser development of our few fat women, but massive with solid beef and streaky tallow; so that (though struggling manfully against the idea) you inevitably think of her as made up of steaks and sirloins. . . . Her visage . . . seems to express so much well-founded self-reliance, such an acquaintance with the world, its toils, troubles, and dangers, and such sturdy capacity for trampling down a foe. (48-9)

The passage got him in hot water, but he let it stand. We may now be less bothered by its fairness (or otherwise) and more interested by the extent to which the image possesses the writer's imagination ('the only figure that comes fairly forth to my mind's eye') and the extent to which he pursues it. This 'mass of earthliness' (50) comes to typify nothing less than the gross body of the world itself, in intimate connexion to its fallen mundane nature.

'John Bull', Hawthorne considers, 'has grown bulbous, long-bodied, short-legged, heavy-witted, material, and, in a word, too intensely English. In a few more centuries, he will be the earthliest creature that ever the earth saw' (64). This is the conclusion to his sketch of Leamington Spa, the first, in the collected version, after 'Consular Experiences', and an essay in which Hawthorne has made it clear he is now observing England not as The Consul but as himself ('I had been holding a position of public servitude . . .' (42)). He has appreciated the 'genuine seclusion' Leamington has offered, especially the seclusion from public demands, so much so that, though Leamington's houses are not really homes, but 'nicely contrived lodging-houses' (47), 'we acquired a homelike feeling towards' the town (41). Having dealt firmly with claimants Hawthorne begins to stake one of his own. 'Leamington Spa' opens with speculations about home: without one there can be 'mad enjoyment' in life—the phrase almost starting from the page—

157

'but no happiness' (41). He considers a row of houses, 'small, old cottages, stuck one against another . . . I presume . . . the habitations of the poorest order of rustic laborers' (52). He worries because 'it seems impossible that there should be a cleanly reserve, a proper self-respect among individuals, or a wholesome unfamiliarity between families' in such surroundings. Nevertheless, 'The cottagers evidently loved the little nests in which they dwelt, and did their best to make them beautiful . . .' (53). Thus at all levels Leamington is habitable England, if under less than ideal conditions. This established, Hawthorne's attention becomes so entirely given over to local churchyards, and especially their graveyards, that he feels the need of apology: 'The article which I am writing has taken its own course and occupied itself almost wholly with country churchyards. . . . And still another church presents itself to my remembrance' (61). He can't leave them alone and the characteristic emblem of these locales, a grim *locus amoenus*, is the soil under his feet: 'The ground must have been dug over and over again, unnumerable times, until the soil is made up of what was once human clay . . .' (54). The very grave-stones are made to seem part of the human clay underfoot. These stones are themselves prey to the same process: 'Time gnaws an English gravestone with wonderful appetite' (55), and Hawthorne speculates on how the worn stones may be put to other uses, and, like everything in England, recycled. He imagines a Church sexton taking the time-worn gravestone away to be used as the 'hearthstone' of a home. We end where we began, in an English home. The closeness of that 'home' to mortality and the grave could not be greater.

Before Hawthorne leaves his 'Leamington Spa' essay, he reflects upon comparable physical symbols of the presence of the human past, 'the influence of hoar antiquity lingering into the present daylight' (58). If at first it fills the American 'with a strange emotion' (59), it soon converts to something else. Hawthorne fixes upon 'the immemorial yew-tree' at Whitnash which has borne witness to hundreds of years of English village history—the device is an embryonic variant of many Hawthorne short stories and sketches, from 'The Town Pump' to Grandfather's Chair, the object which sees the day or history pass before it. The vocabulary darkens, however: 'what a weary life it must have been for the old tree! Tedious beyond imagination!' The air is 'heavy', 'Life is there fossilized. . . .' He turns to the American comparison, the 'Western love of change', as preferable. He suggests, sardonically, that American 'tenderness' (60) for 'the stone-encrusted institutions of the mother-country' comes partly because 'he recognizes the tendency of these hardened forms to stiffen [England's] joints and fetter her ancles. . . .' At this point, then, the heaviness of fallen nature can still be projected onto England and the English, and the American (as in Emerson) can somehow exist outside of it in a purer medium.

Hawthorne is already attracted to what he is, Americanly, repelled by, and he is hard put to explain it:

> Almost always, in visiting such scenes as I have been attempting to describe, I had a singular sense of having been there before. The ivy grown English churches . . . were quite as familiar to me, when fresh from home, as the old wooden meeting house in Salem. . . . This was a bewildering, yet very delightful emotion. . . . . Of course, the explanation of the mystery was, that history, poetry, and fiction, books of travel, and the talk of tourists, had given me pretty accurate pre-conceptions. . . . Yet the illusion was often so powerful, that I almost doubted whether such airy remembrances might not be a sort of innate idea, the print of a recollection in some ancestral mind. (63)

For the moment Americans may regard the English as antitypes, though the balance does not necessarily lie with the former, who 'in our dry atmosphere, are getting too nervous, haggard, dyspeptic, extenuated, unsubstantial, theoretic, and need to be made grosser' (64).[12] A cross-breeding, a mixing with the 'material' John Bull may be some way off yet historically, but intellectually, spiritually, Hawthorne is already sounding committed to it; what, in his treatment, will it signify?

Hawthorne wrote the 'middle' seven chapters of *Our Old Home* first, though in a somewhat different order (5th, 6th, 7th, 1st (but revised), 4th, 3rd, 2nd). They tend to represent a more

159

exclusionist, spectatorly American relation to the condition of
England, though not uniformly, and there are interesting trials
of the question as to how the American might yet discover a
legitimate relation to the Old Home.

Characteristic of the more distant mode is the essay 'About
Warwick', where

> The street is an emblem of England itself. What seems new in it is
> chiefly a skilful and fortunate adaptation of what such a people as
> ourselves would destroy. The new things are based and
> supported on sturdy old things, and derive a massive strength
> from their deep and immemorial foundations, though with such
> limitation and impediments as only an Englishman could
> endure. But he likes to feel the weight of all the past upon his
> back. . . . He presents a spectacle which is by no means without
> its charm for a disinterested and unencumbered observer. (69–
> 70)

Here a visit to Leycester's Hospital, which was to have been the
locale of much of the significant action of the abandoned
Romance, becomes a direct escape into the past, 'such a
pleasant kind of dream for an American to find his way thither,
and behold a piece of the sixteenth century set into our prosaic
times . . .' (84), but even as he leaves, he feels it 'will never be
accessible or visible to him any more'. The Warwick chapter is
really part of a double essay, which continues with
'Recollections of a Gifted Woman', a memoir of Stratford-on-
Avon which frames a long section on the American Delia
Bacon, who believed Sir Francis Bacon wrote the plays of
Shakespeare. While this inset 'recollection' might seem simply
part of a casual and associative essay-style, it bears directly
upon the matter of 'claimancy', now beginning to be handled in
a more indirect but less detached manner. Delia Bacon is
Hawthorne's symbol of the American claimant whose claim is
not to the physical 'estate' of England, but to possession of its
literary and cultural past. She enters at the point where
Hawthorne has put himself down for such an attempt by
carrying us to Stratford and the birthplace of Shakespeare. If a
substantial claim like the Connecticut shopkeeper's is an
'absurdity', is an imaginative one legitimate? Perhaps so long as
you keep your wits about you, noting the realities of the
situation and avoiding the tendency to idealize them. But this

guarded realism, like the Consul's reasonableness, can carry
the American to an opposite extreme:

> After wandering through two or three streets, I found my way
> to Shakspere's birth-place, which is almost a smaller and
> humbler house than any description can prepare the visitor to
> expect; so inevitably does an august inhabitant make his abode
> palatial to our imaginations, receiving his guests, indeed, in a
> castle in the air, until we unwisely insist on meeting him among
> the sordid lanes and alleys of lower earth. (96)

So destructive is this reality of the imagination that it provokes
in Hawthorne a conservative 'moral from these unworthy
reminiscences and this embodiment of the poet, as suggested by
some of the grimy actualities of his life' (100). It is, he suggests,
best not to make such matters known—though he has just done
so, and is in the process of doing so—'because a common mind
cannot properly digest such a discovery. . . . Thence comes
moral bewilderment, and even intellectual loss in regard to
what is best of him.' In fact, such is Hawthorne's coldness of eye
and response, his self-protection against the mania of
claimancy, that 'I was conscious of not the slightest emotion
while viewing ['Shakspere's house'], nor any quickening of the
imagination' (99). The alternatives are the 'peculiar insanity' of
imagining a repossession of the Old Home on the one hand, and
a rational, imaginationless absence of response on the other.
From the birthplace, which he also calls 'Shakspere's house',
Hawthorne proceeds to Shakespeare's burial-place, 'the next
step, of course' (100). Again his imagination is not touched.
Shakespeare's is 'the commonest-looking slab of all, being just
such a flag-stone as Essex-street in Salem used to be paved with,
when I was a boy' (101). Consideration of the bust, the tombs
and the supposed grave leads directly to Delia Bacon—'a fitting
frame-work to some reminiscences of a very remarkable
woman' (104).

Not only did Miss Bacon have her theory of authorship, she
believed that its proof lay in Shakespeare's grave with (or
without) his bones. Hawthorne describes minutely her desire to
effect the opening of the tomb, her progressive haunting of the
site, the 'New England orderliness in her character, and, . . . a
sturdy common sense, which, I trusted, would . . . keep her from

161

any actual extravagance' (109), such as grave-robbing. It does, but Miss Bacon's imaginative claimancy leads to progressive insanity. Hawthorne has, however, been sufficiently touched to have assisted in the publication of her *magnum opus*—perhaps less for its Baconian heresy than for the 'deep political philosophy' she had explored, 'concealed beneath the surface' of the plays (106), and perhaps most of all for her symbolic significance:

> Unquestionably, she was a monomaniac; these overmastering ideas about the authorship of Shakspere's plays, and the deep political philosophy concealed beneath the surface of them, had completely thrown her off her balance; but at the same time they had wonderfully developed her intellect, and made her what she could not otherwise have become. It was a very singular phenomenon; a system of philosophy growing up in this woman's mind without her volition—contrary, in fact, to the determined resistance of her volition—and substituting itself in the place of everything that originally grew there. (106)

Hawthorne sees in her an attempt at intellectual possession which compels respect: she is the tragedy of imaginative claimancy. She cannot be too rationally dismissed, and indeed we know that Hawthorne paid to have her book published. It is therefore with relish that he is able to add that she may not go wholly unappreciated: 'since my return to America, a young man of genius and enthusiasm has assured me that he has positively read the book from beginning to end, and is completely a convert to its doctrines' (116). Nevertheless she has died mad and hers is 'too sad a story'; 'to lighten it' (117) Hawthorne, leaving Stratford, considers Charlecote Hall and the life that has historically been lived there, 'a perfection of comfort and domestic taste, an amplitude of convenience, which could have been brought about only by the slow ingenuity and labor of many successive generations' (119).[13] The hankering after an Old Home which offers such 'perfection' goes on in Americans because 'our philosophers have not yet taught us what is best, nor have our poets sung us what is beautifullest, in the kind of life that we must lead' (119). There is then a lesson in England, if rightly only an analogy.

While Delia Bacon mediates Hawthorne's relation to

Shakespeare, Hawthorne goes in his proper person, and without a mediator, to Westminster Abbey's Poet's Corner. The Abbey is his Home of Homes, 'a spot which I had dreamed about more reverentially, from my childhood upward, than any other in the world' (264). The relation to his own condition is made explicit:

> It seemed to me that I had always been familiar with the spot [Poet's Corner]. Enjoying a humble intimacy—and how much of my life had else been a dreary solitude!—with many of its inhabitants, I could not feel myself a stranger there. It was delightful to be among them. There was a genial awe, mingled with a sense of kind and friendly presences about me . . . together, in fit companionship, mutually recognized and duly honored, all reconciled now. . . . I have never felt a similar interest in any other tombstones, nor have I ever been deeply moved by the imaginary presence of other famous dead people. . . . We neither remember nor care anything for the past, except as the poet has made it intelligibly noble and sublime to our comprehension. . . .
>
> In the foregoing paragraph, I seem to have been betrayed into a flight above or beyond the customary level that best agrees with me, but it represents fairly enough the emotions with which I passed from Poet's Corner into the chapels. . . . (266-67)

When Hawthorne follows this with his appreciation of Leigh Hunt, he is clearly offering the poet the tribute which the now crowded conditions of the Corner may deny him and his fellow modern authors. Hawthorne's portrait of Hunt is an epitaph, not least in that it is standing in for a physical tombstone. And Hawthorne's own hunger for a legitimate fame ('What other fame is worth aspiring for? Or, let me speak it more boldly, what other long-enduring fame can exist!' (267)) is patent: he is coming here as close as he dare to writing his *own* epitaph, to enrolling himself in the company of the poets whose 'ghost is the only one that survives for his fellow-mortals, after his bones are in the dust. . . .'

Henceforth Hawthorne confronts the 'massive materiality' of England in a new way. He returns to the Liverpool and London of his own day, and as if speaking with a new voice finds he can deal directly with matters from which he has perhaps been so far averting his eyes. The 'Outside Glimpses of English Poverty' may still be *English* poverty, but as Hawthorne now sees it, it belongs to him and to all mankind, not excluding Americans. The material substance of England here finds a universal emblem in 'Dirt . . . the symbolic accompaniment of the foul encrustation which began to settle over and bedim all earthly things as soon as Eve had bitten the apple . . .' (277). From this point England, Our Old Home, is seen as the human condition itself, mortality, the dust from which we have come and to which we return. All the previous imagery of graves and gravestones, and of death, comes home in this climactic chapter.

As Emerson had partly preceded Hawthorne on English materiality, so Herman Melville had suggested the dimensions of an English poverty so great as to implicate all of mankind. The eponymous hero Redburn (1849) finds in Liverpool 'Poverty, poverty, poverty, in almost endless vistas: and want and woe staggered arm in arm along these miserable streets.'[14] The conclusion to 'What Redburn Saw in Lancelott's-Hey' points towards Hawthorne:

> again I looked down into the vault, and in fancy beheld the pale, shrunken forms still crouching there. Ah! what are our creeds, and how do we hope to be saved? . . . Surrounded as we are by the wants and woes of our fellowmen, and yet given to follow our own pleasures, regardless of their pains, are we not like people sitting up with a corpse, and making merry in the house of the dead?[15]

For Hawthorne, as for Melville, it is not finally a narrow comparison of American and English manners or institutions, but a general spiritual questioning which presses towards the heart of religious faith in the Victorian age. By now, Hawthorne is writing less a travelogue or a Blue Book than a testament in which he questions the grounds of faith and fairly takes on 'the opaque substance of today'.[16] Americans too, in a condition of Civil War, must come to terms with such mortality, and as he comes to the last phase of *Our Old Home* he offers them the opportunity.[17]

Speculating on 'the drama of low life' in 'a great English town', Hawthorne arranges a theatre exhibiting 'the classic rule' of 'unity of place'. The whole of human life thus occurs within its compass: 'Courtship, quarrels, plot and counterplot, conspiracies for robbery and murder, family difficulties or agreements—I doubt not—are constantly discussed or transacted in this sky-roofed saloon . . .' (281). What this life suggests, however, in its casual, squalid vitality,

> might almost make a man doubt the existence of his own soul, to observe how Nature has flung these little wretches into the street and left them there, so evidently regarding them as nothing worth, and how all mankind acquiesce in the great mother's estimate of her offspring. For, if they are to have no immortality, what superior claim can I assert for mine? . . . Ah, what a mystery! Slowly, slowly, as after groping at the bottom of a deep, noisome, stagnant pool, my hope struggles upward to the surface, bearing the half-drowned body of a child along with it, and heaving it aloft for its life, and my own life, and all our lives. Unless these slime-clogged nostrils can be made capable of inhaling celestial air, I know not how the purest and most intellectual of us can reasonably expect ever to taste a breath of it. The whole question of eternity is staked there. (281-82)

There is no source for this passage in Hawthorne's journals. The startling image of the 'half-drowned body of a child' is used to foreshadow the deformed, probably syphilitic child Hawthorne comes across in the West Derby Liverpool workhouse, who attaches himself to the visitor, supplicating his attention, sympathy, even comfort. Though Hawthorne when taking the workhouse incident from his journal transfers the child's attention from himself to 'one member of our party', and evenly calls the solicitation 'a singular incommodity', the repulsiveness of the child-pauper is emphasized—'a wretched, pale, half-torpid little thing . . . sickly, wretched, humoreaten . . . the offspring of unspeakable sin and sorrow' (300). The person whose attention is solicited, in 'a perfect confidence that it was going to be fondled and made much of', is, we are told, a man susceptible to beauty, 'burthened with more than an Englishman's customary reserve, shy of actual contact with human beings, . . . and, furthermore, accustomed to [the] habit of observation from an insulated standpoint . . .' (300-1). This is Hawthorne the isolated outsider, apart from experience, but a symbolic American, representing his countryman and possessed of his countryman's innate shrinking from this pathetic example of ancient wrong. But the damaged[18] child is not, for all its pitiful symbolization of inherited social depravity, simply a function of English injustice, and Hawthorne's emphasis falls as largely on the 'visitor' as on the child.

When 'our friend' overcomes his repulsion and 'took up the loathsome child and caressed it as tenderly as if he had been its father', Hawthorne reckons the act as 'heroic' and perhaps having 'effected more than he dreamed of towards his final salvation'. This was, Hawthorne speculates, 'the child's mission in reference to our friend',

> to remind him that he was responsible, in his degree, for all the sufferings and misdemeanors of the world in which he lived, and was not entitled to look upon a particle of its dark calamity as if it were none of his concern; the offspring of a brother's iniquity being his own blood-relation, and the guilt, likewise, a burthen on him, unless he expiated it by better deeds. (301)

The world is thus the 'intimate brotherhood' on which he had just before reflected, 'the flow and reflux of a common humanity pervades us all . . .' (299).

As the child has his mission, so the Consul/writer has his, and it is not to rest secure in 'isolation' from a common humanity which his instincts, his *métier*, and even his nationality conspire to make only too natural. He who comforts the 'little Wretchedness' (301) is an American ('with more than an Englishman's customary reserve'), and the American can not hold himself aloof and independent from the Old World's wrong, he is part of the same mortal humanity, and he must embrace it. He must abandon his innocence and eat of the tree of knowledge.[19] The child who must be saved, if we are to be saved, is a transposed image of the writer himself, whose need for the sympathy of his fellows had just before been stated in Poet's Corner and in the memorial of Hunt, and of us all.

Hawthorne gave J. T. Fields the chapter which concludes *Our Old Home*, 'Civic Banquets', to make up for the withholding of 'Consular Experiences' for book publication. It was a tailpiece to the serial publication and is such in the published book.

If its appearance, a page from the symbolic and spiritual matters of 'Outside Glimpses of English Poverty', seems odd or even callous, it may have been intended as a return to the world after the purgation of the previous essay. Our Old Home is finally no longer to be pursued to madness or rejected in cold inhumanity. Hawthorne can thenceforward deal with Anglo-American comparisons from a new standpoint, and nowhere else in the book is he perhaps so gay and witty. The image of Kierkegaard's 'Knight of Faith' shines here, a return to ordinary living following an act of religious abnegation. The book ends with a feast, with 'Dinner' and 'the idea of Dinner'. Down-to-earth as are the proceedings at English civic banquets, after the resolutions and struggles of the previous chapter this one seems like an image of communion. Hawthorne *writes* now like a man who has come through, who can be at peace with himself and with the world. The Lord Mayor, much to the American Consul's affected chagrin, proposes a toast which Hawthorne must answer:

> He wanted to induce me to fling myself . . . into the chasm of discord between England and America, and, . . . had resolved to shove me in with his own right-honorable hands, in the hope of closing up the horrible pit forever. On the whole, I forgive his Lordship! He meant well by all parties—himself, who would share the glory, and me, who ought to have desired nothing better than such an heroic opportunity—his own country, which would continue to get cotton and breadstuffs, and mine, which would get everything that men work with and wear. (344)

The Lord Mayor is a representative modern Englishman of the stripe of Emerson's Macaulay. The Consul rises to his feet to reply to the toast: can he deal with it without either an aesthetic and national American shrinking detachment, without becoming imbued in the same material philosophy of life or without hankering after a lost vision of the Old Home? The writer, who has indeed managed just this difficult balance, taking a book to do it, sets his Double Ganger 'upon his legs to save both countries, or perish in the attempt' (345), but by 'a strategem of sage policy . . . to close these Sketches, leaving myself still erect in so heroic an attitude', he puts down his pen. The Consul will remain forever speech-less; the author has had his say. It was the last word the public was to read from

Nathaniel Hawthorne in his lifetime. Nine months later he was dead.

NOTES

1. *Our Old Home*, Centenary Edition of the Works of Nathaniel Hawthorne, Volume 5 (Ohio State University Press, 1970), p. 9. Subsequent page references will be placed parenthetically in the text, using *C5* as identification where necessary.
2. *The Scarlet Letter*, Norton Critical Edition, eds. Sculley Bradley, Richmond Croom Beatty and E. Hudson Long (New York, 1962), p. 32. Subsequent page references will be placed parenthetically in the text.
3. Edward H. Davidson, Claude M. Simpson and L. Neal Smith (eds.), *The American Claimant Manuscripts*, Centenary Edition of the Works of Nathaniel Hawthorne, Volume 12 (Ohio State University Press, 1977).
4. Of the American drafts, there are fewer such breakdowns in the later 'Grimshawe' manuscript than in the earlier 'Etherege', but 'Grimshawe' becomes flatter and more melodramatic, See pp. 495-506 of the 'Historical Commentary' in *The American Claimant Manuscripts*, which concludes: 'the tale Hawthorne wished to tell receded into the shadows. . . . [I]t became an old-fashioned gothic romance filled with creaky machinery that he could never manage. The story line was never satisfactory, no matter how often he rehearsed it. . . . It was his search for an elusive core of meaning that left Hawthorne baffled and ultimately defeated' (p. 506). For a good recent treatment of Hawthorne's successive failed attempts at an English Romance see Nina Baym, *The Shape of Hawthorne's Career* (Ithaca and London: Cornell University Press, 1976), especially pp. 219-56. Ms. Baym calls the English Romance 'the great albatross of his last years' (p. 222).
5. 'I want $100 awfully and immediately', NH to J. T. Fields, 5 October 1862. For Fields' payments to Hawthorne see *Our Old Home*, pp. xviii-xix.
6. The words and phrases are from *English Traits* (Boston: Houghton Mifflin Company, 1903), Centenary Edition of the Complete Works of Ralph Waldo Emerson, Volume 5, pp. 62, 63, 65, 66, 121, 125, 128. This characteristic vocabulary is so constant and frequent as hardly to require citation.
7. Quotation from pp. 135 *and* 299.
8. Quotations from pp. 234, 111-12, 221, 239, 243.
9. Quotations from pp. 275, 255, 304, 305, 300, 314.
10. *The House of the Seven Gables*, Norton Critical Edition, ed. Seymour L. Gross (New York, 1967), p. 116. Subsequent page references will be placed parenthetically in the text.
11. *English Traits*, p. 130.
12. Emerson too had compared English solidity with American 'spirituality'. Hawthorne follows him in this, though often doubtful whether the

advantage lies with the American: '[O]ur own ladies of autumnal life' are 'so thin, care-worn and frail' (p. 48), in fact, downright 'haggard' (p. 49). On the 'need to be made grosser', *cf.* Hawthorne on Judge Pyncheon, whose comparative complexion, 'nervousness', 'quicker mobility', and 'keener vivacity' than his English ancestor suggests that 'This process, for aught we know, may belong to the great system of human progress, which, with every ascending footstep, as it diminishes the necessity for animal force, may be destined gradually to spiritualize us by refining away our grosser attributes of body' (p. 121).

13. Compare Hawthorne on Roman Catholicism: 'Rome has a certain species of consolation readier at hand, for all the necessitious, than any other spot under the sky. . . . To do it justice, Catholicism is such a miracle of fitness for its own ends, many of which might seem to be admirable ones, that it is difficult to imagine it a contrivance of mere man', *The Marble Faun*, Chapter XXVIII.

14. *Redburn* (New York: Doubleday Anchor Books, 1957), p. 194.

15. Ibid., p. 178.

16. Baym, *op. cit.*, writes that in *Our Old Home* Hawthorne 'says goodbye to romance as a mode of authorship. . . . Hawthorne experiments here—not unsuccessfully—with the voice of the socially aware Victorian narrator' (p. 276), and she writes of 'a start at Trollope's kind of writing' (p. 277). While I agree with the farewell to romance, I believe it is not just a matter of 'voice'. Nevertheless her remarks on England 'as a great symbolic expression of the Actual, before which the imagination has no recourse but retreat. . . . [V]ictory almost always goes to the actual' (pp. 269, 270) are suggestive, and I have tried to extend their meaning.

17. In this regard it is of interest that Henry James would write of Hawthorne's horror and depression (his terms) at the onset of the Civil War, 'it cut from beneath his feet the familiar ground which had long felt so firm, substituting a heaving and quaking medium in which his spirit found no rest. Such was the bewildered sensation of that earlier and simpler generation of which I have spoken' (*Hawthorne*, London, 1879, p. 144). James then speculates that the war 'introduced into the national consciousness a certain sense of proportion and relation, of the world being a more complicated place than it had hitherto seemed, the future more treacherous, success more difficult. . . . [T]he good American, in days to come, will be a more critical person than his complacent and confident grandfather. He has eaten of the tree of knowledge' (*loc. cit.*). For James, however, 'The good American of which Hawthorne was so admirable a specimen was not critical . . .' (*loc. cit.*). This essay is contending that he became 'critical', and that *Our Old Home* is the evidence.

18. I find it impossible not to use James Agee's characteristic adjective. See *Let Us Now Praise Famous Men* (Boston: Houghton Mifflin Company, 1941, 1960). I compare not only the children—especially Burt and Valley Few Gudger—but the two writers' only superficially different attempts to apprehend the appalling poverty they have seen and the spiritual burden it places upon them, and upon mankind.

19. See James, quoted n. 17. The image of the 'fortunate fall' is more than once suggested in *The Marble Faun* only to be repudiated by Hilda ('"Oh, hush!" cried Hilda. . . . "Do you not perceive what a mockery your creed makes, not only of all religious sentiments, but of moral law . . ."' (Chapter L)). It is embraced in *Our Old Home* by Hawthorne *in propria persona*.

9

Nathaniel Hawthorne and the Dream of Happiness

by ERIC HOMBERGER

At the age of thirty-eight Nathaniel Hawthorne was unwilling to tell his mother and sisters that he planned to get married. He wrote to his fiancée Sophia Peabody in February 1842 that this 'incapacity of free communion' within his family was not due to stubbornness, nor to inordinate love of secrecy. An 'involuntary reserve' prevented him from opening himself fully to others.[1] He had already rented a house, the Old Manse at Concord, before the news was given to his family. The way it came, in a letter to his mother from Sophia, gave considerable offence. None of Hawthorne's relatives attended his wedding in July 1842; and he waited over two years before bringing Sophia to meet his mother. Hawthorne's biography is filled with examples of his attachment to seclusion, though few are as painful as this. He happily avoided social occasions when he could, and, outside a small circle of old college friends, generally gave the impression that he was taciturn and withdrawn. His childhood passion for the vast woods of Maine has an explanatory weight; as does a 'coldness of intercourse' which he noted had long existed between himself and his mother.[2]

Temperament and family life gave Hawthorne his great theme, the interplay of solitude and what he called 'sweet society' in *The Marble Faun*. The terms were substantially Emersonian. Hawthorne might have found little to quibble at in Emerson's *Society and Solitude* (1870); but there was an almost

171

complete divergence between the two. Emerson thought little of Hawthorne as a novelist, and Hawthorne remained indifferent to Emerson's philosophical ruminations. Living as they did at opposite ends of Concord village in the 1840s, they suggested to F. O. Matthiessen 'a perfect symbol for the age of extreme individualism'.[3] Matthiessen attributes this in part to Hawthorne's 'unconquerable reserve'. Such an unrelenting withholding of self is not to be understood in terms of literary or intellectual influence, nor does it come in any important sense from the broader current of society. The taciturn New Englander was by Hawthorne's time a well-established American stereotype. Hawthorne's reserve was like a dust in the blood; it was a part of reality. And in virtually everything he wrote the consciousness of isolation and solitude converts every issue and concern to its own terms.

Fanshawe (1828) was Hawthorne's first extended attempt to portray solitariness. The proud and haughty hero is led to glimpse 'the possibility of earthly happiness' and yet knows he cannot possess it. Fanshawe first appears in the novel on horseback with a triumphant expression on his face, 'like one who was a ruler in a world of his own, and independent of the beings that surrounded him'.[4] A Romantic and Byronic hero, Fanshawe's face is thin and pale, and he has the general air of a tortured soul. What in Arthur Dimmesdale rises to heights of self-laceration in Fanshawe is suspect, a pose masking other ambitions:

> Fanshawe had hitherto deemed himself unconnected with the world, unconcerned in its feelings, and uninfluenced by it in any of his pursuits. In this respect he probably deceived himself. If his inmost heart could have been laid open, there would have been discovered that dream of undying fame, which, dream as it is, is more powerful than a thousand realities. But at any rate, he had seemed, to others and to himself, a solitary being, upon whom the hopes and fears of ordinary men were ineffectual.
>
> But now he felt the first thrilling of one of the many ties, that, so long as we breathe the common air (and who shall say how much longer?) unite us to our kind. (III, 350)

The awful reality of isolation in Hawthorne's subsequent work soon replaces the adolescent pride and self-deception of Fanshawe. At the end of the story Ellen Langton, bravely rescued from her captivity by Fanshawe, appeals to him: 'will it not be happiness to form the tie that shall connect you to the world? to be your guide . . . to the quiet paths from which your proud and lonely thoughts have estranged you?' (III, 458). When Hester makes a similar plea to Dimmesdale, the relationship is more complex, the psychology stronger and more accurate. *Fanshawe* represents a simpler working out of these concerns and reminds us of the powerful and opposing presence of solitude and the promise of 'sweet society' at the beginning of Hawthorne's career.

By the time he wrote *The Scarlet Letter* (1850) Hawthorne's long seclusion was over: he had worked in the Boston Custom-House, lived at Ripley's Brook Farm community, published a collection of tales, and married Sophia Peabody. The growth in maturity and psychological complexity is everywhere abundantly visible in his work. The solitude which young Fanshawe hugged about himself is, in *The Scarlet Letter*, diffused throughout the Puritan community itself. And it is the community, in its fully totalitarian and repressive aspect, which Hawthorne shows to be the profound enemy of the 'sweet society' possible between individuals. The faces of the Puritans show a 'grim rigidity'; unseemly behaviour or levity, a too supple expressiveness, were frowned upon. For the Puritans civil and spiritual law were indistinguishable, and implacable in their severity. Twentieth-century life knows Hawthorne's Boston, with its thought-control, heretics, public punishments, and official ideology. But it is a perplexing question why Hawthorne, alone in the 'commonplace prosperity [and] . . . broad and simple daylight' (IV, 3) of Boston in the 1840s, should have imagined it with such brilliant clarity. *The Scarlet Letter* is a novel dominated by deception and secrets. The incessant riddling uncertainties of interpreting the world, the Puritan conventions of allegory and typology, the variousness of symbol and sign, have drawn attention away from the more literal problem posed by the plot. A great crime has been committed. Hester Prynne's adultery has been punished by a symbolic gesture, a badge of shame. Her deed, and punishment, forcibly isolates her from the community; in Hawthorne's imagination, isolation is the most terrible consequence of sin. But Hester isolates herself in more complex ways than that imposed upon her: she refuses to betray the name of her child's father. When her long-absent husband, Chillingworth, reveals himself to her, Hester agrees to protect his true identity. Hester's secrets are at the centre of deception: she deceives Dimmesdale and protects his own act of deception. The web of secrets establishes an invisible connection which they must keep hidden from each other and from public view. Hawthorne's characters live in a closed world of secretiveness. Hester's isolation is more ruthless and terrifying than that experienced by any other character in Hawthorne's novels:

> Every gesture, every word, and even the silence of those with whom she came in contact, implied, and often expressed that she was banished, and as much alone as if she inhabited another sphere, or communicated with the common nature by other organs and senses than the rest of human kind. (I, 84)

The loss of her femininity, the 'marble coldness' (I, 164) of her face, suggests the further price she must pay for her isolation.

One of the most important and surprising consequences of the isolation and secretiveness which pervades the book is the way change and inner development are enhanced and speeded up. As if to compensate for the 'disastrous efficacy' of Hester's isolation, she is shown as gaining a richer insight into other people. Hester's intellectual development is courageous and speculative, and in her needlework that part of her which was 'rich, voluptuous, Oriental' (I, 83) was given free play. Hester has been freed by her isolation in the sense that she glimpses a moral and intellectual life far removed from Puritan Boston. The process of change works as if in reverse on the minister Dimmesdale and the physician Chillingworth. At first the physician's face seemed merely 'ugly and evil' (I, 127) when he began to prove Dimmesdale's soul. After seven years with his obsession, Chillingworth had transformed himself into a devil (I, 170). Dimmesdale's frail health steadily declined. Yet, as with Hester, there were compensations for the guilt burning in his heart: Dimmesdale's 'intellectual gifts, his moral perceptions, his power of experiencing and communicating emotion, were kept in a state of preternatural activity by the prick and anguish of his daily life' (I, 141).

The contrasting changes within Hester and Dimmesdale are pointed up when they meet in the forest seven years after

174

Hester's punishment. Dimmesdale remained an essentially conservative theologian, a man within whom 'the reverential sentiment [was] largely developed' (I, 123). Isolation has given Hester a freedom of perspective denied to the minister:

> For years past she had looked from this estranged point of view at human institutions, and whatever priests or legislators had established; criticising all with hardly more reverence than the Indian would feel for the clerical hand, the judicial robe, the pillory, the gallows, the fireside or the church. The tendency of her fate and fortunes had been to set her free. (I, 199)

The minister, who retreated to safe orthodoxy of opinion before Chillingworth's copious and speculative bent of mind, could not suddenly breathe 'the wild, free atmosphere of an un-redeemed, unchristianized, lawless region' (I, 201) which Hester dangled before him. This 'glimpse of human affection and sympathy, a new life' (I, 200) left Dimmesdale stunned, exhilarated. Plans were quickly made for them to flee the Colony. The sudden dissolution of the minister's isolation deprived him of the iron certainties of his life; all values became uncertain. He can barely control an urge to speak improperly and blasphemously to people he meets on his way home. As he had done in *Fanshawe*, Hawthorne observed that despite the clergyman's great power of introspection, he was 'misterably deceived' (I, 215) in this heady new freedom. The established rule of theology, and a life spent at its service, could not simply be shrugged off. Dimmesdale's growth did not culminate in the forest, but upon his return when he realizes that he had been tempted by a 'dream of happiness': '—he had yielded himself with deliberate choice, as he had never done before, to what he knew was deadly sin' (I, 222). In the renunciation of his 'dream of happiness' and the acceptance of his sin, Dimmesdale believes salvation would be found. He tells Hester that *her* 'dream of happiness' was a deception: 'it was thenceforth vain to hope that we could meet hereafter, in an everlasting and pure reunion' (I, 256). Observing Dimmesdale's weakness and uncertainty, it had previously crossed Hester's mind that the hope of recreating the bond between herself and Dimmesdale was a 'delusion' (I, 240). Although in Hawthorne's world only the sympathetic impulse can transcend the frozen isolation of the individual, Dimmesdale is too conventional and too weak

('Thou wast not bold!—thou wast not true!' (I, 157)) to either free himself or to allow himself to be freed through Hester. The tragedy of isolation is that in the end it destroys the capacity for sympathy, and thus dissolves the human bonds which make the 'dream of happiness' possible.

In the world of seventeenth-century Boston, the 'dream of happiness' was potentially subversive, threatening both the divine and secular order. But in a world in which the Enlightenment and Romantic movements had occurred, in mid-nineteenth century Boston, the constraints are of a different order, and the threat less credible. Although he referred to the Puritans frequently in shorter pieces, Hawthorne's subsequent novels are all set in the milder social and theological climate of his own day. The effect generally is to lighten the gloom, and to give freer play to Hawthorne's vein of relaxed social comedy. In each of the novels following *The Scarlet Letter* isolation remains a central aspect of the lives of his characters, as is the threatened impairment of sympathy and blighting of the 'dream of happiness', but always in a context in which the state, the civil authority, has withdrawn.

The House of the Seven Gables (1851) shows greater variety of tone that *The Scarlet Letter*, and may have been harder to write. The lighter and more jocular scenes, such as Hepzibah's attempt to open a shop, the uncertain treatment of Phoebe (Hawthorne cannot decide whether she is to be regarded as sprite and 'dewy maiden' or practical American teenager), and the general weakness of the story-line, leave it a lesser performance.

Hawthorne's use of Maule's curse ('God will give him blood to drink') demands not only that the very notion of curses be made credible, but that the line, the Pyncheon family, be sufficiently sustained through time to bring the story to the present day. The discussion of the decline in worldly eminence of his Hawthorne ancestors in *The Scarlet Letter* suggests that this had a personal meaning as well as a political one. Hawthorne was a supporter of Andrew Jackson in the 1824 presidential election while he was at Bowdoin College, and had a bust of Jackson in his consular office in Liverpool in the 1850s. He wrote frequently for the *Democratic Review*, and was asked to do a campaign biography for the Democratic candidate in 1852, his old friend Franklin Pierce. Hawthorne was a political appointee in both the Boston and Salem Custom-Houses. Whilst not aggressively partisan, Hawthorne was closely identified by contemporaries with the Democrats.[5]

His second novel is coloured, or at least strikingly tinged, by the spirit of Jacksonian democracy, particularly in Hawthorne's treatment of the Pyncheons as representative specimens of American aristocracy. The political dimensions of the conflict between Maules and Pyncheons, though transposed back to the seventeenth century, would have been abundantly clear. The Maules are Common Man: they 'were generally poverty-stricken; always plebeian and obscure; working with unsuccessful diligence at handicrafts; laboring on the wharves, or following the sea' (II, 25). The Pyncheons, while failing to satisfy their family claim upon vast tracts in Maine, ascended to comfort and social prominence and remained there. Over generations, as the house fell into decay, the family line began to fail. Though infrequently sustained by merited social position, the Pyncheons were Pyncheons:

> There is something so massive, stable, and almost irresistibly imposing, in the exterior presentment of established rank and great possessions, that their very existence seems to give them a right to exist; at least, so excellent a counterfeit of right, that few poor and humble men have moral force enough to question it, even in their secret minds. Such is the case now, after so many ancient prejudices have been overthrown; and it was far more so in ante-revolutionary days, when the aristocracy could venture to be proud, and the low were content to be abased. (II, 25)[6]

The characterization of Hepzibah, resolving between hysterical giggles and sobs to earn her own food or starve, comically emphasizes the false pride, social exclusivity and isolation of the aristocratic Pyncheons. The Daguerreotypist Holgrave (like a character in a Soviet Five-Year-Plan novel) encourages Hepzibah's feeble efforts: 'Hitherto, the life-blood has been gradually chilling in your veins, as you sat aloof, within your circle of gentility, while the rest of the world was fighting out its battle with one kind of necessity or another. Henceforth, you will at least have the sense of healthy and natural effort for a purpose, and of lending your strength—be it great or small—to the united struggle of mankind' (II, 44-5). Holgrave's pomposity, Hepzibah's caricatured mannerisms, and the practical young Phoebe, prevent Hawthorne's strictures against aristocracy from becoming overly serious. The rather protracted comedy of Hepzibah and her youthful customer pulls the narrative towards a Dickensian note. When her brother Clifford is seriously endangered by their cousin, Judge Jaffrey Pyncheon, in the sixteenth chapter, Hepzibah's isolation is meant to bear a hint of tragic meaning:

> In all her years of seclusion, she had never felt, as now, what it was to be alone. It seemed as if the house stood in a desert, or, by some spell, was made invisible to those who dwelt around, or passed beside it. . . . . In her grief and wounded pride, Hepzibah had spent her life in divesting herself of friends;—she had wilfully cast off the support which God has ordained His creatures to need from one another;—and it was now her punishment, that Clifford and herself would fall the easier victims to their kindred enemy. (II, 244-45)

The intensified consciousness of isolation, as in *The Scarlet Letter*, quickens the pace of inner development. During their flight from the Judge, Hepzibah and Clifford board a train. Hawthorne contrasts their reaction to new experiences: Clifford seems alert, hopeful, energetic: 'He had been startled into manhood and intellectual vigor' (II, 258). Hepzibah, on the other hand, seems confused and withdrawn. Their roles have been reversed, and at least for a little while it is Clifford who attends to Hepzibah. Hawthorne presents isolation in the context of dislocation and danger: they are all shocks, challenges, to the self which will either make an individual or break them. (Miriam regretfully notes in *The Marble Faun* that Donatello 'might have had a kind of bliss in the consequences of this deed, had he been impelled to it by a love vital enough to survive the frenzy of that terrible moment,—mighty enough to make its own law, and justify itself against the natural remorse' (IV, 199).)

Clifford Pyncheon is a considerably more subtle portrayal of the aristocrat in decay. While still the embodiment of an unexplained mystery, his 'wasted, gray, and melancholy figure' has about it hints of an 'indescribable grace', 'a charm of wonderful beauty', and a refined and 'softly imaginative' expression (II, 104–7). It is a nature undisturbed by the claims of the moral life. Long estranged from beauty, he has become little more than a selfish appetite. He was made to sample and savour, and to devote himself to the cultivation of sensibility: 'Such a man should have nothing to do with sorrow; nothing with strife; nothing with the martyrdom which, in an infinite variety of shapes, awaits those who have the heart, and will, and conscience, to fight a battle with the world' (II, 108). Henry James saw more deeply than Hawthorne the moral corruption of the Sybarite. It is quite revealing of Hawthorne's lighter purpose in *The House of the Seven Gables* that Phoebe should be the agent for Clifford's restoration within the 'sympathetic chain of human nature' (II, 141). Clifford's 'dream of happiness' in his blighted state was as impalpable and undirected as his appetite. 'I want my happiness!' (II, 157) he cries out, standing before the garden. Like Carlyle, Hawthorne advises Clifford to look about him!

> Fate has no happiness in store for you; unless your quiet home in the old family residence, with the faithful Hepzibah, and your long summer-afternoons with Phoebe, and these Sabbath festivals with Uncle Venner and the Daguerreotypist, deserve to be called happiness! (II, 158)

Where Clifford was vague in his thoughts of happiness, Holgrave was precise and radical. The corrective which Hawthorne offers to Holgrave's hope is no less clear:

> It seemed to Holgrave—as doubtless it has seemed to the hopeful of every century, since the epoch of Adam's grandchildren—that in this age, more than ever before, the moss-grown and rotten Past is to be torn down, and lifeless institutions to be thrust out of the way, and their dead corpses buried, and everything to begin anew. (II, 179)

Hawthorne had seen more than enough of 'lifeless institutions' and his comments on the somnolent Salem Custom-House, and its superannuated inhabitants, had caused something of a scandal when *The Scarlet Letter* appeared. Holgrave's error, Hawthorne advises us, lay in preferring a sudden trans-formation of society instead of a more measured, gradual and piecemeal process of reform. The *volte-face* by which Holgrave abandons his radical views was effected by Phoebe, that sweet and tedious heroine who has brought Hepzibah, Clifford and now the radical Daguerreotypist within the circle of reality and sympathy as she defines them. A domestic and narrowing sense of the real world increasingly became Hawthorne's touchstone and guide for human endeavour. The taming of Holgrave has a hint of politics about it. Holgrave is perhaps too balanced, too generous in his impulses, to join the Abolitionists in their bitter campaign against conservative Democrats of Hawthorne's persuasion.[7] Holgrave (like Hester Prynne) belongs to the Party of Hope and is reminded by Hawthorne (as Dimmesdale was constrained to remind Hester) that 'it was thenceforth vain to hope.' The blissful domesticity of the end of the novel, when Maule and Pyncheon have settled down together on the Judge's pleasant country estate, in which Holgrave's idealism has been tempered by reality, Hepzibah and Clifford restored to the circle of humanity, and Maule's curse lifted, suggests that the subversive 'dream of happiness' of *The Scarlet Letter* had ceased to carry the substance of tragedy. In Hawthorne's society it was material more suited for domestic comedy or melodrama.

In the Preface to *The Blithedale Romance* (1852) Hawthorne declined to 'illustrate a theory, or elicit a conclusion' in respect to the principles on which the utopian community was based. The Blithedale experiment recedes to the background of the story as the narrator becomes increasingly obsessed by the puzzling relationship between Zenobia, Priscilla and Hollingsworth; the fate of the community, and that of the emotional ties of the main characters, *are* ultimately related, and greatly enhance the sense of desolation in the final scenes. This happens despite the narrator, and his typically ironic tone. *Blithedale* is the only one of his novels to have a narrator, and he presents himself as a failed poet who has sunken into self-satisfied middle-age ('. . . I live very much at my ease, and fare sumptuously every day . . .' (III, 246)). The portrait is characteristically self-deprecating. Coverdale's mockery is good-humoured: 'If Kossuth . . . would pitch the battlefield of Hungarian rights within an easy ride of my abode, and choose a mild, sunny morning, after breakfast, for the conflict, Miles Coverdale would gladly be his man, for one brave rush upon the levelled bayonets. Farther than that, I should be loth to pledge myself' (III, 246-47). (Kossuth's visit to Boston in 1852 left

Hawthorne feeling 'about as enthusiastic as a lump of frozen sand'.)[8] In Coverdale we see an ironist whose irony undermines itself, but it is difficult to discount the facile, systematic irony which touches all aspects of the idealistic communitarians. The characteristic tactic is the use of 'reality', whether psychological, climatological or economic, to reveal the foolish naïveté which Coverdale sees in the others—and in himself as well. The free-thinking Hester Prynne and Holgrave convey their message, their 'dream of happiness', without being subjected to such incessant irony. What we see of the community comes through Coverdale. Even Zenobia's thoughts in the early chapters appear in his summary:

> . . . she made no scruple of oversetting all human institutions, and scattering them as with a breeze from her fan. A female reformer, in her attacks upon society, has an instinctive sense of where the life lies, and is inclined to aim, directly at that spot. Especially, the relation between the sexes is naturally among the earliest to attract her notice. (III, 44)

The deeper levels of *The Blithedale Romance* have little to do with the attempt to create a 'sweet society' as an actual institution. Attention is focused upon a puzzling, intensely observed struggle between two women, unequally matched at first sight, for the affection of Hollingsworth. Coverdale fears that Zenobia was being cynycally used by Hollingsworth in a plot to acquire the real estate of the farm. Coverdale increasingly becomes fearful for Priscilla, caught up in a situation she does not understand and seemingly without a will of her own. But he fails to establish frank and open relations with Zenobia, and rejects Hollingsworth's powerful and emotive plea to join his scheme to reform criminals by appealing to their higher instincts. (Hollingsworth's monomaniacal plan reverses Jeremy Bentham's model prison, the Panopticon, which was designed to cure criminal behaviour by the manipulation of the inmates' self-interest.) Having lost his early enthusiasm for farm labour, and for the Blithedale experiment generally, Coverdale feels doubly isolated by his failures with Zenobia and Hollingsworth. He withdraws to an 'inner circle of self-communion' (III, 89). The secluded 'hermitage' formed by wild grapevines and several trees becomes for Coverdale a symbol of his individuality; it also stands for his isolation. Beginning with the hope of a revitalized community, Coverdale's real self is now hidden and protected. Attempts to enter the closed world of Priscilla and Zenobia are rebuffed: Priscilla innocently says that everything is fine, and Zenobia does not trust Coverdale. All that is left him is to observe their lives, and through intuition reach an understanding of their secret. He is embarrassingly recognized while watching Zenobia through a boarding-house window. With a sudden, brilliant gesture she waves in recognition, then pulls the curtain. After Priscilla goes off with Zenobia and the ominous Westervelt, Coverdale, fearing that some great wrong was being planned, seeks out Old Moodie: he learns that the two women were half-sisters. Coverdale sees them all together for a final time at Blithedale. Zenobia has lost Hollingsworth, and her money. Hollingsworth, the man against whom she would hear no criticism, now stands revealed to her as a 'cold, heartless, self-beginning and self-ending piece of mechanism' (III, 218). In a magnificent and devastating self-analysis, Zenobia presents herself as

> . . . a woman—with every fault, it may be, that a woman ever had, weak, vain, unprincipled, (like most of my sex; for our virtues, when we have any, are merely impulsive ard intuitive,) passionate, too, and pursuing my foolish and unattainable ends, by indirect and cunning, though absurdly chosen means, as an hereditary bond-slave must—false, moreover, to the whole circle of good, in my reckless truth to the little good I saw before me—but still a woman! (III, 217-18)

Blithedale itself now seemed a 'foolish dream' to Zenobia:

> . . . I am weary of this place, and sick to death of playing at philanthropy and progress. Of all varieties of mock-life, we have surely blundered into the very emptiest mockery, in our effort to establish the one true system. I have done with it. . . . It was, indeed, a foolish dream! (III, 227)

Coverdale kisses her cold hand, recording his deep sympathy in a gesture; but of course Zenobia was beyond sympathy. Her 'dream of happiness' has ended in disaster. The hope for 'sweet society' at Blithedale has been pushed aside by more aggressive and possessive instincts—the need for love—which knows nothing of Fourier and co-operation. 'You stood between me and an end which I desired', Zenobia said to Priscilla. 'I wanted a clear path' (III, 220). *The Blithedale Romance* touches deeper levels of passional life than Hawthorne had done in his earlier novels. He has come close to the point where the 'dream of happiness' demands the abandonment of any kind of social hope ('It was, indeed, a foolish dream!'), and threatens, if all goes wrong, an isolation so impenetrable that even suicide seems preferable.

Though Italy affords Hawthorne 'a sort of poetic or fairy precinct' in which to set *The Marble Faun* (1860), the story itself is lurid. At different times in the romance two characters contemplate suicide; for two others innocence has well and truly been lost. A murder triggers off an experience of guilt and remorse which stains the consciousness of three of the four principal characters. The sculptor Kenyon, like Miles Coverdale and Holgrave, remains an observer of the course of events. Hilda and Donatello, the innocents, are drawn without premeditation into the tragedy of Miriam's struggle to liberate herself.

The novel begins with a relaxed discussion in an art gallery, in which topics in art, human nature and ethics are easily mingled. But Donatello's murder of the Capuchin monk tears apart the affectionate pattern of relationships. Both Donatello and Hilda turn away from Miriam in revulsion. 'With an involuntary repellent gesture' (IV, 207) Hilda removes herself from Miriam's touch. To Donatello, she has become 'an object of horrour' (IV, 281). With her tormentor the Capuchin now dead, Miriam expressed the hope that she and Donatello would be 'released from the chain of humanity' (IV, 1735–75) sufficiently to enable them to form a new bond. To the young Italian it was indelibly poisoned, a bond cemented with the dead monk's blood. Miriam, perhaps echoing Zenobia's experience with Coverdale, detecting a 'certain reserve' (IV, 128) in Kenyon, is unable to speak openly to him. The shock of being denounced as 'cold and pitiless' makes him more genuinely sympathetic, but it was too late. Even before the murder, isolation was Miriam's nightmare:

> Standing on the utmost verge of that dark chasm, she might stretch out her hand, and never clasp a hand of theirs; she might

strive to call out—'Help, friends, help!'—but, as with dreamers when they shout, her voice would perish inaudibly in the remoteness that seemed such a little way. (IV, 113)

Hawthorne goes on to reflect that this perception 'of an infinite, shivering solitude' which resulted when 'any accident, misfortune, crime, or peculiarity of character' puts an individual 'ajar with the world'. Hester's sin was voluntarily committed, but Miriam's seem to have emerged from her nature without conscious thought. The terror at the heart of *The Marble Faun* lies here, in the possibility that an individual could be plunged into sin and isolation not for what you did, but for the darkest and most secret wishes which might, as in Miriam, suddenly emerge and bring about one's destruction. When the monk, dressed as Miriam's rustic model, appears at the pleasure grounds near the people's gate of Rome, Donatello greets him with an animal rage.

> 'I hate him!' muttered he.
> 'Be satisfied; I hate him too!' said Miriam.
> She had no thought of making this avowal, but was irresistibly drawn to it by the sympathy of the dark emotion in her own breast with that so strongly expressed by Donatello. Two drops of water, or of blood, do not more naturally flow into each other, than did her hatred into his. (IV, 91)

This scene anticipates the complicity in the murder which Hilda and Donatello attribute to Miriam: 'a look of hatred, triumph, vengeance, and . . . joy at some unhoped for relief!' (IV, 210) crossed her face at the moment when the murder occurred. Like the sympathy of the 'dark emotion' which flowed towards Donatello in the gardens, the response was involuntary. It reveals an inner truth, and will; the complicity Hawthorne suggests is at a deeper and more fundamental level. In discussion with Donatello, who shares Miriam's dread of moral isolation, Kenyon suggests that isolation was more the punishment for sin than its consequence:

> . . . perhaps this is to be the punishment of sin . . . Not that it shall be made evident to the Universe, (which can profit nothing by such knowledge,) but that it shall insulate the sinner from all sweet society by rendering him impermeable to light, and thereby unrecognizable in the abode of heavenly simplicity and

truth. Then, what remains for him, but the dreariness of infinite and eternal solitude. (IV, 304-5)

As we saw in *The Scarlet Letter*, there is another consequence of sin and isolation: it serves as 'an instrument most effective in the education of intellect and soul' (IV, 435). The transformation of Donatello is the more dramatic instance, but the subtle changes wrought upon Hilda by her knowledge of evil have the no less important effect of drawing her back from an utter self-sufficiency (IV, 121) to the point where she gains a capacity for love. The price she has paid is a modest one: Hilda loses her sensitive intuition into works of art, and feels for the first time the pangs of the exile. Like Donatello, she has been transformed and humanized. Miriam has lost the most, and her subtle gesture of benediction at the Pantheon carries with it the unmistakable warning that Hilda and Kenyon should keep their distance. An abyss still separated them. Kenyon was the least touched by the events of the book, and his plan to enshrine and worship Hilda as a household saint has survived intact. Donatello has been transformed and become a man, subject to the guilt and remorse which to Hawthorne defined the human condition.

It would be difficult, perhaps impossible, to extrapolate from Hawthorne's reserved and taciturn nature the deep structure which informs his novels. But it is hard to see how the structure can be accounted for otherwise. The consciousness of isolation, whether caused by social exclusivity (Hepzibah), a sinful act (Hester), or a complicity of will (Miriam), stands at the centre of the pattern. As we have seen, the consequences of isolation can be positive and negative. Donatello and Clifford Pyncheon, in their different ways, are startled into manhood by their ordeal of isolation. Hester follows an unpredictable and astonishing path of self-liberation. Chillingworth and Hollingsworth, on the other hand, are deformed and eventually destroyed by monomania and self-deception. Isolation becomes a metaphor in Hawthorne for the possibilities of choosing to be human.

Hester and Miriam touch on the margins of tragedy. They

are bold, free spirits, capable of penetrating the veil of respectability with which society cloaks its power and demands. Their fates, like that at a lower level of Holgrave, have a cautionary weight. They stand at the heart of Hawthorne's secret communities, under continuous threat of inquisitors (Chillingworth, Judge Jaffrey Pyncheon) or merely curious observers (Coverdale, Kenyon); and in their heroism and error make the domestic settlements and 'dream of happiness' of Phoebe and Hilda seem very bland indeed.

NOTES

1. Arlin Turner, *Nathaniel Hawthorne: A Biography* (New York: Oxford University Press, 1980), p. 124.
2. Turner, p. 188.
3. F. O. Matthiessen, *American Renaissance* (New York: Oxford University Press, 1941), p. 194.
4. Nathaniel Hawthorne, *The Blithedale Romance* and *Fanshawe* (Columbus, Ohio: Ohio State University Press, 1964), p. 346. Further references to Hawthorne will be made to the Centenary Edition, by volume and page. The relevant volumes are: I (*The Scarlet Letter*); II (*The House of the Seven Gables*); III (*The Blithedale Romance* and *Fanshawe*); and VIII (*The American Notebooks*).
5. Matthiessen discusses Hawthorne's politics, pp. 318-19.
6. Holgrave's 'lack of reverence for what was fixed' unsettles Phoebe (II, 177). In *The Scarlet Letter* Hawthorne noted the decline in 'the quality of reverence' since the seventeenth century (I, 237).
7. In his notebooks Hawthorne reflected that 'On the whole, I find myself rather more of an abolitionist in feeling than in principle' (VIII, 112). The editor of the notebook comments that this sums up his settled attitude towards slavery.
8. Turner, p. 236.

10

Power and Law in Hawthorne's Fictions

by ERIC MOTTRAM

1

Frankenstein creates a monster and becomes himself monstrous; the two figures are popularly taken as one. Aylmer becomes monstrous by manipulating his wife before the laughing 'underworker', the shaggy, smoky and earthy Aminadab. Hawthorne writes guardedly of the possibility that 'the Eve of Powers' might be converted to 'a monster'. Intellectuality and sexuality are shown in dubious relationship as the Aylmer house is turned into a laboratory, as other fictional nineteenth-century houses are turned into asylums or houses of correction or assignation. The wife becomes a patient first, and then a victim murdered for scientific curiosity and erotic self-satisfaction. The repressed returns in the disguise of science, and the professional gets away with it once again: it is the continual theme of Hawthorne's fictions of professionals. Here and in 'Rappaccini's Daughter' the Renaissance seventeenth-century scientist returns as the nineteenth-century inventor manipulating energy, human and nonhuman, for and against the social, ambivalently a figure of exploitation and enterprise (the business man is not fully used until Dreiser's Cowperwood). The scientist inventor, supposedly the generative centre of technological progress and trade, is morally negated. The relationships of desire to production, of desire to public and private interests, and therefore to law, are

187

repeatedly proposed in Hawthorne's fictions. But in both 'The Birthmark' and 'Rappaccini's Daughter' the victim is a woman. Hawthorne's contemporary, Karl Marx, wrote in the 1844 *Economic and Philosophic Manuscripts:*

> The direct, natural and necessary relation of person to person is the relation of man to woman. . . . It therefore reveals the extent to which man's natural behaviour has become human . . . the extent to which man's need has become a human need; the extent to which, therefore, the other person as a person has become for him a need—the extent to which he is his individual existence is at the same time a social being.[1]

Hawthorne repeatedly collapses and reinstates, sometimes in variable forms, male dominance figures parallel to the partial emergence, and sometimes the total suppression, of female figures. Obedience and disobedience between men and women fascinate him; for him, the cannibal and vampire steal energy, take over, expropriate wherever the class structure permits it. But his sense of the inevitable action of predatory will is that it cannot be halted, let alone eradicated, because it is 'evil'. He asks the crucial questions: What is control, what is counter-control, and who operates their system? What values conflict? What is the nature of alienation and its relations with isolation and community? But he asks them in a particular structure of actual and imagined inheritance, still thinking of the production of relationships as a theological theatre rather than a political factory. 'Historical fixatives' control his ethics or 'traditional bonds'; he feels bound to confront the American seventeenth-century origins with mid-nineteenth century industrial capitalist democracy in terms of an unchanging, unchangeable manichean battle.[2] Deleuze and Guattari put the force of the secular instances in such fictions in post-Reichian terms:

> The strength of Reich consists in having shown how psychic repression depended on social repression . . . social repression needs psychic repression precisely in order to form docile subjects and ensure the reproduction of the social formation, including its repressive structures . . . civilization must be understood in terms of a social repression inherent in a given form of social production.[3]

Hawthorne comes near to asking his questions of repression

within the crucial question—particularly in *The Scarlet Letter*
and *The Marble Faun*—how does it come about that we desire
our own repression? But his questions are taken up with a
constant reminder that Americans are helpless, that Emerson's
characteristic *dicta* of self-reliance are mistaken. Helplessness is
a main source for gothic, horror and science fiction systems, the
oscillations between voluntary and involuntary behaviours.
Seventeenth-century New England society can be used as the
instance of a group which knows it is corrupt but knows, too,
that, short of prayer, penitence and Jeremiads, it is condemned
to the manichean battlefield, the prior inhuman system of God
and Devil. Life polarized into punishment and blessing,
confession and concealment, marks the presence of the
repressed in continuous dialectic with the public surfaces,
partly euphoric drive and partly exhausting depression.
'Confidence in America' could be the endlessly punning title of
the history of New World fictions. Confidence is undermined in
Hawthorne's contribution by his fast conviction that the
Unpardonable Sin is utterly wrong and inevitable. His work is
therefore a criticism of *all* manipulative power between human
beings. Since religion and capitalism infer manipulation, his
work has to be a criticism of the American structure itself (in
1981, we have President Reagan attacking Communists for not
believing in an afterlife). So that the inevitability of America as
a euphoric prophecy, reaching fulfilment in the mid-nineteenth
century, is confronted with the regressiveness of the manichean
permanence. Hawthorne moves out from concepts he hardly
changes; it is both a strength and an inhibition. His characters
are liable to be obliterated by an ideological scheme in which
they have to be exemplary. This is his peculiar legalism, his own
totalitarian pattern, which, curiously and especially in *The
Marble Faun*, needs the Unpardonable Sin just as he defined it in
his *American Notebooks*—'want of love and reverence for the
Human Soul; in consequence of which the investigator pried
into its dark depths, not with a hope or purpose of making it
better, but from a cold philosophical curiosity... the separation
of the intellect from the heart.' But what exactly are the risks?
The desires of the heart are notoriously as possibly cruel as the
desires of intellect may be beneficent. Hawthorne's framework
of enquiry initiates but clings to a prohibitive social ethos. The

preface to his children's *Wonder-Book* (1851) asks 'Is not the human heart deeper than any system of philosophy?' But what does 'deeper' infer as value? A spatialization of ethical images does not make the differentiations any the more 'natural'. 'System' apparently must be a surface action in its artifice. It is a fatal and mistaken separation, since theory and coherence are as 'deep' a need as automatic feeling, and both are equally liable to be programmatic.

But Hawthorne properly resists an over-interiorization of behaviour motivations and sequences. He knows that the so-called individual is, as Marx postulates it, 'as social product (as is even the language in which the thinker is active): my *own* existence *is* social activity. . . . The Individual's manifestations of life—even if they may not appear in the direct form of *communal* manifestations of life carried out in association with others—*are* therefore an expression and confirmation of social life'.[4] But the effect of using 'Puritan seventeenth-century New England' (his own artefact, in fact) as an exemplary field of events, images and explanations through which to compose nineteenth-century fictions is to universalize that field by dehistoricizing it—as if the theocratic state were *the* archetype: just as Freud creates a universal Law of the Father out of parts of an Oedipus story in one ancient Greek writer, refusing to describe 'the unconscious' as an historically determined phenomenon, variable in different societies with differing modes of production. Dehistoricization is mystification. Hawthorne resorts to an onward-going explanatory scheme—in effect, an ideology—of good and evil which is a manichean structure beyond dialectical change, a diachrony carried forward in a vocabulary of inheritance and inevitability, partly Christian, partly medieval, and partly heretical. It is hardly surprising that the nineteenth-century and the seventeenth-century intervention into this scheme is the woman who will not submit to male usage, unlike Aylmer's Georgiana and Rappaccini's Beatrice. Psychological analysis is a politics rather than a science. The anxiety over Mesmerism everywhere in Hawthorne has to be poised between fear of hypnotic domination and submission from one man (a singular source of energy control) and a sense that something beneficial might come from it.

Mesmerism is the type of all procedures that control sub-liminally, whether through religion or education or psycho-logical persuasion within desire and the erotic. Hawthorne is well aware that interference with another self infers the presence of the Unpardonable Sin immediately the process becomes sheer usage for production—a perverse desire to move in on someone's life and use it, perhaps to use it up. The popular seventeenth-century context for Ethan Brand is male witchcraft. But Brand himself believes that the Devil can only use 'half-way sinners'. His full sin is to have sacrificed everything to the claims of 'an intellect', 'a high state of enthusiasm' (Hawthorne uses the term in the late seventeenth-century and Augustan usage). A girl, Esther (from the same source as Hester), is 'made the subject of a psychological experiment' through which she is 'wasted, absorbed and perhaps annihilated'—or, as William Burroughs would say, 'assimilated'. Brand's 'powers', his 'star-lit eminence' in the intellectual world, are detached from that 'moral nature' which is the basis of 'brotherhood'. But Hawthorne withdraws from the actual processes of experi-mental control. The fiction remains visual and theoretical, a discourse on an abstract theme. The erotic desire at its centre is barely hinted. But at least the story reaches towards a point where we can say 'psychoanalysis is a soul murder'.[5] The detective story, like science fiction and fantastic fiction, must be a book of philosophy.[6]

Hawthorne is haunted by a further seventeenth-century image-event—the ability of Comus to change men into beasts in 'the forest' (his name means 'revelry' and he is the son of Bacchus or Dionysus, the enemy of Christ, and Circe), a figure of Control by total transformation. But Hawthorne's mode is not Milton's (the redemptive Lady channel is not available to him) but a different enquiry into the verbal and visual forms and the political-religious dogmas of Control. The manner of transformation may be visually symbolic but, like the burning A and its several interpretations, its effects are concrete enough. Hawthorne explores how much and what should be repressed by oppression to produce a society, and asks long before *Civilization and its Discontents*. 'Young Goodman Brown' proposes that Christ and the Devil may control equally well in terms of daily co-ordinated moral living in a town, and that

191

dogmatic exclusivity may produce deadly isolation. The Mars/
Indian leader at the head of the rebel Comus rout looks directly
at Robin, and his gaze is the challenge of counter-control from
revolt in the State. The rout may be docile, but it is the
American future. Power operates on the frontier crossings of
legality, crime and sin. Transgression and innovation move
together. In the words of Deleuze and Guattari (*Anti-Oedipus*):

> We docile subjects say to ourselves: so that's what I wanted! Will
> it ever be suspected that the law discredits—and has an interest
> in discrediting and disgracing—the person it presumes to be
> guilty, the person the law wants to be guilty and wants to be
> made to feel guilty? One acts as if it were possible to conclude
> directly from psychic repression the nature of the repressed, and
> from the prohibition the nature of what is prohibited . . . what
> really takes place is that the law prohibits something that is
> perfectly fictitious in the order of desire or of the 'instincts', so as
> to persuade its subjects that they had this intention corres-
> ponding to this fiction. This is indeed the only way the law has of
> getting a grip on intention, of making the unconscious guilty.

This is the casual plot of Hester Prynne's obedience and
disobedience between the law of marriage and transcendental
law of erotic desire, with 'a consecration of its own' (Chapter
17). Hawthorne is further to dramatize the transmission of
repression, from the seventeenth century to the nineteenth,
from Europe to New England, in the palimpsest of his Rome, in
Blithedale with its Fourierism and Mesmerism and Benthamite
panopticon, in all those who use 'natural science' to tamper
with the human body and soul. The Devil is the repressed
working through the ages and needs human souls, and working
especially in the utopian ambivalences of Westervelt and
Hollingsworth, the classic double figure of repression/
oppression in *The Blithedale Romance*. Woody Allen's self-
lacerating comedy takes up guilt and neurosis into an anti-
intellectual series of routines; his standard figures are sceptical
and paralyzed into indecision and endless verbalizations.
Hawthorne's professionals are decisive in control but still
neurotic, and equally cut off from the masses. The ritual
sacrifice of intellectuals and artists lies well within the traditions
of the Paleface, in Rahv's terms, and the celebrated thin pale
face of the American intellectual.[7]

In fact the repressed returns in Hawthorne's fictions largely if not altogether through the Comus intellectual with or without his rout, or her dark erotic pressures. And there is an accurate sense that energies are repressed in American as in any other western culture, at least since the Salem witch-hunts. Sexual energy, and its transference into creativity, is repressed towards the ideal which haunts nineteenth-century American fiction: the robot, the automaton, the slave without human limitations which interfere with productivity, who is so totally balanced that he can be used as an it. The woman is repressed towards subordinate passivity and away from assertion, creativity and organizational responsibility. Children's impishness is inter- preted as devilry and educated out, for future labour usefulness. In America the repressed appears as the Indian, the Black Man in the forest, wilderness and wildness, the Devil, uncontrolled libido in any form—so that religious and capitalist relationships can be imposed. Sects flourish but they are rarely liberatory. Hawthorne can easily use the seventeenth century as a con- tinuous present in which the repressed returns, since what is feared continually is the coherence of a particularly thrustful energy imaged as the Adversary. Certain salient sections of that past are given key powers, certain events become metonymic instances. The resulting fiction is employed to analyze the nineteenth-century lacks and suppressions, especially the deterioration of professionals in law, science, the church, and so on, which erodes confidence in society. What thrusts past the censor, what threatens normality, is presented as monstrous, a villain, the natural threatening state forms. The overwhelming emphasis on self-reliance, individual enterprise and personal aggressiveness is countered by the chances of being trans- formed in this process into a criminal, a sinner, a monster or a deprived recluse at the very moment of self-realization. Brand commits suicide in the Devil's fire, and Clifford Pyncheon emerges from false imprisonment as an enfeebled eccentric. A man may live with a snake in his body or facially concealed beneath a long black veil. A woman may be turned into an adulteress just as a black woman is turned into a negress. Innocence is everywhere emergent as experience because of the determinate need to conquer energy. Women and sexuality are nervously shown by Hawthorne moving against their relegation

193

in Christian capitalist society to the utilitarian and subordinate, to the reality principle which devours pleasure. Pearl's position proposes that the innocence of children may no longer be assumed (the educational system had long ago given up such a belief). 'Possession' haunts Hawthorne's pages as a challenge to both reason and innocence and is signalled by displays of intellectual and physical passion. It is 'Rome' in *The Marble Faun* to such an extent that 'New England' becomes a shadowy place for the chastened American lovers to return to. In Hawthorne's fictions heroes and heroines have all but vanished as figures of dominant revolutionary apparatus. Threats to the State and to the family, the nucleus of the State have to be put down as 'Merry England', maypoles and garlanded lords of misrule are put down. But the threats remain. All Endicott can do is have the May Lord's hair cropped and throw a wreath of roses over his head.

Some of the reasons are clear. The creative/subversive must somehow be given permission: the dilemma of the State. Within Hawthorne's critique of the exceptional man or woman lies a fear that the masses may produce nothing new, do not produce through disobedience or breaking laws. The power of the social group in 'My Kinsman, Major Molineux' and 'The Artist of the Beautiful' is clear: the rout may have destructive leadership. Lonely work is fearful to the mob, but that is a major source of change. The rout's leader in 'Molineux' is the figure of choice in law-breaking to which Robin is invited to contribute his energy for a new stage in social production—in effect, the future of New England and of the United States lies with the Mars/Indian at the head of a lynch mob. And here the tar-and-feathering is laid on the governor rather than Southern blacks or the keepers in 'The System of Doctor Tarr and Professor Fether'. Nostalgia for a feudal order in hierarchy, a class-structured unity, confronts the new, the forward movement in revolt. Within the writing confidence of the tale, the author is puzzled by the possibility of two orders of control in conflict which seems to be inevitable. But he finely shows how they lie on either side of the moment where the paradigm is forcibly changing. The fiction is generated from and generates the question so frequently posed in Hawthorne's career: where does change come from? The individual and the masses conflict precisely here. Hawthorne's thought is not evolutionary, as Whitman's is, nor is it an organicist longing for the unity in which 'the everlasting universe of Things/Flows through the Mind . . . from secret springs.'[8]

Shelley Mont Blanc

So he works within fictional methods which are voyeuristic and manichean. An obsessive basis in the visual, the placing of crucial events within the single perception, demands a voyeuristic mode, and the fiction becomes spectatorist. The complete *oeuvre* is an equivalent of a panopticon, with Hollingsworth, the author, at its centre, gazing into each cell holding its captive. Or Henry Ford dreaming of being able to survey each assembly-line operative, and then follow him home. Hollingsworth the egotistic reformer has to be defeated and converted to love of a passive woman. Following a leader almost certainly means you yield to him or her. The continuing power of this programme, within the manichean control system, is still highly valid in the polarizations of Mailer's *Why Are We in Vietnam?* in 1967, where the plot includes, essentially, the reaches of cosmic energy, still imaged as the divine or the satanic into the human brain, 'in the deep of its mysterious unwindings', 'the deep mystery which is whatever is electricity'. This is no great distance from that Poe-like entry in the *American Notebooks:* 'questions as to unsettled points of History, and Mysteries of Nature, to be asked of a mesmerized person'. Like Mailer, Hawthorne grasped the need of the fantastic mode in order to work in these interfaces between possibility, probability and the present:

> In a world which is indeed our world, the one we know, a world without devils, sylphides, or vampires, there recurs an event which cannot be explained by the laws of this same familiar world. The person who experiences the event must opt for one of two possible solutions: either he is the victim of an illusion of the senses, of a product of the imagination—and laws of the world then remain what they are; or else the event has indeed taken place, it is an integral part of reality—but then this reality is controlled by laws unknown to us. Either the devil is an illusion, an imaginary being; or else he really exists, precisely like the other living beings—with this reservation, that we encounter him infrequently.
>
> The fantastic occupies the duration of this uncertainty. Once we choose one answer or the other, we leave the fantastic for a

neighbouring genre, the uncanny or the marvellous. The fantastic is that hesitation experienced by a person who knows only the laws of nature confronting an apparently supernatural event.[9]

But in fact it may be possible, and Hawthorne certainly found it possible, to oscillate between a secular and a theological usage of what Todorov calls 'illusion', 'supernatural'. Inside these defining procedures lies, therefore, a further decision: the writer may hesitate or he may not, and his reader may hesitate or not, according to prior belief, knowledge and experience. Science fiction and science non-fiction may be experienced as possible or improbable or probable accordingly. The 'fantastic' uses 'the laws of nature' to extrapolate a fiction from scientific hypotheses as well as scientific discovery. The writer may compose to a formulaic procedure which produces money-spinners out of tidy moral plots or shiver-causing plots of indecision. In the nineteenth century, the nature of already rapidly accelerating cultural change could frequently be experienced as 'fantastic'—and the decision to place it theologically or not would have to follow. Ignorance and indecision are made within apparent knowledge and decisions. Fictional products imitate. 'The wonderful world around us in harmony' of the Romantics may be poisonous and incurably so, or at least governed, as Rappaccini's garden is, by the Roman god of change (and Hawthorne uses the language of 'adultery' for the hybrids there—'no longer of God's making, but the monstrous offspring of man's depraved fancy, glowing with only an evil mockery of beauty'). Legalistic Nature is the fiction of the Law of the State. Fallout kills Lucy in Cumbria. The apparently inexplicable may be an apparent killer in the real world, and without 'hesitation'. Explanation may 'hesitate' but existential and manmade events happen to real people. You have to believe it, as today's Americans say, to counter the fantastic. Laws kill in the hands of class, caste and intellect or brute force. The victim's innocence may be proved later by other laws. The event is not fantastic unless you believe in singular god-permitted control which is infallible everywhere and at all times—so that you can shift between centuries without shifting gear.

Who in fact 'hesitates' between descriptions of events? Todorov gives the formula which sums up the spirit of the fantastic as 'I nearly reached the point of believing.'[10] Total faith or total incredulity would lead beyond the fantastic: it is hesitation that systains life, he says. Or in Kuhn's terms, the paradigmatic closure is penetrated, and only then generates. But Hester Prynne's risk in sexuality is fantastic only to the unpassionate and the timid, the forever obedient and the academic in whatever class of caste, the utterly law-abiding. Decisions about her action lie between reading fiction and the reader's life praxis. He who hesitates may well be lost, as Miles Coverdale is, rather than sustained. And sustained where? In *The Scarlet Letter* Hester survives in an Atlantic shore cottage—'within the verge of the peninsular, but not in close vicinity to any other habitation'—in order to become a new social power in a tired and hesitant community. But the penalty would have otherwise been worse—Edmund Wilson quotes Sophocles in his essay on the 'Philoctetes': 'Everything becomes disgusting when you are false to your own nature and behave in an unbecoming way.' The hero with a suppurating wound is abandoned on his peninsular—'exacerbated by hardship and chagrin'—but becomes sacred, acquires superhuman powers and 'is destined to be purged of his guilt'. And Gide's version says: 'I have come to know more of the secrets of life than my masters had ever revealed to me.'[11]

So the monster created by a society or by and through its invented gods—and this is a major basis of all fiction since Defoe, and cuts across the genres—elicits sympathy because he or she or it is the form of the repressed and oppressed. The illegal becomes a category of necessity and therefore strangely legal.

Fear in the legal citizen relates to power, control, authority, the State, the gods, all forms of the One and its agents and agencies. The practical counter is in the matter-of-factness of Mistress Hibbins, who knows what Hester has been up to. In one of the few comic scenes in the book (Chapter 22):

> 'Fie, woman, fie!' cried the old lady, shaking her finger at Hester. 'Dost think I have been to the forest so many times, and have yet no skill to judge who else has been there? . . . Thou wearest (the token) openly; so there need be no question about

that. But this minister! Let me tell thee, in thine ear! When the Black Man sees one of his own servants, signed and sealed, so shy of owning to the bond as is the Reverend Mr. Dimmesdale, he hath a way of ordering matters so that the mark shall be disclosed in open daylight to the eyes of all the world!

So Arthur's A may be psychosomatic or it may be diabolic. But more important is that this passage indicates another judge, outside the law and inside the community. What is more, it is a woman to whom Hawthorne gives central words on the way the repressed inevitably returns. And she speaks without hesitation. If, as Todorov believes, quoting Lovecraft, 'a tale is fantastic if the reader experiences an emotion of profound fear and terror, the presence of unsuspected worlds and powers', Mistress Hibbins partly allays those fears in her familiarity with 'the forest' as a daily pattern, as daily as the Church, and she certainly is not perplexed.

Hawthorne understood something of how laws exemplify active ideology—in Colin Sumner's terms:

> As the (passive) reflections of certain social relations, ideologies can become embodied in laws which, when applied, involve their intrinsive ideologies as (active) determinants of other social relations. The legal process also admirably illustrates the theoretical point that, once embodied, ideologies do not *necessarily* (re-)structure our practice; sometimes they need reinforcement to make them effective. . . . New ideologies, new uses for old ideologies, old ideologies—all are thoroughly social products.[12]
>
> A legal enactment is a hybrid form combining power and ideology: an ideological formation sanctioned, according to fixed and hallowed procedures for the creation of Law, by the instituted executors of social power. . . . An ideology of legality develops which celebrates and elevates The Law to an exalted status as the expression of unity in the nation.[13]

Curiously, Hawthorne felt the need to 'establish a theatre, a little removed from the highway of ordinary travel, where the creatures of his brain may play their phantasmagorical antics, without exposing them to too close a comparison with the actual events of real lives.' In fact, his patterns of guilt, shame, power and law dramatize the real.

2

Prefacing his collection of documents in *Ideology and Power in the Age of Jackson*, Rozwenc presents those forty years as typical of the 'psychic and social strains' in a society undergoing rapid economic growth and increase in technological innovation. Emerson believed that such a society, on the contrary, could relax earlier tensions:

> Our forefathers walked in the world, and went to their graves, tormented with the fear of Sin, and the Terror of the Day of Judgement. These terms have lost their force, and our torment is unbelief, the uncertainty as to what we ought to do.[14]

Hawthorne interprets: the moral control of wealth and technology has left the force of theocratic terror. What control now exists as to what we ought to do and by which obedience can be ensured in the State? Individual morality cannot be trusted; the very energy in new enterprises in technology and finance create forceful persons in a disarrayed class structure in which people are left with anxiety for professional power in exploitation and aggression. The closed-shop world of the Pyncheons is catastrophically invaded only by chance, egalitarian ideas and new technics; Hawthorne's romance, and much of the rest of his fiction, is like an analysis of De Tocqueville's passage on law in *Democracy in America*:

> When an individual or a party is wronged in the United States, to whom can he apply for redress? If to public opinion, public opinion constitutes a majority; if to the legislative, it represents the majority and implicitly obeys it; if to the executive power, it is appointed by the majority and serves as a passive tool in its hands. The public force consists of the majority under arms; the jury is the majority invested with the right of hearing judicial cases; and in certain states even the judges are elected by the majority.[15]

Jackson's extension of presidential veto, based on his being the people's representative, impregnates Hawthorne's work, as it does Melville's—and Pound's sense of the nature of organizatory centralism against the dangers of aristocratism. Hawthorne is a reflection on the kind of belief stated by George Bancroft in 1840—five years before the first part of De Tocqueville and ten years before *The Scarlet Letter*:

> The opinion which we respect is, indeed, not the opinion of the
> one or the few, but the sagacity of the many. It is hard for the
> pride of the cultivated philosophy to put its ear to the ground,
> and listen reverently to the voice of lowly humanity; yet the
> people collectively are wiser than the most gifted individual, for
> all his wisdom constitutes but a part of theirs . . . (truth) owns no
> safe interpreter but the common mind; she knows no court of
> appeals but the soul of humanity. It is when the multitude give
> counsel, that the right purposes find safety . . . theirs is the heart,
> of which the largeness is as the sand on the sea-shore.[16]

But the American's pride in being part of a country pre-
eminently of self-made men invaded this kind of 'natural law'—
in the words of Calvin Colton's *Labor and Capital* (1844): labour
is free, 'with the exception of African slave labour'—which is
not discussed further—and this generates a market for 'talents,
prudence, and personal exertions'—'this is a country of *self-
made men*, than which nothing better could be said of any state of
society.' But Colton warns Americans of 'the love of one man
power' or 'demagogueism', a 'relapse' into a repetition of the
1829 to 1841 years under 'the dictation of a Chief, and by the
aristocratic assumptions of his menials'. But it could hardly be
claimed that the next president, Harrison, instituted democratic principles beyond mere populist rhetoric.[17]

But beneath the rhetoric of freedom and enterprise lay that
magma force represented by Charles Brockden Brown and Poe,
the strife between manichean fears and anarchic individualism,
the need for community and the actualities of self-reliance, and
what Senator Fulbright as late as 1966 could still call 'the fatal
arrogance of power' in the Republic. Hawthorne lived through
the 1812 to 1866 years of war—the war of 1812, the Mexican
War, the Civil War—which, to use Fulbright's terms, were
'unjust or unnecessary or both'. These were the years in which
dissent grew to a central issue. Hawthorne, like the other major
writers of Matthiessen's 'American Renaissance', confronted
the tripod of power—law, disobedience, and punishment—and
urged themselves towards plots which could at least hint at the
sado-masochistic issues of domination and submission, in
which 'the face of "evil" is always the face of total need'.[18] In
this social scene, *The Scarlet Letter* is simply a representative text.
Inside its use of 'forest' lies steady anxiety in the nation

concerning the wild, the unkempt beyond the garden and field, the 'Black Man' shaped as devil, Indian or Negro, and the erotic, elements which resist the rusting prison door, Governor Bellingham and the formulations of law. Pearl is explicitly a child of the Lord of Misrule (Chapter 8)—an early worry that continues into the second half of the twentieth century. The counter-urban and counter-dogmatic feels the forest eroticism as sacred, but the A is explicitly the 'mark' of the Black Man, his holy sign. The brook's 'black depths' are as daunting as the swamp in 'Big Two-Hearted River'. 'The minister' has the mark right in his heart, his 'inward . . . black reality', an A which in him 'burns in secret'. Chillingworth's 'authorized interference' confronts Dimmesdale's duplicity, 'alienated from the Good and True'. Hawthorne is firm: this is 'insanity'; passion in the manichean system is 'the portion . . . which the Devil claimed'. Both men are publicly part of the theocratic state. Dimmesdale can admit 'shame' and indelicacy', but it is Hester, like Eve in Milton, whose arrangements in this field of power Hawthorne used continually, sets up disobedience—adultery is the serpent. She cries out warily, 'Let God punish! Thou shalt forgive!'—but in this fiction the woman ends her days in internal exile, charismatic with a talismanic A, a sophisticated punishment quite beyond the manichean god. Nor does the Devil win, since Hester's loneliness is melancholy, like Carrie Meeber's, but not diabolic.

But 'the polluted priest' is nothing to the overtly devilish and erotic revenge of the doctor. The nineteenth-century component here is that romantic forgiveness is possible since sexual love is superior to the 'dark passion' of revenge, that violation 'in cold blood' in Chapter 17. The 'consecration' of adultery challenges the bourgeois values of alienation through marriage, family and the state. The doctor's explicitly Mephistophelian design—to cause Dimmesdale to die in a state of sin—curiously fails. Faust here speaks of public 'fame', 'honour' and 'sacred profession', but he is in fact a lawbreaker who wants the production of love and an illegal child to be a way to God—'Thy power is not what it was! With God's help, I shall escape thee now!' (Chapter 23). But public confession of adultery and an appeal to God's mercy beyond 'the law we broke' does not break the dualistic universe which is the premise of Hawthorne's fiction. It is the women

201

who gain a measure of victory. Pearl's 'spell' is broken and she moves from 'elf' to woman doing 'battle with the world'. Dimmesdale remains trapped in Hawthorne's scaffold ambivalence: 'maybe' God was forgotten when Arthur and Hester violated their 'reverence for each other's soul'. That soul versus sexuality remains unresolved conflict in the male leader who is supposed to stabilize state law. 'The arrogance of power' is scarcely eroded by his 'shame'—and Hawthorne does not say 'guilt' here.

By 1850 Americans were well into their search for singular identity through which to straddle the dualisms of a Christian capitalist democracy and its primary valued thrusts of individual verticality. Guilt follows not succeeding as an individual rather than not succeeding as a convivial communalist. Shame follows disobedience, but is not entirely absorbed by guilt, because to feel guilt would be to accede entirely to the precepts of enclosed desire 'New England' demands:

> The scene was not without a mixture of awe, such as must always invest the spectacle of guilt and shame in a fellow creature, before society shall have grown corrupt enough the smile, instead of shuddering, at it.

Hawthorne's 'and' is not resolved as Hester mounts the scaffold in the nineteenth century. The seventeenth-century version represents popular 'simplicity', as she feels the 'thousand unrelenting eyes' of simplicity 'almost intolerable to be borne' and comes near to shrieking 'with the full power of her lungs', or going mad. Shame and guilt move the book because Hawthorne feels the differences and ellisions. The gaze of the Other, as Lacan would put it, controls subjectivity, but the subject controls the Other's gaze too. Actaeon changed into a stag; 'truth . . . runs after truth.'[19] But a useful entrance into the interrogative scene is through Lynd's On Shame and the Search for Identity, a deeply American book since it searches right into the private and public instabilities coupling shame and guilt— 'guilt, or self-reproach . . . based on internalization of values, notably parental values'—that is, social conscience, following Freud's discussion in Civilization and its Discontents—in contrast to shame, 'based on disapproval coming from outside, from other persons', the gaze of populist simplicity. (Hawthorne calls

202

the A 'the child of its father's guilt and its mother's shame'.)
Lynd reminds us that 'experiences of shame appear to embody
the root meaning of the word—to uncover, to expose, to wound.
They are experiences of exposure, exposure of peculiarly
sensitive, intimate, vulnerable aspects of the self.'[20] And
nothing is more shameful to Christian utilitarian sexuality than
the exposure of innate pleasure in erotics.

But lawbreaking and the transgression of taboo are forms
of social cement. Dimmesdale somewhat atones by confession
and death in public, but Hester lives on with shame because
shame is irreversible and has no code.[21] Condemnation or
punishment establishes communication—'the very law that
condemned her . . . had held (Hester) up through the terrible
ordeal of her ignominy' (Chapter 5). It is Chillingworth who is
totally alienated: 'The pursuit and systematic exercize of
revenge', 'that evil principle', is 'Devil's work' which once
completed, sends 'the unhumanized mortal' to Hell and 'his
Master'. Hawthorne is fascinated by the 'sensitive, intimate'
aspects, the 'intimacy and heart knowledge' of love and hatred
cemented by private passion and public confession, alienation
and death. Even Chillingworth is pardoned a little since he does
the decent bourgeois thing and bequeaths Pearl enough
property 'both here and in England' to make her 'the richest
heiress of her day'—enabling her to marry into British nobility.
But as Dreiser with Carrie, so Hawthorne with Hester: he
refuses her happiness, preferring 'life-long sorrow'. Her desire
to be 'the destined prophetess' of a new 'mutual happiness'
between the sexes is prevented because of her 'sin' (not, be it
noted, her crime). And society does not punish the doctor: the
Devil does and will. *The Scarlet Letter* can be read as an exercise
in legal nostalgia for the good old theocratic days of unchanging
enclosure placed in tension with Lord Coke and what one
American in 1839 called the 'old Blackstone Moorings',[22] and
with the danger of which Lincoln spoke in 1838 on the Illinois
frontier:

> Is it unreasonable then to expect some man possessed of the
> loftiest genius, coupled with ambition sufficient to push it to its
> utmost stretch, will at some time, spring up among us? And when
> such as one does, it will require the people to be united with each
> other, attached to the government and laws, and generally intel-
> ligent, to successfully frustrate his designs.[24]

Ahab, the United States navy in *White Jacket*, Ethan Brand, Hollingsworth, and even that descendant of Pearl, the girl from Schenectady whom Henry James killed off with a disease caught in the Coliseum in Rome. . . . It repeatedly comes to 'genius' and its 'caesarism' versus 'the people' within a 'science of justice'[24] grounded in respect for individual success leading to power—for that is what the Protestant Ethic comes to as capitalism. The conflict between Common Law and equity fought out in confusion—that is the gist of Miller's section on law in *The Life of the Mind in America*. Cooper's last novel in 1850, *The Ways of the Heart*, proclaims that the American jury is ignorantly incapable of 'judging either law or fact'[25]—that is, law could not be left to nature or instinct in 'the people'. In 1846 a lawyer, later Chief Justice in Georgia, openly scorned 'the infallible mob' and its criticism of the law; lawyers, like any other professionals, must be trusted until found to be corrupt: 'The physician can be in a family like the serpent in the garden of Eden. . . . These evils all flow from the fact that the medical profession, like the legal, is one of confidence . . . in the secret bethel of the homestead the confiding heart may find that the black cloth and the white cravat are but disguises assumed by the traitor to his God and to his fellow-man.' It sounds like a Hawthorneian recipe for fiction, but it is James Jackson placing law between 'the modern rabble' and tyrannic 'genius'.[26] The undermining of confidence in professionalism in medicine, law, church and politics is obviously a Hawthorneian preoccupation, the gaps between private and public life, or, in Lynd's terms, the nature of concealment and exposure. His fictions detected or, as Robbe-Grillet puts it, *excavated*, 'the law under which punishment is inflicted (which) has not the same facilities of information as private individuals.'[27] Hawthorne 'burrows deeper and deeper to reach some ever more intimate strata . . . finally unearthing some fragment of a disconcerting secret.'[28] His 'neutral territory . . . where the Actual and Imaginary meet' is excavated but the limits of revelation cause him, and his age, to mask the confrontations of power revealed in chronic, highly suggestive withdrawals. In Robbe-Grillet's words:

> Having descended into the abyss of human passions, he would send to the seemingly tranquil world (the world on the surface) triumphant messages describing the mysteries he had actually

touched with his own hands. And the sacred vertigo the reader suffered then, far from causing him anguish or nausea, reassured him as to his power of domination over the world.

As James Jackson averred, 'if all the evidence is to be indiscriminately admitted, then the most perjured villain has the most spotless character completely under his control.'[29]

The characteristic heart/head dichotomy motivating Hawthorne's fiction is stated in contemporary American law too. In 1824 James Kent, professor at Columbia and Chief Justice of New York, stated, 'wisdom is as much the offspring of the heart as of the head'—and heart is associated with 'the people'. When Abner Kneeland was convicted for libel against God in 1833, he appealed in the name of 'the right of conscience', 'the privilege of the freedom of speech' and 'the liberty of the press'. But Chief Justice Shaw decided that the Common Law incorporated Christianity. Emerson, Channing and Alcott, among 167 Massachusetts intellectuals, petitioned and lost. Shaw was a Unitarian, Kneeland a pantheist. The law was as uncodified as relationships between self and community. The assassin's cry in 1865, '*sic semper tyrannis*', is a motto for the major writers of the 'American Renaissance', and echoes its anxiety at least through to 1980. When Rufus Choate addressed the Harvard Law School in 1845 on the duty of law to preserve 'obedience and reverence and justice' over 'the fitful will of the individual and the crowd', and in the name of Burkean 'organic forms' in the political system, we are in the presence of Captain Vere's judgement on Billy Budd.[30] Vere's allegiance to Orpheus the tamer is perhaps founded in the very quotation Choate cites from Coleridge on the power of law as 'guardian angel' and 'avenging fiend':

> This is the spirit of Law,—the lute of Amphion,—the harp of Orpheus. This is the true necessity which compels man into the social state, now and always, by a still beginning, never ceasing force of moral cohesion.

For Choate, God's voice and the people's are one and manifest in absolute State law, 'the wisdom of America'.[31] This is the context for the conclusion of *The Marble Faun* fifteen years later, when the Republic was entering the war between the states:

Human beings of Donatello's character, compounded especially for happiness, have no longer any business on earth, or elsewhere.

So sin educates, changes and elevates him, while not committing him to the Comus rout. Through Kenyon, Hawthorne proposes a Miltonic usefulness for sin 'which we deem such a dreadful blackness. . . . Did Adam fall, that we might ultimately rise to a far loftier Paradise than his?' Hilda protests, as it were, in the name of Shaw and Choate, that this is 'a mockery of all religious sentiment' and 'moral law'. Kenyon hastily backs down: 'I never did believe it! But the mind wanders wild and wide.' He lives without a 'pole-star'; Hilda's heart's 'white wisdom' is supposed to guide his head. The couple fall by sufficient proxy and only interesting because highly indicative of American legal and intellectual confusion concerning the natural and the educated, nature and the state, sin and crime, law and freedom, and 'evil' and 'happiness'. Melville roots Claggart in the 'mystery of iniquity', with a Chillingworth sort of fire 'eating deeper and deeper into him', his 'conscience' operating as 'the lawyer to his will', until he is like Guy Fawkes but with 'a depravity according to nature' and 'peculiarly subject to the law of reason' and a heart which 'riots in complete exemption from that law'. He is made, like so many figures in Melville and Hawthorne, or edging that way, with 'the mania of an evil nature . . . firm and innate'. Such superstition exempts Melville from the proper analysis of the master-at-arms as a nineteenth-century product. He is in fact a typical predator imaged as a vampiric force, part of an imagic field that haunted Marx as well as Poe and Hawthorne: the figure of dominant energy-sucking. After Dimmesdale's death, Chillingworth's 'vital and intellectual force' deserts him; he withers, shrivels, once his 'material' and 'support' is withdrawn. The nineteenth-century lawyer frequently lost faith in humanity, being 'too apt to believe the depravity of man innate and natural, allowing of no cure, and beyond the reach of reform'.[32] Lawyers took up theocratic postulations of an evil force in the universe in order to justify impositions of restraint on the people. In 1830 Mr. Justice Washington claimed the Supreme Court as 'the regulatory power of the complicated machine or our government' against 'confusion and ruin'. The old fear of a possible

American return to barbarism was never exorcized by Whitman's gentle appeals for an agrarian yawp as against, for example, Theodore Sedgwick's 1857 fear of 'the power of a majority taking the shape of unjust law'—by which he meant the 'vested right' of property over life and liberty.[33] In 1852, the year of *The Blithedale Romance*, James Walker put it for the legal profession: 'Power is human will',[34] and this is the ground the 'American Renaissance' excavated from Brown through Poe to Hawthorne, to expose the conflict in Common Law. Americans had to ask where the sources of power/will sprang, both locally and historically—and, especially after 1857, radically and biologically. Since law controlled the peaceful order of unequally distributed wealth and property, and unequally allocated personal ability, it had to be totally enforced. But the bases of this action were only thoroughly examined in fictions. Meanwhile lawyers resisted codified law because code would be unnatural whereas the chaos of human law was natural. The major American codifier, David Dudley Field, proposed regulation in order to protect property, and won a measure of victory in the states only after 1865.[35] Perry Miller neatly compares him to Hank Morgan trying to fix up Camelot. Today we may ruefully recall the Kennedy days of Camelot in the White House, or even Nixon's proposals for Ruritanian uniforms to be sported by White House guards.[36] The manichean and apocalyptic language of Hawthorne's judgement scene is stronger than ever in America, but lacking his scepticism and ambivalence.

3

His writing necessity presses out from a vocabulary of law, witchcraft, judgement, science and medicine, and theology—towards the Sin the Passion could not redeem, the Sin which it is therefore permitted to eradicate. In *An American Tragedy* this Sin still haunts American crime at the point where abortion, law, and criminal justice for homicide intersect with sex, class, religion and the press. But Dreiser hesitates between the determinist motivations and explanations from Freudian complex, character 'chemisms' and economic pressures, until he doubts both law and personal moral decision, and the church is scorned as an opportunist soul-catching operation. Hawthorne does not have the wretched press to bother him, or psycho-analysis, or materialist behaviourism. His determinisms are inherited ethics. Young Goodman Brown is destroyed into morbid alienation within his community: knowledge brings weakness, and it is irrelevant whether he is right or wrong. The programme in the woods certainly does not make the citizens wicked in their daily affairs. In Sara Good's curse on John Hathorne, a helpless woman resorts to a peculiar threat against a judge—sooner or later the curse—'God will give you blood to drink'—will be effective in your family. Her confidence meets the witch judge, and his nineteenth-century descendants. Maule's curse penetrates Pyncheon Street as 'the germ which may and must produce good or evil fruit' (Chapter 1). The curse is therefore organically imaged from the inevitabilities of Nature as law. Colonel Pyncheon had Matthew Maule executed for witchcraft to gain his land, as part of the way the property-military class tyrannized the common settler, and 'the influential classes', 'leaders of the people', rejoice like 'the maddest mob':

> Clergymen, judges, statesmen—the wisest, calmest, holiest persons of their day—stood in the inner circle round about the gallows, loudest to applaud the work of blood, latest to confess themselves miserably deceived.

Under such lynch law Maule is 'hunted to death', his only revenge a curse on the scaffold in Sarah Good's terms, appealing to a law beyond class justice, to a power structure of inevitable inheritance beyond property inheritance, disguised as another kind of determinism. What else could he do against 'the inner circle'? The eighteenth-century Pyncheon reclaims his house from confiscation, as a Royalist. When renunciation of property and responsibility for its origins is possible, as it becomes in *Go Down, Moses* for McCaslin, the rich old bachelor Pyncheon is found murdered. But 'the energy of disease', the need for property, are not so easily expunged. The nephew is life-imprisoned for murder, a man of aesthetic sensibility and taste, refined features and gentleness up against a cousin who has 'a natural tendency towards office', studies law, becomes a judge, a congressman, a power in the state legislature. In other words, a prime member of 'the inner circle'. Clifford is reduced to

POWER AND LAW IN HAWTHORNE'S FICTIONS

a feeble hysterical ghost confronted by a judge with rich estates. The last Maule, disguised as Holgrave, takes up Fourierism and early photographic techniques, and thereby becomes Hawthorne's example—before Hollingsworth and Westervelt—of a possible alternative society; mutual attraction could be a universal law backing Fourier's belief that 'all societal arrangements must be started afresh' so that, in new associations, the passions may be converted to positive harmony. After all, a number of such communities had flourished for a time in the Republic, and as George L. Mosse puts it: 'European inventors of utopias saw the unsettled vastness of North America as an experimental station for their ideas.'[37] The laws of competition, alienation and property might be alleviated there. Hawthorne's scepticism is, of course, firm. The last Maule is committed to utopian communalism; two of the last Pyncheons attempt to escape the judge by a railroad that reduces them to inertia; and the Fourierist daguerrotypist can marry Phoebe Pyncheon because she is country-bred and therefore outside the inner circle. But Hawthorne cannot leave the action secular.

The curse is 'probably' the first Maule's knowledge of a Pyncheon family 'predisposition' or 'heriditary liability' (Chapter 20), but Hawthorne adds 'inward criminality', so that the professor of law is countered by another law. The book opens by separating 'moral right' from 'legal tenure in the context of land, property and class rule, as the foundation for his probing through 'the fantastic'. His 'time-stricken virgin' in her genteel shopkeeping end to inheriting the 'princely territory at the eastward' fits into 'inner circle' round the scaffold through her 'circle of gentility'. The 'stain' of her earned money, a coin, is a new bond, 'a little circlet', 'a galvanic ring'. She has then to confront Holgrave's circle—'reformers, temperance lecturers . . . cross-looking philanthropists, community men . . . who acknowledged no law'. But Hepzibah lets Phoebe know that she presumes Holgrave 'has a law of his own'. Part of that law is to 'make pictures out of sunshine' (Chapter 6), a law fused into 'a certain magnetic element' in the artist's nature. The shifts in the field of 'law' are Hawthorne's action.

Official law turns Clifford into an imbecile (Chapter 9) with 'an electric sparkle of ill-humour'. But he is punished also because his nature 'tends to feed exclusively upon the Beautiful'. Like Owen Warland, he is pathetic rather than diabolic, for Hawthorne a creature of Providence, an abrupt shift from the social and psychological to the theological, once again (Chapter 10). But in Chapter 17, Clifford is allowed sense that only appears mad because it is original—but this, too, fits Hawthorne's image framework: 'the facilities of locomotion are destined to bring us round again to the nomadic state . . . all human progress is in a circle; or, to use a more accurate and beautiful figure, in an ascending spiral curve. . . . The past is but a coarse and sensual prophecy of the present and the future . . . (Railroads) annihilate the toil and dust of pilgrimage.' Facile transport releases us from being 'a prisoner for life in brick, and stone, and old worm-eaten timber'. We can now live 'wherever the fit and beautiful shall offer . . . a home'. The 'polluted life of households', like Seven Gables, could be exchanged for 'a wide sweep and frequent change of it'. But such beliefs break the law of stable property in households, and by holding them Clifford is as undermining as Holgrave. He shares Holgrave's concern for Mesmerism (and we know the important effects of Mesmer from the excellent documentation in Darnton's book[38]), and claims a faith in electricity creating a global brain that sounds rather familiar: 'by means of electricity, the world of matter has become a great nerve, vibrating thousands of miles in a breathless point of time . . . the round globe is a vast head, a brain, instinct with intelligence. . . .' The electric telegraph is 'an almost spiritual medium'. Hawthorne presents such statements as enfeebled speculation. The 'broken links of brotherhood' have left Clifford culpable in a house-dungeon of which he is, ironically, the jailer. Hawthorne takes pleasure in a careful scrutiny of decay. On what terms, then, is 'a public lecturer on Mesmerism' and a Fourierist allowed success?—because Holgrave 'had never violated the innermost man, but had carried his conscience along with him'. This is his law, his 'integrity to whatever law he acknowledged' (Chapter 12). He is therefore permitted to tear down 'lifeless institutions' and 'begin anew'. But he is also presented in Whitmanian terms as a figure of 'crude, wild, and misty philosophy and . . . magnanimous zeal for man's welfare . . . in a country where everything is free to the hand that can grasp it'. He therefore opposes the law of inheritance as the dead judging the present and future—'a family should be merged into the great, obscure mass of humanity, and forget about its ancestors. Human blood, in order to keep its freshness, should run in hidden streams.' Holgrave is Hawthorne's limited hostage to progress.

The Judge appears, then, as the ruling class's intervention with what it assumes to be 'duty and conscience' and 'the force of law'—that is, tyranny masquerading as 'public justice' and therefore beyond any claim 'to stand in the ring of human sympathies', the counter-ring to the 'little circlet' and 'the inner circle'. His respectability' is sanctioned (legalized) by the church and state but not by Hepzibah and Clifford or Holgrave. Pyncheon is typical in an egotism so unaware of his guilt and in being a man, like Captain Vere, and Rufus Choate, 'to whom forms are of paramount importance', and fundamentally the forms of management and manipulation, largely visual and external—Hawthorne's controlling images are a marble palace containing an entombed, decaying human being, and 'splendid rubbish' which paralyzes conscience (Chapter 15). 'Public' here means the hypocrisies of a life which 'seldom or never looks inward'. Beyond prison he can offer Clifford the life sentence of a public asylum, and prison and asylum are the notorious containers of dissent and revolt against church and state in whose wealth Pyncheon has shares (real estate, railroad, bank, U.S. stock). But Hawthorne has to give him, as well, heart trouble and relate his tall oaken chair to *Comus*. In the final tidying chapter he stabilizes his plot back into the very social and medical/curse structure he apparently traced to initial damnation and the need for radical legal reform. With something like glee, he makes Holgrave, 'the sworn foe of wealth', become rich through Phoebe among the Pyncheons, and accept a house of stone instead of the transitory forms of Chapter 12. The parchment hidden by a Maule and signed by Indian sagamores, conveying a vast territory to the Pyncheons—that basic land-curse Faulkner was to employ—is discovered by the latest Maule. Wealth and land are redistributed in the ruling class, reinforced by intellectual know-how, backed by legal documentation. Hawthorne's conservatism remains ill at ease with the belief he gave Holgrave: 'the word owes all its onward impulses to men ill at ease'. And he offers even less leeway in his next romance, in which Fourierist methods are visible and tentatively active.

George Ripley termed Brook Farm a community 'to ensure a more natural union between intellectual and manual labour than now exists; to combine thinker and worker, as far as possible, in the same individual', as a preparation for liberal life 'amidst the pressure of our capitalist institutions'.[39] Emerson's response came characteristically: 'I wish to break all prisons.' Hawthorne regarded his seven months' utopia 'the most romantic episode' in his life—that is, an interface between reality and imagination—and, if *The Blithedale Romance* is any clue, discovered what Charles Nordoff concluded by 1875, that 'the fundamental principle of communal life is the subordination of the individual's will to the general interest or the general will: practially, this takes the shape of unquestioning obedience by the members toward the leaders, elders or chiefs of their society.'[40] Robert Owen played into one part of American prejudice when he informed the President and a large audience in 1825 that he would eliminate evil by changing their environment. Even Emerson resorted to the unreal performance of Brook Farm in his *Journals*, envisaging a time when, after days of 'honest labour', 'having filled up all the hours from sun to sun with great and equal action (a man) shall lose sight of this sharp individuality which contrasts now so oddly with nature.' But in fact utopia came to a ghastly amorphous refusal of high technology and the *polis* under leadership—about which William Alfred Hinds stated the actuality in 1878: leaders must possess 'rare qualifications, such as freedom from selfish ambition and the genuine spirit of service'.[41] On the other hand, the great seal of the United States bears the words '*Novus Ordo Seclorum*, a new order of the ages'.[42] Hawthorne's analysis of the actuality of Brook Farm and its type begins with the capitalist wealth of the father, the failed support behind the daughters in *The Blithedale Romance*—Zenobia the witch figure and Priscilla the white innocence figure. The centre of vulnerability is, as usual in Hawthorne's main novels, the female condition. The impotent observer intelligence, Coverdale, sees some of the issue in Chapter 9—a male outsider's view: 'I could not suspect that, if merely at play with Hollingsworth, she was sporting with a power which she did not fully estimate.' Of her earlier power relationship with Westervelt and his class, Hawthorne gives us, in Chapter 12, 'No passion save of the senses . . . the real womanhood within her has no corresponding part in him. Her deepest voice lacks a response; the deeper her cry, the more dead his silence'. The father, Westervelt and Hollingsworth destroy the social, defined by Hawthorne as something that extends passion into respect and intellect. *Blithedale* concerns the failure to guide energies of mutuality and destruction towards love and the creative. The law of the dream commune is not the law of American actuality. Coverdale, too, is depleted by Blithedale and his legalistic language shows how: 'Our souls, after all, are not our own. We convey a property in them to those with whom we associate. . . . Hollingsworth, Zenobia, Priscilla . . . had absorbed my life into themselves' (Chapter 23). The deterioration of the commune in these hands is paralleled by Westervelt's performance, which Coverdale witnesses in the 'Lyceum Hall', the centre of cultural communications in the district, a sign of the 'mystic sensuality of this singular age'. Westervelt's act is clear: 'the miraculous power of one human being over the will and passions of another'—the Carwin theme, the major product in Poe, and Hawthorne's Unpardonable Sin. Mesmerism, love and social organization unite at this point of moral ambiguity: control—for which Coverdale's soul-as-property is unequal.

In 1852 Hawthorne decided to write the campaign biography of a future president of whose administration Emerson observed that it was so 'miserable' that it 'admits of but one excuse, imbecility. Pierce was either the worst, or he was the weakest, of all our Presidents.' Hawthorne admitted it. Pierce was a weak compromiser, supporting the South on constitutional grounds, to prevent what Hawthorne called 'the ruin of two races' by fanaticism—a version of 'the individual soul . . . virtually annihilated', in *Blithedale* Chapter 23, by 'mutually conscious brotherhood'. And Hawthorne yet praised Pierce for placing the Union above 'the mistiness of a philanthropic theory', and, no doubt reflecting on his experience ten years earlier, broadly dismissed reform (the first British Reform Act had been passed in 1832):

There is no instance, in all history, of the human will and

213

intellect having perfected any great moral reform by methods which were adapted to that end; but the progress of the world, at every step, leaves some evil or wrong on the path behind it, which the wisest of mankind, of their own set purpose, could never have found the way to rectify.

But progress comes from breaking the established, the paradigm, the law: and it is the gist of Emerson and Thoreau. And Hawthorne well knew that he himself could be swamped in the laws of the commune—'a man's soul may be buried and perish under a dung-heap, or in a furrow of the field, just as well as under a pile of money', he wrote to his future wife from Brook Farm. Coverdale merely echoes Pierce (Chapter 29): 'As regards human progress . . . let them believe it who can, and aid in it who choose.' Where he is empty of purpose, and feels it, Hollingsworth is morally ruined by an 'overplus' of it. Coverdale's one approved example is Kossuth, the Hungarian hero, who became Governor-President in 1849.

In spite of Zenobia's sacrificial suicide within the circumstances of utopia, Hollingsworth's manipulations are exonerated, as Westervelt's are not, because of a redemptive element in 'the whole power of his great, stern, yet tender soul'. Westervelt, like Chillingworth, uses the psychosomatic potentiality of the body to commit the Unpardonable Sin; but the ex-blacksmith 'pours (the) warm tide of his benevolence', his 'rich juices' into 'one channel', 'an overriding purpose'. Such angelism denies community reciprocity. A caesarist relationship connects his schematic prison—for the study and reform of 'our criminal brethren'—and the Blithedale experiment. But both men intervene in the scene of capitalist inheritance exemplified by the irresponsible Fauntleroy, a speculator from the Middle West who squandered wealth and used his wife as 'another jewel'. Then he resorts to a socially unpardonable crime—unnamed, but possibly that of John Gabriel Borkman in 1896, and certainly part of the very 'constitution' of society. His first daughter, Zenobia, 'enthralls' the second, Priscilla, into becoming part of Westervelt's spurious commercial experiments, 'a blindfold prisoner within the sphere (of) this dark earthly magician', with his false inauguration of 'a new era . . . one great, mutually conscious brotherhood'—a parody of Blithedale. Wealthy upbringing and intellectual power causes Zenobia to exercise vampiric powers, wasting Priscilla's 'soul and body . . . by her spells'. Then she in turn accuses Hollingsworth of being 'a monster, a cold, heartless, self-beginning and self-ending piece of mechanism'. Once again, the repressed returns as the Comus rout (explicit in Chapter 24); but Zenobia's terms for her enthrallment to the monstrous Hollingsworth are legal—she is 'on trial for her life' with him as 'judge, jury, and accuser'. Where the Comus rout is open, his is closed 'self-deception'. Imitations of Bacchus, Circe and the Devil are again enacted among forms of sensuality under Christian legal suspicion and criticism—Indian chief, Diana, Jim Crow, Kentucky 'woodsman', Arcadian shepherds, the Witch of Lynn, gypsies, and so forth, 'the dust of deluded generations' in New England. Chillingworth's 'dark necessity . . . our fate' has resisted the democratic egalitarian agrarian economy again. But to Hawthorne these imaginative programmes of guilt, punishment and limited survival are an 'education' for Americans.

The governing phrase in *The Marble Faun* is 'the education of intellect and soul.' The shift from 'Tuscany' to 'Rome' is an educational journey from aristocratic pastoral innocence to urban imprisoned experience: a 'dark necessity', to Hawthorne. Miltonic disobedience is necessary if men and women are to progress from Eden puppets. Even spectators of sin are sufficiently contaminated to return to 'New England' chastened by 'Rome', leaving the Europeans to stoic misery, since the Fortunate Fall falls heaviest on them. Europe is purgatory for the Americans, but hell for the natives or the adopted. Donatello's crime is his opportunity for 'a new intelligence' (Chapter 31) to penetrate his 'former simplicity'. As Irving Howe puts it, Hawthorne is a man 'so eager for experiment in personal life that at times the "inquisitive tendency" becomes sheer hunger' and he is drawn to moral outlaws 'who dare what he himself never even desired to dare . . . some great liberating transformation which will bring him, for the first time, into full vibrant life'.[43] But in effect (Chapter 43) the price of 'the growth of a soul' is too high for Kenyon, the American, for whom the Faun is transformed into 'one other morbid and remorseful man among millions that were cast in the same indistinguishable mould'. But this alternative view is lost in the plot's visual melodrama and symbolic plausibility, the gaming with human life as intolerable as Chapter 28 of *Blithedale*—Coverdale keeping Zenobia's shoe for ever, Hollingsworth's hook 'close by the heart', and Westervelt's verdict on her heart, 'that troublesome organ' which prevented her from becoming 'controlling genius'. The 1860 stereotypes exist in a schema whose moral, legal and sexual detail is nearly a surface statement of totalitarian judgement. Mystification and gloomy suggestion take the place of information. Ruins are too easily equated with moral decay. The Arcadian 'monster' is a 'simpleton' to be pressed into dungeon incarceration, a good place for the educated soul, or a revenge on a late Noble Savage whose 'coarser animal portion' is his sensuous exceptionality.

Miriam's crime or sin or shame is an unstable racial and cultural origin in the early and late members of the Comus rout: she is either a rich Jewish banker's heiress or an oriental-looking German princess or the daughter of a Southern planter and an African slave or a noble English woman. She is also sensuous and aristocratic and an artist and therefore ready to be damned for witchcraft. Her darkness is transferred, for example, to obsessive drawings of women 'acting the part of a revengeful mischief towards man' (Chapter 5), a tendency enacted to 'educate' the Faun. The dark stranger who follows her in Europe is some wild lawless frontiersman, bearded and satyric, dressed in a buffalo hide cloak and goatskin breeches, a parody of the Arcadian. This association of blackness is placed against Hilda's 'white soul'. Miriam's 'terrible guilt' (hints of incest by way of the Beatrice Cenci portrait) and secret 'doom' lead to her post-murder sexless union with Donatello, a stoic sterility the educated must suffer. Like Melville's Claggart, the stranger is motivated from a destructive element he shares with non-human existence, an 'influence such as beasts and reptiles of subtle and evil nature sometimes exercize upon their victims'. This is offered in support of a vocabulary of the 'tie' of 'fate', 'destiny', 'labyrinth of midnight paths' and 'crimson stain'. Miriam also has an animal 'odour of guilt and a scent of blood'—and Hawthorne throws in a reminiscence of Lady Macbeth for good measure (Chapter 11): 'I have known hands as white, which all the water in the ocean would not have washed clean.'

When Unpardonable Sin is translated as Original Sin, human beings are trapped against social or self reform. As a result of Miriam's darkness, the Faun's soul grows from 'natural to sinful', but the law-breaking is encased in the legalisms of theology and moral highmindedness, not to say downright superstition. The four main characters are supposed to inherit some of Cellini's demonic experience in the Coliseum—and Miriam's 'blackness' is part of the 'ancient dust' of ritual sacrifice there. The murder itself is located with Curtius's prophecies of the fall of Rome and the traditional fate of traitors at the Tarpeian Rock, so that it is European, pagan and Roman Catholic. Donatello's transformation is melo-dramatically immediate—'an intelligence' destroys the 'simple and joyous creature'. Serpentine guilt immediately coils him with Miriam into a parody of marriage: guilt, 'by its terrible contractile power' is 'closer than a marriage-bond'. By a pure Hawthorneian pun, contraction and law are fused. The outlaws become original outlaws in a universal condition with slightly obscene rapidity. The language of intimacy, humanity and alienation is highly familiar:

> So intimate, in those first moments, was the union that it seemed as if their new sympathy annihilated all other ties, and that they were released from the chain of humanity; a new sphere, a special law, had been created for them alone. The world could not come near them; they were safe.

This is a severe advance on Chapter 17 of *The Scarlet Letter* and the sacred permissions law-breaking offers lovers. And else-where, those who annihilate ties with 'humanity' (an undis-cussed purity of 'the people')—Goodman Brown, Ethan Brand, Owen Warland, Major Molineux—are not permitted this moral ecstacy, this fanaticism to alleviate their dooms. The safety here is criminally angelic in its elevation above 'humanity': Hawthorne does not believe that Adam and Eve were the parents of ordinary people, as the first outlaws. The rebirth of Miriam and Donatello is such a threat to the social and law that the couple must not be allowed to live together and have a family, the nucleus of the State. In a key paragraph in Chapter 19, they experience 'fiery intoxication' from the past, 'rapture' in guilt, 'ecstatic sense of freedom' following 'broken law', 'bliss' from 'a human corpse'—'bliss, or an insanity', and a passion that 'lent them (as it does meaner shapes) its brief nobility of carriage'. That corpse parodies the sacrificed human being or god in the curse knows as religion. 'Meaner shapes' or elevated shapes, it hardly matters; the politics of damnation are the same, and 'Rome' claims its own: the guilty couple enter the host of 'majestic and guilty shadows, that from ages long gone by have haunted the blood-stained city'. Ecstatic union follows transgression; intimate oneness follows murder; the couple are 'shut out of heaven' beneath Hilda's 'snowy curtain'. In Chapter 23, Hawthorne rubs it in: the murder is a 'commission' from Providence.

Yet Hawthorne has Miriam accuse Hilda of being 'merciless', 'severe', needing sin to 'soften' her—a judgement on virgin aristocratism Melville would have called 'marblization'. In fact, Hilda is in some ways Hawthorne's Pierre, looking for the return of the repressed white father, and becoming a monster in the process. But Hawthorne wants her limitedly tainted: 'Every crime destroys more Edens than our own!'

In Chapter 26, the Faun and the American share a Hemingway drinking ritual with a wine called Sunshine, but its Golden Age 'joyousness' cannot be regained, cannot bring back Bacchus and his lynxes—as Pound knew as he trailed Zagreus through *The Cantos*. Faun's ears and being a descendant of 'the Pelasgic race' do not help. Donatello was once like Pearl, 'handling all the elements of nature so fearlessly, nothing had either the power or the will to do him harm.' But now 'the genial wine-god' leaves Paradise, and enters the world of the Comus rout and Hawthorne's region of danger: 'a purpose in life . . . a complicated scheme of progress . . . a colder and drearier region.'

The book plays with 'free will' and 'destiny' to create the conditions of law against the ebullience of what should remain repressed. The ambition is large but the coherence is suspect as 'the iron rule in our day' destroys the 'healthy life of animal spirits' in some peaceable kingdom. But ill-health and murder are part of a schema not simply of 'our day'. The Faun's tower in fact retained crucifixion and death emblems from its former use as a prison (Chapter 28), and Hawthorne actually states 'each generation has only its own sins and sorrows to bear'

(Chapter 33). In one stained-glass window the American, who is given the latter remark, sees God's love and Donatello sees God's wrath. The destructive centre of the text is here in ambivalence of Providence as itself a manmade fiction. Hawthorne needs the scheme of religion and its vocabulary of ambivalent terror from a loving tyrant quite as much as Donatello takes his hope from the bronze statue of papal authority in Perugia (Chapter 35).

But 'Rome' has to be maintained as the vice in the final fourteen chapters: 'a half dead serpent on Hilda's limbs', 'a decaying corpse' within the 'spring' of her heart. Art loses 'consecration' in the Catholic 'machinery', and after hysterical confession to an American priest in 'the world's cathedral'—a primary disobedience to 'New England'—she starts to copy images of Virgin, saviour and saint. Miriam at the same time is condemned for 'mixed race' (Chapter 47)—a primary disobedience of the law of racial purity—as well as 'freedom of thought and force of will' which stem from such disobedience. Her past proposed husband has, like Chillingworth, evilly insane traits, which Cenci-like, have the incestuous quality of 'old, close-kept races of men, when long unmixed with new blood'. The whole language structure is highly tendentious—'insanity', 'original composition', 'depravity', 'self-inflicted penance' . . . once again, the isolated professional is criminal.

The Roman carnival, to Kenyon, is a manichean 'battle' among the 'lawless' with its own laws—one last Comus rout in Hawthorne's career, in which Kenyon parodies a man assassinated by a monster female. Hawthorne has him hit by a cauliflower. Has he concluded that his American artist is *that* ludicrous?

In Chapter 50, Hawthorne pretends to tell a little of what happened to Hilda in the hands of state-religious 'power', but actually, like Melville, repeatedly withdraws from information which might confer documentary evidence on his schema. We might recall here that his courtship letters express disgust for 'earth', by which he means 'dirt', 'excrement', 'sex'—'what delusion can be more lamentable and mischievous than to mistake the physical and material for the spiritual?' He and Sophia Peabody will live on a cloud six inches above the 'mud and mire'.

Hawthorne's dark intellectual beauties disobey a law which has to be reinforced by judge, surveillance and punishment. They line up with Chillingworth, Hollingsworth and Brand as dangers to community and simplicity east of Eden. Scientists, artists, reformers, certain clergy and other superior people exert power through professions which demand analysis and probe, rather than obedience to the law of the god that guards the Tree of Knowledge for himself. Did the snake sneak in or is it the god's agent? Was the snake's entry into Roderick Elliston's bosom welcomed or can it be charged with entering and breaking? The bosom was ready for the mouth to let it in: did the lips and tongue suck it in voluntarily? Retreated, reclusive characters—Fanshawe, Coverdale, Clifford, Aylmer—are crippled and defeated, can even be accused of murder or commit it. After the 1860 war which split America, under soldiers and lawyers, Hawthorne believed, with a prescience Henry Adams would agree to in 1906, that 'one bullet-headed general will succeed another in the Presidential chair', but that at least that would be 'more real and genuine' than other claims to leadership. When Emerson and Thoreau claimed John Brown a martyr for Abolition, for Hawthorne he was a fanatic murderer. He opposed slavery but emancipation left him sceptical, and during the war he visited both Union and Confederate prisoners. So detached was his *Atlantic Monthly* article, 'Chiefly About War Matters', in July 1862, that the editor suppressed certain passages and criticized him for saying John Brown was 'justly hanged'.

Given the failure of exceptional men in his fictions, with their implied model of a balanced heart and head action, it is surprising that the lawyer Lincoln became so nearly his ideal—an intellectual man of action, a figure of contemplative leadership. But here again, Hawthorne's visual susceptibility takes over, in order to create a fiction of non-urban sagacity, suppressing his cunning and intellectuality:

> The whole physiognomy is as coarse a one as you would meet anywhere in the length and breadth of the States but, withal, it is redeemed, illuminated, softened, and heightened by a kindly though serious look out of his eyes, and an expression of homely

sagacity that seems weighted with rich results of village experience. A great deal of native sense; no bookish cultivation, no refinement; honest at heart, and thoroughly so, and yet, in some sort, sly—at least, endowed with a sort of tact and wisdom that are akin to craft, and would impel him, I think, to take an antagonist in flank, rather than to make a bull-run at him right in front. But on the whole I like this sallow, queer, sagacious visage, with the homely sympathies that warmed it; and for my small share in the matter, would as lief have Uncle Abe for a ruler as any man whom it would have been practicable to put in his place.[44]

Later, the language includes the 'comical twist of his face', 'utmost cordiality' to everybody, 'wholly without pretense', and 'natural dignity': nothing on how Lincoln escaped the necessary 'education of intellect and soul' the Tuscan count required. A year later, *The Dolliver Romance* returns to central obsessions: a man in search of knowledge, the distilling of virtue from waste and 'evil'. An aged apothecary hopes for renewal from an elixir (while the Civil War brought no hope, Hawthorne was suffering from a disease undiagnosable, perhaps, like Chillingworth's diagnosis of Dimmesdale's condition, 'a symptom of some ailment in the spiritual part'). He would like to commercialize it but is ignorant of one of the elements in the stranger's gift. Old Colonel Dabney greedily gulps down this natural resource which should be common property. Retribution is bound to be Hawthorne's outcome but the inference is a social chaos of no commonly held moral confidence, and law reduced to little more than ritual judgement. (The judges in *The Marble Faun* were hidden Vatican city state authorities working for undiscovered ends.) The visible judgement is by non-authoritarian human beings on themselves. The rest is futurity: presumably women like Hester Prynne, men like Lincoln, a democratic community of art, love and law. But, given the continuing return of the repressed within the manichean system, there must be a consistent pathos in Hawthorne's fictions, the gap between schematic analogues and desperate solutions in an unrealized, unrealizable future. Seventeenth-century 'New England' is the site of a scheme of probable solutions and absolute analogues, where any professional had his guarded place, where church *was* state, where a snake at the synod in

1648 was a metonymy of Satan and the black caterpillar epidemic of 1646 could be vanquished by 'a day of humiliation', and everything would be all right, or wrong, on the Night, the Day of Judgement, where Wigglesworth would come true.[45] But in Europe, a scholar had committed a deed of darkness: 'For the Virtuoso's Collection—the pen with which Faust sign away his salvation, with a drop of blood dried on it', writes Hawthorne in his *American Notebooks*; and in Europe and America, a further sin: 'All slavery is reciprocal, on the supposition most favorable to the rulers.' American law had to control this field, 'the kingdom of power', and the immediate instance was that state of America under President Jackson:

> Jacksonian spokesmen drew upon exhaustive repertory of the moral plots which might engage the political attention of nineteenth-century Americans: equality against privilege, liberty against domination; honest work against idle exploit; natural dignity against factitious superiority; patriotic conservativism against alien innovation; progress against dead precedent.[46]

The terminology of manicheism, and its semi-secularization in 'gothic' romance and science fiction, could very well be used to dramatize these plots—Marx's terminology of alienation is packed with it: 'Vampire thirst for the living blood of labour', parasites as 'the ideologists of the vegetable world', 'a werewolf's hunger for surplus-labour', capitalists as 'flesh agents', commodities as 'necromancy', and so forth. As Endicott unmasks the leader of 'the crew of Comus' before the 'flower-decked abomination', he addresses the Reverend Mr. Blackstone as 'priest of Baal', and has the May Lord's hair cropped. Instinctual drives must be categorized and de-eroticized away from the 'systematic gaiety' of that 'sad forest'. Desire must be channelled into a war between the Covenant and Baal. But Endicott is in armour at 'the centre of the circle' of monster-costumed New Englanders to hold back 'the black surrounding woods'. Marx's incubus within us and Freud's repressed press for power. Robin Molineux may choose the Comus rout under 'the double-faced fellow' but the 'visionary' march and the 'inactive' spectators will not change. At eighteen he can answer 'I have authority', but the 'infernal stranger's gaze' and the gaze of the tar-and-feathered 'kinsman' will divide its potentiality. In 'The Golden Touch' murder is a mystic desire for gold as gold, in the line of Volpone, but necessitates the temporary sacrifice of a daughter; the beneficent alchemic stranger is simply a moral counter-power. The stranger's intervention in 'The Gray Champion' is a counter-justice within historical relativity: Hawthorne's moral is a hope that Americans will not renege on this 'hereditary spirit', the Lockeian permission to challenge tyranny. But then the theological details of 'The Gentle Boy' hold the conflict between 'popular antipathy' and individual dissent; between 'enthusiasm', 'responsibility' and 'martyrdom', the violence is atrocious. 'Bigotry' and 'persecution' engulfs both leaders and 'the common people', but the veiled mother's pulpit outburst is equally 'inspiration', 'imagination hopelessly entangled with her reason', and her black hair, beauty and intelligence fit her back into Hawthorne's anxiety. Her 'white' appearance belies her 'violence' in opposition to the violence of the theocrats, the government. The outcome is a characteristic language for the nonconformist anarchist in the United States—'sanctified by her love and her affliction', 'the apostle of her own unquiet heart'—the language of holy sacrifice in a political vacuum. Fanaticism rules both sides, according to Hawthorne; it is the pattern worked out in *Light in August* in 1932, and in practically everything that other follower of Hawthorne, Norman Mailer, ever wrote. 'The Gentle Boy' is an analogue of bases for a possible civil law which unites a community with that 'miraculous power of the human being over the will and passions of another' in *The Blithedale Romance*. Aylmer moves from the *physis* of science to the moral *physis*, from 'chemical' to 'spiritual' affinities in his bid to exceed Nature, to produce out of ecological stasis. Discoveries have opened science to 'the region of miracle' where a professional may 'lay his hand on the secret of creative force and perhaps make new worlds for himself'. *For himself* is the issue. Love for his wife and desire for power over origins causes a laboratory murder (and Aylmer dreams of removing Georgiana's heart with a knife) in the tradition of the Renaissance magus who hoped to gain 'from physics a sway over the spiritual world'. For 'laboratory' the professional will soon need to read 'society'. The moral of 'The

Artist of the Beautiful' is that a man cannot 'spend his labour upon a reality'—blacksmithing or clock and watch repair—and at the same time dream of 'the spiritualization of matter'. Warland informs Danforth 'I am not ambitious to be honoured with the paternity of a new kind of cotton machine', and his 'moral cold' is thereby caused by any professional's 'insulation' from Nature's supposed limits and 'the people'—and Hawthorne includes his guilty self: 'the prophet, the poet, the reformer, the criminal, or any other man with human yearning'. Genius must be exorcized into utility before diabolism destroys it or society. Hawthorne shares Hovenden's alarm: Warland 'would turn the sun out of its orbit and derange the whole course of time, if . . . his ingenuity could grasp anything bigger than a child's toy.' On the other hand, Baglioni may criticize Rappaccini as 'a vile empiric . . . not to be tolerated by those who respect the good old rules of the medical profession', but experimental medicine is the necessary equivalent of Warland's inventiveness. Rappaccini accelerates evolution, and changes its course, to modify ecology. His daughter is the sacrificial guinea-pig for the science of immunization. She becomes an 'an angel or demon' by such law-breaking, such transgression. The politics of science must take place in the politics of morality, is Hawthorne's issue: Control under Permission, Power from Agency. The question is dramatized equasively: are controls to be placed on any exceptional human praxis, and, if so, in the name of what ethic of leadership responsibility to the people? Hawthorne's fictions repeatedly exemplify the chaos of democratic principles as they necessarily resist dogma and yet rest in prejudice, aware that 'obedience, Bane of all genius, virtue, freedom, truth, Makes slaves of men and of the human frame A mechanized automaton.'[47]

Like McCaslin with his family ledger in *Go Down, Moses*, so Hawthorne with the past's documents in 'The Custom-House': he works back into origins, obsessively, to find causes, a singular cause, what lies behind the A, the alpha, before the beginning of the A to Z sentence of Authority. His hunting around in the cobwebbed room is the dire analogue of his fictions' motivation. The Acts of Congress, the Digest of Revenue Laws, 'the original Briton', 'the first ancestor . . . with

224

his Bible and sword . . . soldier, legislator, judge . . . ruler . . . bitter persecutor', the 'curse'—the writer accepts this legacy, as few writers have ever accepted it. But it is 'the dreary and unprosperous condition of the race', in spite of his hope that his own children, 'so far as their fortunes may be within my control, shall strike their roots into unaccustomed earth'. So he enters the House with the President's commission as 'chief executive offiicer', a political appointee on the edge of the sea, looking east to Europe. But the 'legacy' he turns up denies the idea of 'a refuge and sanctuary of liberty and freedom'; it proclaims slavery, 'wildcat manipulators of mythical wilderness town sites', bankers, 'the bellowing of politicians, the mellifluous choiring of self-styled men of God', and all the other manifestations of Law. The pattern is 'Promiscuity. Violence. Instability and lack of control. Inability to distinguish between mine and thine': the 'heritage'. Fortunately, 'the law of political warfare' found him on the losing side, so that the heat from the A in the legacy generates a 'sacred consideration' in the moonlight, sunshine, firelight and candle-light of the 'neutral territory'. But the dominant image is that bloody ancestral footstep in *Dr. Grimshawe's Secret*, 'blood running in such intricate currents',[48] from past to present. The enquirer puts his own foot in the mark and it enters his imagination. In 1855 he encounters the dissenter of 1555. Two years later, in the British Museum, he recognizes in the huge South American spider the form of natural entanglement which humanity cannot escape. The American in the web is the curse theme, and cursed for Hawthorne because he had no harness in confident moral or religious order, no Aquinas map, as Pound was to call it. He could not firmly relate his fascination with images, emblems and analogues with a dogma. The narrative plot only generates within Hawthorne's equasiveness and the readers' belief and knowledge. Edward H. Davidson understands Hawthorne as the artist groping for a 'central effect' among the Grimshawe fragments. Yet his sense of entanglement and the mark, the print, is impeccable. The cobwebs in the hall of the Protestant footprint meet the spider from South America, resulting in 'unjust violence' but in a natural web:

> 'I have seen,' said the old man, 'a great spider in South America that would have gratified your friend. The interior Indian

thought it a devil, and that by possessing it, and tracing out its web, a man could see what was to be the course of any event.

'How strange!' said Etheredge. 'The friend I speak of had that same fantasy, and died in a singular way, in accordance with it'.[49]

Tracing the web is Hawthorne's impulse, but he hesitates before the totality of such an enterprise, since it and the impulse are diabolic, the work of power maniac, an isolating will to probing to utter completion. He yields to the interior Indian who refuses total possession and constructs an archaeological site of tremendous energy, its past pressing through to conquer the present. In reply to Rosemary Jackson's dismissal of Hawthorne as 'excessively conceptual', fearing desire and eliminating it, and 'petrified' into allegorical usage, we have to expose such simplifications, reiterate his complex enquiry, and recall Jameson's statement on the necessity of thinking carefully about this kind of work:

> . . . if interpretation in terms of expressive causality or of allegorical master narratives remains a constant temptation, this is because such master narratives have inscribed themselves in the texts as well as in our thinking about them; such allegorical narrative signifieds are a persistent dimension of literary and cultural texts precisely because they reflect a fundamental dimension of our collective thinking and our collective fantasies about history and reality. To such a dimension correspond not only those cobwebs of topical allusion which the ahistorical and formalizing reader attempts desperately to brush away—that dry and intolerable chitinous murmur of footnotes reminding us of the implied references to long-dead contemporary events and political situations in Milton or Swift, in Spenser or Hawthorne; if the modern reader is bored or scandalized by the roots such texts send down into the contingent circumstances of their own historical time, this is surely testimony as to his resistance to his own political unconscious and to his denial (in the United States, the denial of a whole generation) of the reading and the writing of the text of history within himself.[50]

NOTES

1. Karl Marx, *Economic and Philosophic Manuscripts of 1844* (London: Lawrence and Wishart, 1961), p. 101.
2. G. Deleuze and F. Guattari, *Anti-Oedipus* (New York: Viking Press, 1977), . p. 256.
3. Ibid, p. 118.
4. K. Marx and F. Engels, *Collected Works,* Volume 3 (London: Lawrence and Wishart, 1975) pp. 298-99.
5. G. Deleuze, 'Four Perspectives On Psychoanalysis', *Language, Sexuality and Subversion* eds., P. Foss and M. Morris (Darlington, Australia, 1978). Working Papers Collection, p. 138.
6. Colin Gordon, 'The Subtracting Machine', *I & C: Power and Desire—Diagrams of the Social,* No. 8 (Oxford: I & C Publications, 1981), p. 34.
7. Philip Rahv, 'Paleface and Redskin', *Image And Idea* (New York: New Directions, 1957).
8. Shelley, 'Mont Blanc'.
9. Tzvetan Todorov, *The Fantastic: A Structural Approach to a Literary Genre* (Ithaca, New York: Cornell University Press, 1975), p. 25.
10. Ibid., p. 31.
11. Edmund Wilson, *The Wound and the Bow* (London: Methuen, 1961), pp. 254-55.
12. Colin Sumner, *Reading Ideologies* (London, New York and San Francisco: Academic Press, 1979), pp. 22-3.
13. Ibid., p. 293.
14. Edwin C. Rozwenc, *Ideology and Power in the Age of Jackson* (New York: Anchor Books, 1964), p. xi (Ralph Waldo Emerson, *Works* (Boston: 1870), Volume 1, p. 154).
15. Ibid., p. xiv.
16. Ibid., p. 298.
17. Ibid., pp. 353, 356-58.
18. William S. Burroughs, 'Interview', *Journal for the Protection of All Beings* (San Francisco: City Lights, 1961), No. 1.
19. Jacques Lacan, *The Four Fundamental Concepts of Psycho-Analysis* (London: Penguin, 1979), p. 188.
20. Helen M. Lynd, *On Shame and the Search for Identity* (New York: Science Editions, 1961), p. 27.
21. Ibid., pp. 65-6.
22. Perry Miller, *The Life of the Mind in America* (New York: Harcourt, Brace & World, 1965), p. 106.
23. Ibid., p. 148.
24. Ibid., p. 163.
25. Ibid., p. 180.
26. Perry Miller (ed.), *The Legal Mind in America* (New York: Doubleday, 1962), p. 277.
27. Ibid., p. 278.
28. Alain Robbe-Grillet, *For a New Novel* (New York: Grove Press, 1965), pp. 23-4.

29. Miller (ed.), *op. cit.*, p. 281.
30. Miller, *op. cit.*, pp. 189, 194-95; Miller (ed.), *op. cit.*, pp. 261, 271; see also Eric Mottram, 'Orpheus and Measured Forms: Law, Madness and Reticence in Melville,' in Faith Pullin (ed.), *New Perspectives on Melville* (Edinburgh University Press, 1978).
31. Miller (ed.), *op. cit.*, p. 264.
32. L. J. Bigelow. Quoted in Miller, *op. cit.*, p. 214.
33. Miller, *op. cit.*, p. 223; see also *The Legal Mind in America*, pp. 297-306.
34. Miller, *op. cit.*, p. 227.
35. Miller, *op. cit.*, p. 260.
36. Miller, *op. cit.*, p. 264.
37. George L. Mosse, *The Culture of Western Europe* (London: Murray, 1963), p. 165.
38. Robert Darnton, *Mesmerism and the End of the Enlightenment in France* (Cambridge, Massachusetts: Harvard University Press, 1968); see also Maria M. Tatar, *Spellbound: Studies in Mesmerism and Literature* (New Jersey: Princeton University Press, 1979).
39. Mark Holloway, *Heavens on Earth: Utopian Communities in America 1680-1880* (New York: Dover Publications, 1966).
40. Charles Nordhoff, *The Communistic Societies of the United States* (New York: Hilary House, 1961), p. 392.
41. William Alfred Hinds, *American Communities* (New York: Corinth Books, 1961), p. 164.
42. Ibid. Introduction by Henry Bamford Parkes, p. v.
43. Irving Howe, *Politics and the Novel* (New York: Meridian Books, 1957), p. 165.
44. Mark Van Doren, *Nathaniel Hawthorne* (New York: Viking Press, 1957), p. 252.
45. Perry Miller and Thomas H. Johnson (eds.), *The Puritans* (New York: Harper And Row, 1963), Volume 1, pp. 141-43.
46. Edwin C. Rozwenc (ed.), *The Meaning of Jacksonian Democracy* (Boston: Heath And Co., 1963), p. 120.
47. Shelley, *Prometheus Unbound*.
48. Nathaniel Hawthorne, *Dr. Grimshawe's Secret* (ed. Edward H. Davidson, Cambridge: Harvard University Press, 1954), p. 37.
49. Ibid.; pp. 13, 73 and 67-8.
50. See Rosemary Jackson, *Fantasy: The Literature of Subversion* (London: Methuen, 1981), p. 100, and Frederic Jameson, *The Political Unconscious: Narrative as a Socially Symbolic Act* (London: Methuen, 1981), p. 34.

11

Hawthorne, Melville, and the Fiction of Prophecy

by RICHARD BRODHEAD

> . . . if we saw the real from hour to hour, we should not be here to write and read, but should have burned or frozen long ago.
> —Emerson, 'Nominalist and Realist'.

1

'Hawthorne interests me considerably. I feel more of a kinship with him than with any other American.'[1] This is Flannery O'Connor speaking; but the interest of her statement is that it could come equally well from a dozen other authors. For Hawthorne has always had a remarkable power to make American storytellers recognize him as an intimate relation. From Melville through James to Faulkner and his successors, the most powerful figures in the tradition of American fiction have all looked back to Hawthorne as the pioneer of their line of work. In their most original creations they have regularly insisted on their derivation from Hawthorne, inscribing his fictions in their own in such a way as to claim him as their source.

The reason Hawthorne has such a hold on later writers has something to do with his situation in literary history. He came early enough in a tradition for his work to take on the exemplary character of a founder's labour. And his exemplary stature was massively reinforced by the institutionalization of an American high culture in the mid-nineteenth century, since Hawthorne alone among native novelists was placed in the ranks of ultimate achievers.[2] But by their own accounts Hawthorne's followers have always been less impressed by his august public status than by the peculiar power he exerts in the privacy of reading. A surprising number of authors have left written records of their first experiences of Hawthorne; almost without exception they use Hawthorne's own idiom of possession and enchantment to describe his peculiar effect. Hawthorne 'fixes and fascinates' Melville, makes him feel 'seized' as by a 'wizard'. Howells's Hawthorne is the same: not a 'person' but a 'remote and impalpable agency', who 'dominate(s)' him with his 'potent spell'. Such was the 'mysterious charm' of *The Scarlet Letter* to the child Henry James, James recalls in his *Hawthorne*, that its physical volume, seen for the first time, 'fixed his eyes as (it) lay on the table'.[3]

The language of potency and fixation suggests that Hawthorne's successors identify him not so much with any particular fictive matter or method but first off with a startling exercise of force. His influence on their writing is in keeping with this, for when his fiction is most palpably present to their minds, it does not merely give them new materials for their work: it opens up new visions of the power their work could possess. Especially among nineteenth-century writers, the discovery of Hawthorne typically involves something like a discovery of literary possibility, such that in their careers renewed responsiveness to Hawthorne's precedents tends to accompany a larger action of self-reformulation: a crisis in which, using Hawthorne as an aid to conception, they re-imagine the authority they could claim as writers, and redesign the shape of their work. When Howells, after writing Howells-ian novels for ten years, starts writing a deeply Hawthornesque one in *A Modern Instance*, the effect of Hawthorne's intrusion is to help him forge that new idea of the novel—the idea of the novel as the history of communal spiritual life—that releases him from his minor to his major work. James seeks Hawthorne's guidance every time he reconstitutes his writing project—as he turns to him to learn how to write as the historian of contemporary social change, in *The Bostonians*; as he returns to study Hawthorne's art of abstract moral representation in the late 1890s, when he begins to work out his own late style.

Hawthorne's importance to other writers, these examples suggest, is that he helps them know what it means to do the writer's work. But it is paradoxical that Hawthorne, of all writers, should provide this sort of service. For one of the peculiarities of his work is that it is silent about its organizing intentions. Emerson, Hawthorne's principal rival among American tradition-founders, leaves no doubt about how he is to be followed, even if his message is the confusing: the way to follow me is not to follow me. By contrast Hawthorne's writing puts forth no statement of what it believes or attempts (the apparent definitions of the prefaces are exercises in evasion), and certainly offers no overt guidance for the work of another. One result is that he frees his followers, to a remarkable extent, to invent his motives for themselves—and in so doing to make his work speak the message their own work requires. So it is that Hawthorne's followers each 'follow' him in a direction of their own—toward the chronicle of local customs, but equally toward the unlocalized fable; toward the symbolic unfolding of moral truth, but equally toward the symbolic encoding of moral mystery; toward the fiction of domestic life, but equally toward the fiction of the occult; and so on. But another result of Hawthorne's failure to express his work's intentions is that the messages others carry away from him are curiously lacking in authority. Having themselves composed the directions they set out to follow in his name, when they look back to Hawthorne they find not confirmation and encouragement but silence: a figure intimating, if he intimates anything at all, that his path is not the one they have adopted but another, possibly even the opposite one.

For the authors who search him most pressingly, the enigma of Hawthorne's intentions becomes the final source of his fascination; and he can affect their work quite as powerfully in his capacity as riddle as he can in his capacity as guide. In one of his aspects Hawthorne precipitates something like self-discovery in his followers, allowing them to grasp and act out new notions of artistic power. But since his work refuses to verify the understandings it occasions, it also retains the power to cast the authenticity of these new notions into doubt—then, possibly, to provoke other discoveries in their stead. This, I take it, is Hawthorne's special gift as a maker of tradition. A founder establishes an authoritative way of doing things, and for the least interesting of his followers that is what Hawthorne does: he teaches them a procedure, outlines a way for fiction to be written. But for his abler students Hawthorne does not prescribe a fictive way. Rather he engages them in the founder's act: the act of reaching into the space of literary possibility, to find anew how fiction can be made. Finally to those who read him with most imagination he gives the further gift of renewed unsettlement. He forces them to question even their own boldest self-inventions, and so to go on unfounding and refounding fiction's founding claims.

2

Melville was the first American author to be influenced by Hawthorne, and his case shows especially clearly how Hawthorne serves to orient, then disorient and reorient, his successors' work. Hawthorne has never found a student more ready for a new direction than Melville was when he met and read Hawthorne, in August 1850.[4] At this point in his career Melville has become extremely proficient at doing one sort of work, but is under intense inward pressure to do not that sort of work but another. These pressures make their appearance in 1848 during the writing of *Mardi*, that extravaganza of free-form composition undertaken for the sake of generating a new writing self. *Mardi* does generate, if not a new self for Melville, then certainly a new idea of himself. In its late chapters we see an author beginning to be haunted by dreams of literary grandeur:

> Yet, things immortal have been written; and by men as me;— men, who slept and waked; and ate; and talked with tongues like mine. Ah, Oro! how may we know or not, we are what we would be? Hath genius any stamp and imprint, obvious to possessors? Has it eyes to see itself; or is it blind? Or do we delude ourselves with being gods, and end in grubs? Genius, genius?—a thousand years hence, to be a household word?

The sense of being singled out for the highest form of literary greatness, however nervously phrased here on its first appearance, haunts Melville with increasing urgency in the years after

Mardi. We see its mark in his sudden obsession, in his letters, with fame and posthumous reputation; or again in the cult of genius that Melville erects in 1849 and 1850, in which he celebrates, through figures like Shakespeare and Emerson, the form of greatness he hopes to make his own.

Along with the fantasy of literary election, the writing of *Mardi* also activates a sense of calling to privileged spiritual office. This is when Melville's messianic streak makes its first appearance: when he begins to brood on the imminent coming of the messiah, as he does in *Mardi*'s late hymns to the incarnation, or in *White-Jacket*'s fits of messianic nationalism; and more particularly when he becomes moved by the idea, not fully manifest until *Pierre*, that the work of the messiah may be his to perform. (Melville's readers usually forget, but Melville I think seldom does, that between 1849 and 1852 he reached the ages of 30 through 33, the years of Christ's active mission.) Melville's messianism is only one strain in a general sense of prophetical calling. The notion that it has been given him to see an order of reality closed off to other men and to speak that reality to an otherwise unilluminated world enters his thinking at this time, and quickly becomes his most driving thought.

All of these new self-identifications focus their pressure on Melville's work as a writer. It will be in his writing, or not at all, that he will discharge his duty to speak neglected truth; his writing will give the proof whether he is indeed equipped with special powers. But it is important to remember that in mid-1850 Melville has not yet reorganized his work to accommodate his new ambitions. One reason for his delay is that his fantasies of special selfhood are still fraught with uncertainty. How can I know that I am what I dream, prospective genius asks itself in *Mardi*: 'hath genius any stamp and imprint, obvious to possessors?' Christhood is, to Melville, another state of promise that cannot evidence itself: 'Not even in the case of one deemed more than man, not even in our Savior,' he writes in 1850, 'did the visible frame betoken anything of the augustness of the nature within.'[5] Another reason for his delay is that even if Melville could be certain that the privileges he dreams of are his to attain, he still has no very clear idea how to implement those privileges in his work—still does not know, in any practical sense, how one sets about writing like a prophet-genius. His sense of promise is sufficiently strong to breed contempt for his earlier, what might be called pre-awakened, writing formats, but not yet sufficiently focussed to enable him to clinch a new identity by making a new kind of work. His remarks on the books of 1849 and 1850, *Redburn* and *White-Jacket*, express his position clearly enough:

> no reputation that is gratifying to me, can possibly be achieved by either of these books. They are two *jobs*, which I have done for money—being forced to it, as other men are to sawing wood. . . . So far as I am individually concerned, & independent of my pocket, it is my earnest desire to write those sort of books that are said to 'fail'.[6]

These are the ambitions and anxieties that Melville brings to his meeting with Hawthorne; and Hawthorne's magic, for Melville, is that he opens a way through this impasse in his work. 'Hawthorne and His Mosses', the essay that registers Melville's shock of recognition, is surely the most excited piece of literary criticism ever written. The ground for its excitement is that as he writes it, from paragraph to paragraph, Melville watches his own uncertain theories of authorship get clarified and confirmed. On the basis of Hawthorne's example Melville moves toward a full articulation of the idea of the artist's activity that he has previously held only in vague forms: recasting and recasting his analysis of Hawthorne's fascinating power, he finally arrives at a comprehensive vision of the author as diviner, a being gifted to penetrate through the apparent and familiar to 'the very axis of reality', then to speak an estranged but 'vital truth' in the face of conventional acceptations. As he comes to see truth-bearing as the author's real work, Melville becomes increasingly confident that literary labour can have the kind of spiritual stature he had previously fantasized: 'Hawthorne and His Mosses' four times equates the great author with the messiah, identifying Hawthorne as an avatar of that 'literary Shiloh' in whom Melville's literary and religious aspirations are both fulfilled. And when he sees this privileged status as a condition actually attained by Hawthorne, Melville gets a powerful boost for his own sense of prophetical calling. The logic of his argument is that if literary Shilohdom is realized now in Hawthorne, then it is available to be realized next by another. His conclusion makes clear his extrapolation from Hawthorne's current to his own coming literary-spiritual incarnation:

> And here, let me throw out another conceit of mine touching this American Shiloh, or 'Master Genius,' as Hawthorne calls him. May it not be, that this commanding mind has not been, is not, and never will be, individually developed in any one man? And would it, indeed, appear so unreasonable to suppose that this great fullness and overflowing may be, or may be destined to be, shared by a plurality of men of genius?[7]

What Hawthorne does for Melville, this self-annunciation suggests, is in a stunning way to resolve his doubts about the sort of author he is to be. And having been emboldened, by Hawthorne's example, to claim for his own what he calls 'the great Art of Telling the Truth', Melville now takes another look at Hawthorne's fiction to discover how an art of that stature gets organized. It is well known that, in the months just after his meeting with Hawthorne, Melville stopped writing the whaling sequel to *Redburn* and *White-Jacket* that he had almost finished, and revised the book so drastically that it took another year of hard labour to complete. Students of *Moby-Dick*'s compositional history have also shown that what Melville added, in redesigning *Moby-Dick*, was the figure of Ahab and the story of his quest.[8] In watching Melville build this figure into the structure of the book we watch him rereading Hawthorne as a guide to composition, watch him identifying, then appropriating, the fictive structures that seem to carry Hawthorne's power.

It is striking how much Melville's vision of Hawthorne gets sharpened in the months between 'Hawthorne and His Mosses' and the first Ahab chapters of *Moby-Dick*. In the essay he is well-disposed to various kinds of Hawthorne pieces—he talks about 'Young Goodman Brown' and 'A Select Party' as is they were equally remarkable, for instance—and he is eager to catch a range of Hawthornesque tonalities: his terrific blackness, but also his genial humour, his white melancholy, and so on. By the time he writes Ahab into *Moby-Dick* his attention has concentrated on a handful of Hawthorne tales, and within them, on a single figure. The identifying mark of this figure, as Melville reconstructs him, is that he has passed through a radical reorganization of selfhood, a process at once of extreme intensification and extreme reduction. In the chapters 'Moby-Dick' and 'The Chart' Melville twice rehearses, in explicating the motive for Ahab's quest, a transformation repeatedly replayed in Hawthorne ('Ethan Brand' and the analysis of Roger Chillingworth in Chapter 10 of *The Scarlet Letter* provide its classic versions)—a self-fracturing or self-fractioning whereby a faculty that has existed alongside others in an integrated personality suddenly separates off and assumes what Melville calls an 'independent being of its own'. This now-independent faculty next extends its domination over the rest of the self, absorbing its collective powers into its one form of agency—as Ethan Brand's 'intellect' absorbs the energies of 'heart'; or as, in the 'furious trope' of *Moby-Dick*, Ahab's 'special lunacy stormed his general sanity, and carried it, and turned all its concentrated cannon upon its own mad mark.' What results is a prodigious concentration of being, in which the desires available for the ordinary self's various projects get fixed and focussed on one object, and the energies available for the self's various moves get redirected into movement toward one end. What was once a person is now a project. Living becomes, for the hero thus transformed, a drive long the straight line toward a goal (so Ahab can say: 'the path to my fixed purpose is laid with iron rails, whereon my soul is grooved to run'). So consolidated are his being and his object that we name him fully in naming his goal: Ahab *is* he who hunts the white whale, as Ethan Brand *is* he who searches for the Unpardonable Sin.

The figure (in a phrase Melville repeats from Hawthorne) mastered by one Idea, and compelled, by his Idea, to the unswerving execution of an inflexible program, is not, of course, Hawthorne's exclusive invention. The structure of selfhood I describe Melville as imitating from Hawthorne Angus Fletcher finds in all of allegory: Fletcher likens allegory's simplified agents to figures possessed by a daimon, that form of intermediate deity whose effect as it descends on the human self is to narrow it to one function and direct it to one end.[9] The consolidation of the self that Hawthorne's fiction displays is also a standard feature of the gothic—I think of Godwin's Caleb Williams, who slips as easily from having ideas to being had by

Ideas as Ethan Brand ('it was but a passing thought. And yet . . . the idea having once occurred to my mind, it was fixed there forever'); or I think of Frankenstein, like Ahab and Chilling-worth, both agent and victim of an idea that converts wholeness of being into a will for one thing ('one by one the various keys were touched that formed the mechanism of my being; chord after chord was sounded, and soon my mind filled with one thought, one conception, one purpose'[10]). But what Melville finds in Hawthorne is the fusion of monomania as a personality type with a peculiar mode of figuration. In Hawthorne the self recentred within a single faculty sees the world recentred in a parallel way. Its attention fixes on a single object, which it lifts out of the continuum of objects and makes into the sign of its obsession. Aylmer, the perfectionist bridegroom of 'The Birthmark', isolates and resignifies Georgiana's facial blemish in this way, projecting his inward preoccupations upon it in such manifold and insistent ways (Hawthorne says that he connects it 'with innumerable trains of thought, and modes of feeling') as to convert it into a figure for the sum of his dreads, 'the symbol of his wife's liability to sin, sorrow, decay, and death'. He is in this the prototype for Hawthorne's idea-possessed men, who in the moment that they succumb to obsession also find an object—Reverend Hooper's black veil, Roderick Elliston's bosom serpent, Arthur Dimmesdale's scarlet letter—in which obsession lodges as an overdetermined meaning. Melville has clearly noticed the conjunction of monomania and figure-making in Hawthorne, because when he recreates Hawthorne's account of the consolidation of self Fletcher calls daimonization in *Moby-Dick*, he insists that its products are a pathology and a metaphor, or more accurately a pathology whose action is the forging of metaphors. According to Melville, Ahab's loss of his leg to Moby Dick generates a rage that activates and absorbs every other possible form of human rage until rage is so intense that it brings about a fusion of previously separate things, makes Ahab 'identify with (the whale) not only all his bodily woes, but all his intellectual and spiritual exasperations'. As if still struggling to grasp this notion Melville runs through every way he can think of to say that Ahab's madness is a madness of metaphor: 'the White Whale swam before him as the *monomaniac incarnation* of all those malicious agencies which some deep men feel eating in them'; or again: '*deleriously transferring* its idea to the abhorred white whale'; or again: 'all evil, to *crazy* Ahab, were visibly *personified*, and made practically assailable in Moby Dick.'

The curious thing about emblem-makers in Hawthorne is that although it is clear, both to themselves and others, that the meanings they read into their chosen objects originate in an act of obsessive projection, once that projection is completed the meaning it generates takes on an oddly objective and authoritative status. Aylmer selects the birthmark as the symbol for a human condition that he cannot accept, but once he has done so neither Georgiana nor Hawthorne can work free of the notion that this is indeed the birthmark's meaning. Reverend Hooper converts a black veil into the symbol of that secret sin the knowledge of which torments him, but when he presents his neurotic emblem before others it takes on an 'awful power'— the power to disclose them to themselves as the secret sinners Hooper claims them to be. Roderick Elliston, the chief case in Hawthorne of what might be called the symbolist as aggressor, thrusts his bosom serpent upon others as their meaning—he 'make(es) his own actual serpent . . . the type of each man's fatal error, or hoarded sin, or unquiet conscience'. But the effect of this energetic self-projection is to bring forward the serpent that is them—'by obtruding his own bosom-serpent to the public gaze' he 'drag(s) those of decent people from their lurking-places'.

Obsession in Hawthorne, this is to say, is associated not just with figuration but with figuration as a means to knowledge. The Hawthornesque obsessive deforms reality, subjects it to a perverse pressure that distorts and violates its familiar contours; but through this deformation he discovers another state of things that is instantly known to be more deeply real, and that is not to be known otherwise than through his obsessive deformations. Similarly the Hawthornesque symbolist is a pure projectionist, writing out onto the world a condition that starts within himself; but through his projections he brings a real and general condition to expression, one that is not available except through his expressive projections.

The descent from here to Ahab is clear: for Ahab is above all a knower, and a knower on the same terms that Hawthorne's heroes are. Like Elliston or Hooper, he is a testifier: he embodies a statement of how things are in the world. Like them, his statement has no referent in the visible world. He knows by his obsession: he knows what he knows by his rage, as Hooper knows what he knows by his guilt. But the lack of objective external sanction for his frantic projection does not make it less authoritative. He is mad and therefore sees another world than the one we see—in Ahab's case, sees strange gods at work where we see only natural process. But although it is known to be the product of insanity, this antithetical vision carries the power to make others recognize its deep or at least potential truth. So it is that Ahab's insane symbolization can make the faithful Starbuck acknowledge life's 'latent horror'; so it is that his insane quest can present itself to Ishmael as 'mine'.

Here it begins to come clear, I think, what Melville is finding in Hawthorne as he writes *Moby-Dick*. When Melville puts aside his earlier form of work in *Moby-Dick* it is in order to practice fiction as an art of divination, fiction as the great Art of Telling the Truth. When he looks at Hawthorne's fiction in the light of this ambition he seems to see exactly such a divination taking place—through the figure of the monomaniac, with his gift of knowing and expressing a reality ordinary reality denies. The monomaniac becomes, as Melville now reads Hawthorne, the secret agent of a great art's greatest task; and in reconstituting his book around such a figure he is seeking to lay claim to literature's deepest powers.

In fact so elated is Melville to discover the visionary aspect of the monomaniac that he has trouble taking other features of Hawthorne's characterization seriously. In Hawthorne to be transformed into a man of one idea is both a privilege and an impoverishment. One gains the power to see through to a hidden reality at the cost of forfeiting the familiar one. To be embraced by a daimon always entails withdrawal from the natural and consensual in Hawthorne—so Richard Digby, the cavedweller of 'The Man of Adamant', moves into the space of revelation by moving out of the world of nature and of others. Also, being mastered by one idea enlarges the faculty of knowing at the expense of other faculties, and so always entails a sacrifice of dimensions of one's humanity—as Roderick Elliston, promoted to an emblem, is also flattened into an emblem; as Brand and Chillingworth, committed to their quests, become not men but 'fiends'. The costliness of obsession explains why Hawthorne surrounds his daimonic agents with those familiar therapist figures who try to coax them back into ordinary humanity—as Hester, midway through *The Scarlet Letter*, tells Chillingworth how he could 'be once more human'; as Rosina, in 'The Bosom Serpent', urges Elliston to 'forget yourself in the idea of another!' It also explains why, having activated the daimonic agents whose missions give it its narrative line, Hawthorne's fiction struggles rhetorically to contain the visionary in the familiar, to re-express the daimon's private significations in a transpersonal language of common wisdom.

Melville's way of understanding the monomaniac's privileges makes him give these restrictions less weight. In *Moby-Dick* Ahab both knows and feels the pain of knowing that he has forfeited other human powers to gain the power of vision: 'gifted with the high perception,' he laments, 'I lack the low, enjoying power.' Nevertheless through this transformation Ahab gains not diminished but increased access to the experience that Melville regards as fundamentally human. In the famous Hall of Thermes passage in Chapter 41 Melville explains that what finally motivates Ahab's quest is no idiosyncracy of pathology but his full recognition of our general condition: his recognition that we are the disinherited offspring of a deposed king; that (in Wallace Stevens's beautiful phrase) 'we live in a place/That is not our own and, much more, not ourselves/And hard it is in spite of blazoned days.' Because his quest is grounded in this sort of knowledge, the humanistic restraint that Hawthorne would subject it to has less containing power in *Moby-Dick*. Starbuck is Ahab's Rosina; when he urges Ahab to relinquish the quest in 'The Symphony' we hear the familiar Hawthornesque exhortation back to nature and the human family: 'See, see! the boy's face from the window! the boy's hand on the hill!' But moving though this exhortation is, it has less authority in Melville's version of things. Ahab cannot lose himself in the idea of an other, ghastly though it is to be unable to do so, because he has already lost himself in the idea of all others—of our common predicament in an unhuman world. The rhetoric of health through nature and community—greatly scaled down

240

in any case in *Moby-Dick*—inevitably appears in this book less like wisdom than like an evasion of superior knowledge. Even while he speaks the cause of 'the soft feeling of the human', Starbuck knows that Ahab describes his own deepest knowledge better than his humane faith does.

Subjecting Hawthorne to the will to divination, then, leads Melville both to identify the divinatory function of Hawthorne's monomaniac and to read the limits Hawthorne sets on that function as less deeply intended. The consequence of this double construction is that in the act of finding a figure who is actually present in Hawthorne's fiction, Melville also creates a figure who was never present there in that form. For when the restrictions Hawthorne sets on the truth-bearing impulse get weakened as they do in *Moby-Dick*, the result is an extraordinary expansion of power. Released from its association with self-restriction, obsession now confers a magnificent enlargement of stature: daimonization as Melville imagines it yields not the two-dimensionality of Hawthorne's human emblems but the expanded selfhood of the hero, the 'great heart' whose giant capacities for knowing and suffering let him 'condense to one deep pang, the sum total of those shallow pains kindly diffused through feebler men's whole lives.' Released from Hawthorne's censure of privatized and antinatural meaning, obsession now confers enlarged moral stature as well. No one else's code of value dictates Ahab's moral meaning in *Moby-Dick*. If the book treats him with final irony, its irony is that his vision is finally not authoritative either, not that someone else's is more authoritative than his. Imitation on Melville's plan both faithfully reproduces certain elements in a configuration from Hawthorne and, by rendering those elements alone, produces a figure Hawthorne never drew: the heroic obsessive, or the monomaniac as superior man.

Ahab's aggrandizement is one possible consequence of Melville's deregulatory reading of Hawthorne. We see another, quite different one in *Pierre*. *Pierre*'s early chapters put squarely at the centre the process of daimonization that Melville introduces into *Moby-Dick* at a later stage. As Melville presents it Pierre's learning that he has an illegitimate sister brings about a wholesale reversal of vision—a discovery that the appearances and arrangements of ordinary social life are so many deceitful constructions, designed to hide the truth about selves and relations from public view. The disruption of ordinary reality that discloses a 'darker, though truer aspect of things' makes Pierre simultaneously the bearer of a vision and the agent of a mission: to know of his sister's existence is to have an 'incipient offspring' born within him, a self within the self that makes him feel 'divinely dedicated' to amend Isabel's wrong through perfect personal obedience to 'the inflexible rule of holy right'.

Pierre's account of how the ordinary and various self gets reconstituted as an inflexible project still thinks that it is telling a tale from Hawthorne. A dense fabric of allusions associates Pierre's project with the Hawthorne project as Melville described it in 'Hawthorne and His Mosses'; and it has often been noted that Isabel, whose 'magnet' reorients Pierre's field of vision, lives in the moss-covered red farmhouse Hawthorne stayed in when he was Melville's neighbour. At the same time in this version of the tale Melville much more clearly identifies daimonization with his own authorial aspirations. Daimonization becomes, as *Pierre* renders it, a promotion to messianic office, or literally incarnation: the 'incipient offspring' that wrests Pierre's ordinary selfhood to its transcendent ends is repeatedly called a 'heaven-begotten Christ'; Pierre's mission, unswervingly required of him but incomprehensible to other men, is explicitly the mission of the Christ, to enact God's law amid the laws of men. Just as clearly, daimonization in *Pierre* expresses Melville's mid-career sense of literary vocation. Pierre's 'accession of the personal divine' is also an accession of literary 'genius', prompting him not just to holy living but to the writing of a 'deep book'. Specifically Pierre feels called to the writing of prophecy, called 'to deliver . . . new, or at least miserably neglected Truth to the world', or as he says elsewhere, to 'gospelize the world anew'. (Compare Melville to Hawthorne: 'Though I wrote the Gospels in this century, I should die in the gutter.'[11])

Melville's dedication to the role of literary Shiloh is thus implicated in Pierre's dedication to enacting the heaven-begotten Christ within him. Where this dedication leads him, every reader of *Pierre* will remember, is into the arms of Isabel. This conclusion is not the irony it seems: for the arms of Isabel is the place of vision in *Pierre*. It is where the artist gets his literary inspiration—as Isabel's sexual presence makes Pierre feel 'chapter after chapter born of its wondrous suggestiveness.' It is also where the prophet learns the truth it is his to deliver: so Pierre, in the moment when he recognizes his incestuous lust for Isabel, also acceeds to prophetical status:

> Ah! now I catch glimpses, and seem to half see, somehow, that the uttermost ideal of moral perfection in man is wide of the mark. The demi-gods trample on trash, and Virtue and Vice are trash! Isabel, I will write such things—I will gospelize the world anew, and show them deeper secrets than the Apocalypse!—I will write it, I will write it!

This scene of incestuous-prophetical inspiration is an extremity, even for a writer who loves extremes as much as Melville. For this reason it is all the more striking that Melville should reach, in this scene, his moment of greatest closeness to Hawthorne. His scene recreates, with uncanny precision, the forest scene in *The Scarlet Letter*. Pierre goes to the city with Isabel, as Hester goes to the woods to Dimmesdale, to execute an obligation he has had to define for himself. But such are the workings of disguise and displacement, in both books, that the will both characters feel to perform a duty gets its real energies from unacknowledged sexual attraction. The concealment of a hidden sexual within a manifest ethical motive explains why, in these scenes, the intended performance of a duty precipitates instead a seduction. The unexpected but quite brazen resurfacing of the most illicit forms of desire the novels know (incest is not more heavily prohibited in *Pierre* than adultery is in *The Scarlet Letter*) gives the scenes part of their thrilling power. But their power comes even more from the fact that, when the illicit reasserts itself, it does so in such a way that it cannot be known if it is truly illicit. The scenes takes place *in extremis*, beyond the bounds of the known world: Pierre reaches his point by 'follow(ing) Virtue to her uttermost vista, where common souls never go'; Hester reaches hers by crossing, by means of the 'passport' of the scarlet letter, 'into regions where other women dared not tread'. When desire resurfaces in this place, it is not only uncontrolled by the law: it is free to rewrite the law on its own authority. So adulterous sexual love, known in another context as transgression against the holy, announces in the

forest scene that it creates the holy: 'what we did had a consecration of its own.' So incest, known in another context as
'monstrousest vice', inspires the declaration here that the
categories of the ethical are collapsible and disposable: 'Virtue
and Vice are trash.'

What Melville recaptures, in this scene from *Pierre*, is not the
literal action of the forest scene so much as its air of moral
vertiginousness, that destabilizing of norms that frees the novel,
all of a sudden, to give the moral world in a new and inverted
form. As such the scene shows a further stage in Melville's
understanding of the nature of Hawthorne's art. In *Moby-Dick*
to write in the manner of Hawthorne is to be engaged in
speaking the gods—in tearing off the masks of nature's
seemings to name the agents behind them. In *Pierre* to do
Hawthorne's kind of work is to do the work of new-seeing and
new-saying the ethical: of unmaking, through the verbal and
narrative action of a fictive text, the ethical significations that
prevail in the world, and then remaking those significations in a
radically altered way.

Such a project does indeed exist in Hawthorne's fiction, and
Melville deserves to be called its discoverer. But here as with
the monomaniac-as-diviner, the prophetical obsessions that let
Melville identify the covert prophetical movements in
Hawthorne also lead him to push those movements in quite
different directions. As Melville sees, *The Scarlet Letter* strives
toward a moment when the usual senses of good and evil, sacred
and unholy, can be radically reversed. But as soon as it reaches
this point it backs away from it—moves back into the town,
back into the legal, moral, and religious world the novel has just
inverted. This return is not a mere submission, real or feigned,
to the priority of communal structures. The book returns as it
does because it is the nature of the antithetical energy liberated
in the forest scene to precipitate its own reversal. Dimmesdale is
freed by Hester's new testament—but freed, first to the perverse
acts listed in 'The Minister in a Maze', then to compose his
prophetical prose hymn to the glories of the New England state,
then to claim for himself the judgement of that old law Hester
had momentarily negated. Hester is freed by her gospel too: not
freed from the community and its significant structures, as she
first thinks, but freed to embrace those structures on altered

terms. On the novel's last page she puts herself back under the sign of the letter the community had imposed on her to express the recognition won from within her private experience, that it is the sign of her 'more real life'.

In Hawthorne's novel as in the lives of his characters the freedom of the broken law becomes finally the freedom to reconstruct the law: the same energy that fuels, at one moment, an inversion of the ethical brings about, in another phase of its action, a reestablishment of the thing it destroyed. This is a move that Melville, in *Pierre*, does not and cannot make. Not that he persists in the illusion, so animating to the novel's middle sections, that fiction actually can seize and articulate ethical 'truth'. *Pierre* pursues this object to the point where it exposes itself as chimerical—pursues the hunger to be in the depths to a point where depth reveals itself as only another kind of surface; pursues the drive to write a 'book of sacred Truth' to a point where Truth reveals itself as only another form of fiction. But when it explodes the notion that it could ground itself on some totally extraconventional truth, *Pierre* cannot move back onto familiar ground. The novel identifies with its hero's fantasies of privileged vision so fully that it consigns the communal and the conventional wholesale to the category of the Lie—the category of that iniquitous thing that refuses to be the Truth. When those fantasies expose their emptiness, then, the book is at a dead end. Where *The Scarlet Letter* can turn from the bold resignifications of the forest scene to yet further acts of resignification, *Pierre* reaches the point where making sense in fiction no longer seems possible, except as a choice between perpetuating the lies of the world and the lies of truth.

This divergence shows what Melville misses in reading Hawthorne as he does. Melville takes Hawthorne as the patron for a purely anticonventional form of art; this means that he regards as genuine everything in Hawthorne that hints that the world is much mistaken in its common acceptations, and as ungenuine everything that pays tribute to the collectively held. What such a reading gets wrong is not so much the degree of Hawthorne's attachment to the communal—this is hard to determine, although he is, obviously, more attached to it than Melville is. Rather what it misperceives is the play of opposed attachments in Hawthorne's thought. Hawthorne's imagination is so organized that antithetical impulses fuel and release one another in it—so organized that an impulse, once activated, moves both to express itself and to activate an opposite one. So, in *The Scarlet Letter*, the expression of a powerful and genuine antinomianism touches off a new respect for the law; so in Hawthorne's politics a recoil into privacy touches off an urge to join in the drama of public life; so in Hawthorne's historical fiction a powerful denial of the past sets off a new insistence that the past fills the present—an insistence that, pressed far enough, sets off a new repudiation of the past; and so on. The consequence is that Hawthorne can fully occupy positions without becoming fully committed to them, since each of his positions, once embraced, calls up another one that reverses it.

Reading Hawthorne in Melville's way wins Melville the greatest measure of encouragement for the most adventurous impulses of his art. But it does so at the cost of sacrificing the protection Hawthorne might have given against the self-destructiveness of adventurous impulses. In Hawthorne extreme possibilities of fictive assertion—like the assertion of fiction's power to disclose more genuine forms of truth—get contained by the counter-assertions they ignite, and this containment serves, exactly, to keep them alive as possibilities. Hawthorne's returns back through the communal and conventional renew the impulse to vision, so that the adventures Melville finds so exciting are always starting up again in Hawthorne's work. When he identifies Hawthorne's intentions with one phase of his fiction Melville extends Hawthorne's most extreme tendencies toward their full expression, but he does so at the expense of those reverses and attenuations that give such tendencies continued life. Construing Hawthorne as a programme for prophecy lets Melville release, in Ahab, Hawthornesque divination in the fullness of its power, but it also commits him to press on to divination's abortive end—to the point, reached in *Pierre*, where the urge to know and speak unfamiliar truth annihilates itself as a possible basis for work or thought.

Since Melville reaches this unHawthornesque extremity by following what he takes to be Hawthorne's own direction, it is not surprising that he now looks to his former mentor with puzzlement, accusation, and shame. A long critical tradition, started by Henry Murray in the Hendricks House edition of

Pierre, has it that Plotinus Plinlimmon, in that novel, is Melville's portrait of Hawthorne after the failure of their friendship. Plinlimmon certainly shows what Hawthorne must have looked like to Melville at the end of his effort at imitation. The author of the lecture 'Horologicals and Chronometricals', Plinlimmon maintains that the ethical meanings that prevail in the world are communal conventions only, and that they displace a different set of meanings that have the superior authority of 'Heaven's own Truth'. But having outlined their contradiction Plinlimmon then embraces both orders of meaning, accepts both schemes as equally legitimate in their place. This power to affirm opposite things together, and specifically to accept the validity of the conventional while also exposing it as merely conventional, is the Hawthorne trick that Melville cannot catch; and Pierre's mystification at Plinlimmon's incomprehensible self-possession surely expresses Melville's mystification at the secret of Hawthorne's poise. Melville confided the secret of his prophetical ambitions to Hawthorne, and he felt that Hawthorne encouraged him in his extraordinary undertakings. When he goes on to find, in the wreck of *Pierre*, where his dream of prophetical authorship leaves him, Melville must see Hawthorne in another way that Pierre sees Plinlimmon: as one who, while keeping the secret of his own authorial intentions, knows the secret of Pierre's, and knows it for a delusion.

Melville's revised portrait shows the author who thought he knew the grand truth about Hawthorne rediscovering Hawthorne as an enigma. Interestingly, this discovery does not end their literary relation: it permits Melville to establish the relation on a new footing. In the summer and fall after he finished *Pierre*, Melville wrote a series of long letters trying to talk Hawthorne into writing a story he had heard in Nantucket, about the return of a deserting husband long presumed dead. In this correspondence Melville singles out as typically Hawthornesque the story 'Wakefield'—an intriguing choice, since this tale renders the same Hawthornesque figure who has always fascinated Melville in a somewhat different way. Wakefield, like Hooper or Brand, or like Ahab or Pierre, is a man found out by a fate, by an idea that descends on him, wrests him from the world of ordinary habits and relations, and compels him to unwavering adherence to a peculiar personal program. This is the familiar process of daimonization; but in 'Wakefield' daimonization is a process almost perfectly opaque. Wakefield's personal program—to live one block away from home for twenty years while never going home—has not the superclarified significance of Brand's or Hooper's symbolic conduct but the enigmaticalness of purely arbitrary behaviour. Living under a special fate makes Wakefield, like Hawthorne's other obsessives, seem like an emblem for some deep truth about our common condition—so at the tale's close he is 'shaped into a figure':

> Amid the seeming confusion of our mysterious world, individuals are so nicely adjusted to a system, and systems to one another and to a whole, that, by stepping aside for a moment, a man exposes himself to a fearful risk of losing his place forever. Like Wakefield, he may become, as it were, the Outcast of the Universe.

This sounds like Hawthorne's usual sententiousness, but in this case the 'as it were' confesses how imperfectly the sentences of common wisdom exhaust the contents of Wakefield's figure. He remains a fascinating freak, fascinating because whatever meaning he embodies can be so little expressed.

'Wakefield' presents Hawthorne's daimonic agent acting in a reversed role—acting as the bearer not of revelation but of mystery itself. The lesson is not lost on Melville, who seizes on this figure to organize a new kind of fiction after *Pierre*. Bartleby, the hero of the first of his new experiments with the tale, resembles Wakefield in his imperviousness to relationship: he is a second instance of what Hawthorne thought was Wakefield's 'unprecedented fate', 'to retain his original share of human sympathies, and to be still involved in human interests, while he had lost his reciprocal influence on them'. But he resembles him even more in his imperviousness to interpretation. He is another irreducible enigma, in his very freakishness an image, we are compelled to believe, for some general truth of our 'humanity', but of a truth neither we nor the tale can undertake to say.

A story like 'Bartleby' suggests that when Melville takes its lessons to extremes Hawthorne's fiction reconstitutes itself, as the model for an art not of prophetic disclosure but of secrecy itself. And this development in Melville's 'career helps show why Hawthorne is so continuingly useful to writers in general. Reading him in the light of their own ambitions, they think they see what he is up to, and they think they can use him as a guide for their work. In fact he eludes them: when they think they have caught him, they do not have him at all. But his elusiveness, it turns out, gives them what his fixed image never could— the chance to keep catching him in a new aspect, and reading him in a new light. Since what they find when they find Hawthorne is a way their own art could be practised, he turns out to be something better than a guide. He becomes part of their equipment for self-renewal: part of the means by which, whenever it threatens to become established in form, their art can go on to recreate itself on altered terms.

NOTES

1. Flannery O'Connor to John Hawkes, 28 November 1961, in Sally Fitzgerald (ed.), *The Habit of Being: Letters of Flannery O'Connor* (New York: Farrar, Straus & Giroux, 1979), p. 457. It is only fair to add that O'Connor continues: 'though some of what he wrote I can't make myself read through to the end.'
2. Neil Harris gives one measure of Hawthorne's place in the nineteenth-century American pantheon by recording the voting for candidates for the Hall of Fame for Great Americans, established at New York University in 1900. Among literary figures, Hawthorne is surpassed only by Emerson, Longfellow, and Irving; a wide gap separates these four from the next figure (Bryant). Among figures in other categories, Hawthorne is out-ranked only by Washington, Lincoln, Webster, Franklin, Grant, Marshall, Jay, Edwards, Morse, Farragut, and Clay—Neil Harris (ed.), *The Land of Contrasts, 1880-1901* (New York: George Braziller, 1970), pp. 304–12. The history of the formation of the American literary canon in the nineteenth century has not yet been adequately written. On Hawthorne's reputation in the late nineteenth century, see Edwin H. Cady. '"The Wizard Hand": Hawthorne, 1864–1900', in *Hawthorne Centenary Essays*, ed. Roy Harvey Pearce (Columbus: Ohio State University Press, 1964), pp. 317–34.
3. Melville, 'Hawthorne and His Mosses', in *The Portable Melville*, ed. Jay Leyda (New York: Viking, 1952). pp. 400, 402, 407; William Dean Howells, *My Literary Passions* (New York: Harper and Brothers, 1895), p. 139; Henry James, *Hawthorne* (1897; rpt. New York: Collier Books, 1966), p. 99.

4. Melville's meeting and friendship with Hawthorne have been frequently discussed in biography and criticism. For the standard account see Leon Howard, *Herman Melville: A Biography* (Berkeley and Los Angeles: University of California Press, 1950), especially pp. 151-79. The fullest revisionary reading is that of Edwin Haviland Miller, in *Melville* (New York: Persea Books, 1975), pp. 19-52, 172-91, 220-24, 234-50, 286-92, and 334-41. Documents pertaining to the Hawthorne-Melville relation are gathered in Jay Leyda (ed.), *The Melville Log: A Documentary Life of Herman Melville, with a new supplementary chapter* (New York: Gordian Press, 1969).
5. 'Hawthorne and His Mosses', p. 401.
6. Melville to Lemuel Shaw, 6 October 1849, in Merrell R. Davis and William H. Gilman (eds.), *The Letters of Herman Melville* (New Haven: Yale University Press, 1960), pp. 91–2.
7. 'Hawthorne and His Mosses', p. 420. The fantasy of joint or plural incarnation is a persistent feature of Melville's thinking about himself and Hawthorne; see for instance his letter to Hawthorne of 17? November 1851: 'I feel that the Godhead is broken up like the bread at the Supper, and that we are the pieces. Hence this infinite fraternity of feeling', *Letters*, p. 142.
8. Leon Howard's demonstration that the Ahab chapters of *Moby-Dick* were written after Melville's meeting with Hawthorne is, so far as I know, universally accepted (Howard, *Melville*, pp. 162-73). For an extremely sensible survey of subsequent work on the compositional history of *Moby-Dick* see Robert Milder, 'The Composition of *Moby-Dick*: A Review and a Prospect', *Emerson Society Quarterley*, 23 (1977), 203-16.
9. Angus Fletcher, *Allegory: The Theory of a Symbolic Mode* (Ithaca, N.Y.: Cornell University Press, 1964), pp. 25-69 and 279-303. The principal limitation of Fletcher's account is not that the daimonic agent does not characterize allegory but that it characterizes so many other literary modes as well: the comedy of humours, for instance; and the grotesque (Anderson's *Winesburg, Ohio* is a casebook on daimonization, as are the novels of Flannery O'Connor); and perhaps the whole of romance, where character is restricted to the performance of a formulaic role. It might be noted that while Melville takes the fictive schema of the daimonic hero from Hawthorne, he reads this schema in connection with a broad tradition of daimonic lore: particularly the classical accounts, in Plato and Plutarch, linking daimonic possession with oracular inspiration; Goethe's association of the daimonic with greatness beyond good and evil—an idea available to Melville, as Mansfield and Vincent noted in the Hendricks House edition of *Moby-Dick*, either directly or from Emerson's extensive translations of Goethe in the essay 'Demonology'; the Romantic poets' association of daimonization with a female muse (an association clearly invoked in the figure of Isabel); and so on.
10. William Godwin, *Caleb Williams* (1794; rpt. New York: Holt, Rinehart, and Winston, 1960), p. 124; Mary Shelley, *Frankenstein* (1816; rpt. New York: New American Library, 1965), p. 47.
11. Melville to Hawthorne, 1 June 1851, *Letters*, p. 129.

Notes on Contributors

HAROLD BEAVER, Reader in American literature at the University of Warwick, has recently been elected to the new Chair of American literature at the University of Amsterdam. He has contributed five editions of Melville and Poe to the Penguin English Library, is a frequent contributor to the *Times Literary Supplement*, and has just completed a book, based on past articles, *The Great American Masquerade*.

RICHARD BRODHEAD teaches at Yale University. The author of *Hawthorne, Melville and the Novel* (1976), and of various essays on American literature, he is now at work on a book on Hawthorne's tradition in American fiction.

KEITH CARABINE is Lecturer in English and American literature at the University of Kent at Canterbury. He is the author of recent articles on Hemingway, Sherwood Anderson, Wright Norris, Dickens and Conrad.

GRAHAM CLARKE teaches English and American literature at the University of Kent at Canterbury.

ARNOLD GOLDMAN is Professor of American Studies at the University of Keele, England, and Associate Editor of the *Journal of American Studies*. His academic specialisms include aspects of American fiction and theatre.

RICHARD GRAY is a Senior Lecturer at the University of Essex. He has edited two anthologies of American poetry and a collection of essays on Robert Penn Warren. He is also the author of *The Literature of Memory: Modern Writers of the American South* (1977) as well as articles on American poetry and the American south.

ERIC HOMBERGER is Lecturer in the School of English and American Studies at the University of East Anglia. Besides articles on twentieth-century English and American literature, he has written *The Art of the Real: Poetry in England and America Since 1939* (1969) and edited *The Cambridge Mind* (1969) and *Ezra Pound: The Critical Heritage* (1972).

MARK KINKEAD-WEEKES is Professor of English at the University of Kent at Canterbury. He is the author (with Ian Gregor) of *William Golding: A Critical Study* (1967), *Samuel Richardson, Dramatic Novelist* (1973) and Editor of *The Rainbow: A Collection of Critical Essays* (1971). He has written extensively also on African literature and aspects of the English novel.

251

A. ROBERT LEE teaches American literature and studies at the University of Kent at Canterbury. He is the Editor of the Everyman *Moby-Dick* (1975) and of two other Vision Press collections, *Black Fiction: New Studies in the Afro-American Novel Since 1945* (1980) and *Ernest Hemingway: New Critical Readings* (1982). Among his recent publications are articles on Melville, George Eliot, Chester Himes, Ralph Ellison, Edward Albee and Robert Penn Warren.

ERIC MOTTRAM is Reader in American literature at the University of London. He has published books on Kenneth Rexroth, William Burroughs, Paul Bowles, William Faulkner, Allen Ginsberg and others, and, with Malcolm Bradbury, edited and contributed to the Penguin *Companion to American Literature*. He has written widely on nineteenth- and twentieth-century America. His last three books of poetry were *1980 Mediate*, *Elegies* and *A Book of Herne*.

BRIAN WAY is Senior Lecturer in English at the University College of Swansea. He is the author of a short study of *Moby-Dick* (1977) and of *F. Scott Fitzgerald and the Art of Social Fiction* (1980) and of numerous articles and reviews, mainly on the American novel.

Index